To

John, Anne and Bee

Hobbit to Hero:

The Making of Tolkien's King

Elizabeth Stephen

ADC Publications Ltd
Unit 8 Wychwood Court
Cotswold Business Village
Moreton in Marsh
Gloucestershire
GL56 0JQ
Tel: UK 01608-812867

Email: info@adcbooks.co.uk
www.adcbooks.co.uk

First Published by ADC Publications in 2012

0-9551900-7-X

A copy of the British Library Cataloguing in Publication Data is available from the British Library

ISBN 0-9551900-7-X   978-0-9551900-7-0

Printed and bound in the UK

Hobbit to Hero:

The Making of Tolkien's King

Contents

Preface

This is a book about J.R.R. Tolkien's writings of a kind which we have not had before, and which I am very glad to see. It is a book for anyone who has ever read The Lord of the Rings and thought, 'I like that; I want to know more about it.'

Elizabeth Stephen has not started, as so many critical studies do, from J.R.R. Tolkien's biography or his professional interests. Nor does she deal with the sort of arcane literary-critical theory whose vocabulary can't be found in either the OED or Webster's. Instead she has started where we as readers do; with Tolkien's best-known book, and one of his best-known characters, Aragorn. Just as Bilbo and Frodo in turn acted as guides through their adventures, characters with whom we could identify in the strange world that J.R.R. Tolkien presented us with, so in this book it is Aragorn who is our guide and torch-bearer through the labyrinth of Tolkien's mythology.

By following one thread in the complex weave that is Aragorn's story, Elizabeth Stephen has been able to unravel the long tale of the making of The Lord of the Rings. Moving on from there, she uses the other threads of Aragorn's tale to take us steadily deeper into Tolkien's thinking. This is a book which ultimately explores the nature of heroism, the links between The Lord of the Rings and Tolkien's other writings, and Tolkien's philosophical ideas - among much else. What might to the more academically-minded seem an odd choice, to explore this huge subject through the lens of a single character, is in fact its greatest strength. Thanks to the fact that we view Middle-earth through the lens of Aragorn and his story, our feet are always on the ground. We never lose sight of where we have come from, we always see how this strange and sometimes complex world relates back to the book and the character that we know and love.

It's very easy for a critical writer to end up baffling their audience, or speaking to only a very small constituency. Elizabeth Stephen is that rare creature, someone who can unravel and expound complex material with clarity, and also with an easily readable grace of expression. She has gone on a long journey from interested reader to writer herself, and now she takes us with her as she retraces the path to show us what she has discovered.

This is exactly the sort of book that I wished I had to hand when I first finished reading The Lord of the Rings and wanted to know more.

Thirty-odd years on, with three-and-a-bit books of my own under my belt (co-written with Alex Lewis, under the pen-name Elizabeth Currie), this book has still taught me things that I didn't know about J.R.R. Tolkien and his writings, and started me thinking about new questions. Elizabeth Stephen's work can offer both enjoyment and enlightenment to people at both ends of that range of knowledge and to everyone in between as well.

Ruth Lacon

Acknowledgements

Bilbo once remarked upon the dangers of heading out of your door and setting off into the unknown. The same could be said of venturing into the field of Tolkien scholarship, especially for one who has never previously attempted so much as a short stroll in the footsteps of those inured to such perils.

It is a daunting prospect, but even the most committed of travellers rarely complete worthy quests without the support of companions. My own journey has been no exception and I have been especially fortunate to receive assistance from several of my talented and inspirational friends in the Three Farthing Stone Smial. In particular, I am indebted to Andrew Compton of ADC Publications Ltd for accepting this book for publication; to Ted Nasmith for allowing his artwork to grace the cover; to author and artist Ruth Lacon for a most generous preface; to Angie Gardner, Tolkien quiz mistress extraordinaire, for her very kind review, and to Carlota da Cunha Parreira for untold incidents of help and encouragement throughout the writing of this book.

I am also most grateful to my mum, Margaret, who, in spite of little interest in the subject matter, nonetheless waded meticulously through the early drafts.

However, my biggest debt of gratitude is reserved for Cathy Fox. It is no exaggeration to say that without Cathy, my tireless support, sounding-board, proof reader and dear friend, who has daily held my hand from across the Atlantic, this project would never have come to fruition.

Introduction

Middle-earth is such a wondrous place, the breadth and depth of its history and geography so vast, the stories of the individual characters can at times seem swamped by the scope of the epic tale that unfolds before us. This is perhaps especially true of *The Silmarillion* where few of the characters attain the level of development usually associated with the traditional novel. While the multitude of players is vital for the realisation of the story as a whole, careful reading is required if the reader is to understand the hearts and minds of characters whose appearance is often tantalisingly fleeting. *The Lord of the Rings*, while labelled heroic romance by Tolkien himself, qualifies as a novel far more than *The Silmarillion*. Even so, there are only a handful of characters possessing personalities of sufficient complexity that we feel we come to know them in any great depth, a matter which is usually a prime consideration in a story if their spiritual journeys are to resonate successfully with our own lives and experiences.

Of all the races we encounter in Tolkien's legendarium, it is the hobbits who feel most familiar to us. Despite their immediate physical differences, we know and understand them with relative ease and it is through their eyes that we predominantly view the main events of the story. We empathise with their frailties and fears; we can imagine ourselves as lost and bewildered by the strange and perilous world into which they venture. We marvel at their achievements and wonder if we could perform as well in the situations in which they find themselves. Similarly, we might respond to Gandalf in the same way. In his persona of an old, grandfatherly figure with his genial companionship and prickly wit, we are easily persuaded that we have met his ilk before. We could happily hold a conversation with him, laugh at the same jokes and find enjoyment in his company. Yet can we really understand the mind of one who has dwelt in the world for millennia? Like the Elves, he is not human, and it is only when we meet him again in his later guise do we begin to comprehend that this Maia is unknowable beyond any but the most superficial of levels.

In a world populated by so many strange and unfamiliar beings, we might reasonably expect the race of Men to possess the most readily identifiable characters. But even here, 'Men' is too broad a definition to describe the diversity of peoples encompassed by this generic term. Characteristics found in all of us are broadly aligned with the traits exhibited by the various cultures, and inevitably we find we identify with some Men more closely than we do others. With their destructive cruelty, the 'evil' men of Harad and Rhûn who worship the Dark Lord exhibit our worst qualities, whereas the Rohirrim, and the men of Bree, are, by and large, 'good' men, certainly in comparison with the more dubious Dunlendings. Théoden is an example of a good man. He lives honourably and rules his kingdom within the moral framework by which his people conduct themselves. Even so, his judgement has been found to be lacking and evil has found its way insidiously into his realm. Butterbur is a good man. He does not possess the wit to see the worth of Strider in the way that Frodo does, but he is honest and kind-hearted, earning a living the best he can within the bounds that he has set himself. Faramir, on the other hand, is an exemplary man. A descendant of Númenor, he is a respected warrior who also demonstrates great sensitivity and wisdom. He exhibits none of the flaws of either his brother or his father and, despite his elevated stature and worth, remains readily accessible to the reader. It could be argued that he comes very close to being a representation of an ideal Man.

However, this position of the most idealised of mortal Men, Tolkien reserves for his King.

Aragorn is without doubt the leading Man of *The Lord of the Rings*. His is the classic fairy-tale of the emerging hero whose identity has long been kept secret, and of the lowly suitor who dares to claim the hand of a princess. As Gandalf tells Frodo in Rivendell, there are few men left in Middle-earth like Aragorn son of Arathorn, and at the end of the Third Age, even among his kin, Aragorn is ultimately set apart from any other mortal. He is after all the king, the supreme leader and ruler of his race, a role that he earns through his many heroic endeavours and yet one that is also his by right, by virtue of his birth. His outstanding personal qualities are unsurpassed by any of his contemporaries. Supremely learned in the lore of both Elves and Men, he is a great captain and a mighty warrior; in fact, the greatest hunter and traveller of the Age. He is undoubtedly the traditional, epic hero of the story, a character whose modest origins belie his great destiny, although, unlike that of some of his literary predecessors, Aragorn's courage is tempered by a demonstrable compassion. His strength is not only found in his sword and the might of his arms, but in his selflessness and his humility, his true power lying in the healing ability of his hands and the clarity of his wisdom.

His impressive attributes have, in part, been acquired and moulded by his substantial labours and efforts, and being of the royal bloodline of that most noble of mannish races, the Dúnedain, he is superbly acquitted to fulfil the role that fate has dealt him. His is an idealised conception and a man so blessed with near perfection should be distinguished from his peers by being as spiritually and morally flawless as is humanly possible.

In Aragorn, Tolkien gives us just such a man.

Yet, of all the principle characters we meet in Middle-earth, Aragorn is arguably one of the most elusive to truly understand. At times, the narrative can leave the reader without the basic intuitive connections necessary to fully appreciate his noble heart. Consequently, we might be forgiven for being less moved by his story than perhaps we feel we should be, especially when we consider his supreme dynastic importance to Middle-earth. The critics, too, have often undervalued Tolkien's great king, even to the point of neglect. The tall and dignified figure of Aragorn son of Arathorn; Elessar Telcontar High King of the Reunited Kingdom first strode onto the literary stage over half a century ago and since then a great deal has been written about *The Lord of the Rings* and the characters that collectively inhabit the pages, but it is by no means unusual for the name of Aragorn to barely receive a mention. Nor have all observations been intended as complementary; priggish, a Tory cabinet minister, a noble horse and the sort of man to support exclusive membership of golf clubs are a few of the more memorable descriptions that have been applied to Tolkien's King over the years.

This omission by the critics and the indifference of some readers can largely be attributed to the story being told primarily from the point of view of the hobbits. Throughout much of *The Lord of the Rings,* the character of Aragorn is shrouded in mystery, a riddle which is only solved as the story gradually unfolds. His is the untold tale in this great story, one initially only perceived through briefly snatched glimpses caught here and there in the text and then possibly by only the most alert of readers. Aragorn's journey runs parallel to that of Frodo's; the success of each in their respective endeavours dependent on the efforts of the other. Aragorn's quest to claim his crown would have ended at the Black Gate if Frodo had not struggled, step by painful step, to Mount Doom. Similarly, Frodo might have come to grief in Bree without Aragorn's timely assistance. Without doubt, his role in *The Lord of the Rings* is crucial for the development of the story and yet, for the most part, we do not read of Aragorn's adventures in the way we do of Frodo's. In full, as Tolkien admitted himself, Aragorn's tale would belong to an entirely different story altogether, *The Saga of Aragorn Arathorn's son.* [1]

Another factor behind this neglect was Aragorn's difficult and slow evolution from his original persona of the hobbit, Trotter, the effects of which persist into the finished work. As a result, most of what we learn about Aragorn is relegated to the Appendices which the reader only arrives at once the main body of the story is completed. To compound matters further, not all the early editions of *The Lord of the Rings* even included the full complement of these enlightening pages. Of course, it can not be assumed that every reader will bother with them anyway, but it is only here, at the very end of this long tale, that much of the riddle of who exactly is Strider can be answered.However, if we are to better appreciate Aragorn's wider purpose and to discover more profound answers to the riddle, we must look beyond *The Lord of the Rings* to the larger picture of Tolkien's mythology. It can justifiably be argued that we must also read *The Silmarillion, Unfinished Tales* and the complete *History of Middle-earth* if our understanding of Aragorn is not to be found wanting.

Even this is not the end of the matter. Middle-earth was not created in a vacuum. Its myths and legends owe their roots to a wealth of actual mythology of which Tolkien was both well versed and acutely aware. These legends not only provided inspiration for Aragorn's creation, but with skilful interweaving of characters found on the fringes of recorded history, Tolkien subtly manages to suggest his ranger-king still exerts an influence today. We must, therefore, spread our net further if we are to develop a complete appreciation of the character.

Aragorn has enjoyed a resurgence of interest in the wake of Peter Jackson's film trilogy and this enigmatic hero shows no sign of fading into obscurity just yet. Tolkien's books are as popular as ever and over the decades his great king has been given new life on stage, screen and radio, as well as in numerous depictions on canvas. With the growth of the internet, it is even possible to read further adventures of Strider as fan fiction archives abound with ever continuing tales of his daring deeds.

Here, the emphasis is firmly upon Tolkien's creation. As we unravel the mystery behind this grim ranger with a great destiny, we shall discover the vital role that Aragorn came to fulfill within Tolkien's mythology. Indeed, far from being the mandatory figurehead king of the 'hobbit sequel' or merely a competent 'extra' who rescues the Ringbearer from the odd tight spot, Aragorn is revealed as an extraordinary literary character of great depth and consequence who provided the means by which his creator chose to illuminate many of his most important themes and concepts.

Chapter 1: The Riddle of Strider

By the end of the War of the Ring, no character in *The Lord of the Rings* is adored quite as much as Aragorn. As the victor in battle, he earns the gratitude and respect of all the free peoples of Middle-earth, and throughout his journey to claim his throne, the depth of esteem in which he is held by those who already know him gradually becomes apparent to the reader. From an early age, he is loved by Elrond as a son of his own; in his youth, he earns the affection and regard of the Rohirrim and the host of Gondor. He has the friendship of Gandalf; the hobbits very quickly realize his worth while Bilbo is already a good friend. Éomer confides that he has loved him since their first meeting; Faramir's love is evident the moment he wakes in the Houses of Healing. Théoden refers to him as great hearted; Legolas and Gimli don't hesitate to follow him. He has the favour of Galadriel and the love and loyalty of the Dúnedain. Éowyn is instantly smitten and, after nearly three thousand years of being unmoved to wed, Arwen falls in love with him.

This is clearly a very charismatic man! Yet on first meeting Aragorn our initial perception is very different from our impression of him once he is king. The contempt for Strider demonstrated by the people of Bree, together with Sam's early suspicions, rather wrong-foots the reader into assuming this is how Aragorn is regarded generally. But Aragorn is not what he seems and his opening scene literally introduces the riddle of his identity. How that riddle unravels with the unfolding of the story is the subject of this opening chapter.

We are nearly two hundred pages into *The Lord of the Rings* before Aragorn makes his first appearance. Although his name appears in the *Prologue* and Gandalf mentions him briefly in the second chapter, *The Shadow of the Past,* none would connect this fleeting reference with the character we meet at *The Prancing Pony.* Nor is it likely that Tom Bombadil's cryptic mention of sons of forgotten kings would be foremost in the minds of most readers when first encountering this hooded loner sitting in the corner of the inn. Yet as soon as we become aware of his existence, Strider immediately earns our attention, and it would be a very indifferent reader who failed to ask the question of just who is this man. There is something vaguely sinister about the mysterious stranger watching the hobbits so intently. His dishevelled and disreputable appearance does not instil confidence. His clothes are dark and dirty, his hair awry. He does not look respectable and the landlord is less than encouraging. He sits alone and does not join in the revelry of the other patrons at the inn. Neither does it allay our suspicions that he goes by what is blatantly an assumed name. His mere presence instantly raises the tension in the story and both Frodo and the reader could certainly be forgiven for thinking they have encountered some sort of rogue.

We quickly discover that Strider knows something of Frodo's secret and has been actively searching for the hobbits, a revelation which only alarms them further. Yet he advocates extreme caution where the Black Riders are concerned and appears to have first hand experience of them himself, the memories so evil they haunt him still. But is he to be trusted? Those who have aided the hobbits thus far on their journey, Farmer Maggot, Gildor, Tom Bombadil, have quickly been identified as the 'good guys'. This dour-looking stranger could hardly be more different from these jolly characters, and Frodo readily admits to having been frightened by him. Sam especially is wary and advises his master against placing trust. The man's motives certainly appear dubious when he demands a reward in exchange for information. And as the conversation continues, the suspicion that the stranger is adopting a disguise is reinforced when Frodo observes that the stranger's manner of speech is inconsistent. However, it seems Strider is prepared to reveal certain details about himself, although, with Butterbur interrupting at that very moment, we never learn precisely what.

The landlord has belatedly remembered that he has in his possession a letter given to him by Gandalf which contains this riddle:

> 'All that is gold does not glitter,
> Not all those who wander are lost;
> The old that is strong does not wither,
> Deep roots are not reached by the frost.
> From the ashes a fire shall be woken,
> A light from the shadows shall spring;
> Renewed shall be blade that was broken,
> The crownless again shall be king.' [1]

Much that we need to know about Aragorn is contained within that one verse, but the hobbits do not immediately associate the lines with their new companion and the moment passes. So, when we later discover that Strider carries a broken sword which, as he says himself, is of little use as a weapon, we are unlikely to revisit the riddle and wonder at its significance. However, from the contents of the letter itself, we do discover that the stranger is a friend of the wizard. This is more promising and actually makes Strider a potentially more intriguing character than if he was merely the villain we are tempted to believe him to be. Also, we are treated to one of those wonderful moments when he grows in stature in the eyes of those around him before declaring himself to be Aragorn son of Arathorn. Since we know nothing of Arathorn, we can deduce little from this other than that his parentage is a matter of great personal pride. Only in his rather touching comment that a hunted man sometimes wearies of distrust and longs for friendship does he reveal anything of his inner self and hint at the loneliness of his existence. Yet the spectre of a hunted man in itself raises more questions than it answers.

Strider clearly possesses a sharp wit, but curbs his impatience with the hobbits' ridiculous behaviour, reserving the bite of his cutting tongue for the hapless Butterbur.Nor is he without humour and is quite capable of laughing at himself when the joke is on him, *'I look fair and feel foul. Is that it?'* [2] In fact, he handles the hobbits with great skill and kindness in spite of his irritation. Furthermore, by stating, *'if by life or death I can save you, I will,'* [3] far from commanding them to do as he says, he is demonstrating his willingness to give even his life in their defence. Our initial perception of Strider is altered greatly by just this one statement. It is an extraordinarily bold yet generous declaration and such humility is surprising given that he has only just met the hobbits. One has to wonder how much he already knows about them; what has Gandalf or Gildor told him. There can be no doubt, however, that by taking the hobbits under his wing that night, he has, at least for now, saved them from the Black Riders. Our suspicions about him are not as dark as they were.

A chapter and a half is devoted to introducing Aragorn to the story, and yet we are none the wiser as to exactly who he is when he sets off for Rivendell the next morning. We know nothing of his background; we do not know of the long years that he has spent guarding the very thing which the hobbits were so careless with the night before, and we know nothing of the significance of the Ring to him personally. Nor do we know what fears are filling his heart or of the intense pressure that he is under at this time. Gandalf is missing, at least five Black Riders are in the vicinity; he must be desperately worried about his men stationed at Sarn Ford and he has a very long trek ahead of him before he can reach the safety of Rivendell. In those empty leagues of Rhudaur, anything untoward could happen and he now has the daunting task of protecting four unworldly hobbits. If Aragorn was ever tempted to take the Ring for himself, then surely it must have been during that long night in Bree, alone with his bleak thoughts, knowing the Ringwraiths were closing in on him at any moment. And yet he does not.

As they set out on the journey to Rivendell, we slowly discover a little more about Strider. In spite of the name calling by some of the villagers, the Breelanders seem wary of the stranger and treat him with a grudging respect. It appears he knows the area well, seeking out secret paths where he will not be followed. He can find food in the wild, and, as the hobbits soon discover, he is learned in lore, something about which they wonder. He is proving a competent ally, but he is not infallible. Already we see glimpses of the doubts and uncertainties which come to the fore later. At Weathertop, when it becomes clear that the Black Riders are hot on their trail, Strider is unsure of how to evade them. They are all in imminent danger but, making do in a desperate situation, Strider does his best to cheer the hobbits by telling them stories. He is rapidly becoming a stalwart friend and we glimpse the softer side of his nature in his chanting of the *Tale of Tinúviel*. With his shining eyes and rich voice, Strider is evidently deeply moved by the story he is telling. However, we have a long wait to learn the significance of this particular tale to his own story since he declines to enlighten either the hobbits or the reader of his own part in the ongoing saga of Lúthien's heirs.

When the Black Riders attack, Strider attempts to drive them away, leaping out of the darkness with a flaming brand of wood in either hand, although his valiant defence fails to prevent Frodo from being stabbed. Then he mysteriously disappears into the night, leaving the injured Frodo to be cared for by his companions. He is gone for a long time, so long, it is small wonder that Sam's suspicions are aroused once more and, on Strider's return, Sam is again wary of the stranger and protective of his master, standing over him with his sword raised. Here, Strider reveals his kind heart as he speaks gentle words to reassure Sam of his own good intent and explains the extent of Frodo's injury before once again disappearing on an unexplained errand. He returns at dawn and comes across the knife that wounded Frodo. The blade seems to melt in his hand but then, placing the dagger on his knees, he *'sang over it a slow song in a strange tongue. Then setting it aside, he turned to Frodo and in a soft tone spoke words the others could not catch'* [4]. Without further explanation, we can only guess at what power Strider is evoking here with his strange words or at what encouragement or blessing he is bestowing upon the injured hobbit by this odd ritual.

We then discover that Strider has spent the night searching for the leaves of the *athelas* plant which he explains was brought to Middle-earth by the Men of the West and is now known only to those who wander in the wild. Who these 'Men of the West' are, we do not yet know. Neither do we know why Strider should be familiar with the benefits of this herb. However, the plant clearly possesses some healing properties since it does as he claims. Almost immediately, Frodo feels his pain lessen and the minds of all present are calmed and cleared by its fragrance. Here Strider's skill could easily be dismissed as that of any wandering ranger and nothing in the scene suggests otherwise. However, as a result of his efforts to protect and aid them, the hobbits gradually begin to accept the help that Strider offers Frodo without question and the incident at Weathertop demonstrably serves to strengthen their trust in him.

The journey from Weathertop to Rivendell is a miserable one with even Strider seeming tired and depressed, perhaps indicating that the encounter with the Ringwraiths has not left any of them completely unscathed by the influence of the Black Breath, a danger we know something about following Merry's experience in Bree. As the journey progresses, Strider becomes increasingly anxious. Frodo's health is failing; the food supplies are running out and he is unsure of the best course to take through land that is less familiar to him than the trails nearer to Bree. Only the incident with the stone-trolls provides any welcome relief as Strider teases the hobbits over their imagined peril. Later, he is encouraged when he finds a jewel in the mud on the Mitheithel Bridge. He takes this as a sign of hope, though he is far from certain of what it portends. We are beginning to see a suggestion of a supernatural element surrounding Strider; first the chant over the blade, then the healing power of the plant and now his interpreting the finding of the jewel as a sign of some sort. We could be forgiven for asking, is this mere superstition or is he in possession of knowledge and skills that we, the reader, have yet to discover.

As the weary companions pass through the derelict lands of Rhudaur, we are given a very direct clue to Strider's identity, although it is one easily overlooked. When Pippin asks Strider how he knows so much lore, he replies: *'The heirs of Elendil do not forget all things past'* [5]. The name of Elendil is mentioned twice by Gandalf in *The Shadow of the Past,* and the hobbits might be expected to have learnt of this great king in their lessons, but it would take a very alert reader to make the connection here. More intriguingly, when Frodo asks if he has been to Rivendell often, Strider replies: *'I have... I dwelt there once, and still I return when I may. There my heart is; but it is not my fate to sit in peace, even in the fair house of Elrond'* [6]. Particularly for readers of *The Hobbit* who are already familiar with the genial Elrond and the welcoming comforts of the Last Homely House, this revelation that Strider has dwelt at Rivendell significantly alters our perception of him. Strider is not quite the loner he appears, and he evidently has the friendship of the Elves. Even without prior knowledge of Elrond, we already know, both from Sam's fascination and from meeting Gildor, that the Elves are exceptional beings, and that associating with them is something greatly desirable although not easily achieved. That this strange man has lived among them immediately elevates his standing in our eyes and begs an answer to the question of precisely why he resided in this Elven dwelling. Yet the answer is only provided in the Appendices and readers who dispense with them will never find out.

Strider's connection with Rivendell is almost immediately reinforced by the arrival of Glorfindel, an Elf-lord from that House. With his white horse and golden hair we have no doubts at all that Glorfindel is one of the good guys. Furthermore, he is obviously well known to Strider who is overjoyed at his unexpected and most fortuitous arrival. Now the hard pressed ranger need no longer protect the hobbits single-handedly. And, given Strider's earlier revelation, it comes as less of a surprise to learn that he speaks the elf tongue fluently as he converses with Glorfindel as one would an old acquaintance.

By this stage in the story, Strider has earned the respect of the hobbits and none of them, not even Sam, questions his methods or his motives. As Frodo tells Gandalf when he finally awakes in the safety of Rivendell, it was only with the appearance of Glorfindel that Sam came to trust Strider completely, and he concedes that they would never have reached Rivendell without him. In spite of this, Frodo is still not entirely sure of what to make of his new ally. He admits to having become fond of him, but Strider's strange grimness is still something of a barrier to true friendship. Yet our inkling that there is something extraordinary to discover about Strider is confirmed in the course of Frodo's conversation with Gandalf. We now find that he is a member of a dwindling race that is not from Middle-earth, but from *'over the Sea'* [7]. Gandalf's words conjure images of nobility with his talk of kings but precisely who these men were and what specifically is their relationship to Strider, we have to wait until the next chapter, *The Council of Elrond*, to discover. Rather than answering questions, the conversation has merely added to the sense of mystery, and before answers are forthcoming, we are given further clues for solving the riddle of Strider, all of which serve to round our image of the character enormously.

A great feast is held in Frodo's honour and it is here that we first meet Elrond and his daughter, Arwen, although Strider in missing. Later this is explained. The sons of Elrond returned unexpectedly with news which he wanted to hear at once, although we are never told what was so urgent that a man who has been surviving on slim rations for weeks should find it necessary to miss such a splendid meal. Strider does, however, turn up for the merrymaking in the Hall of Fire afterwards, but he has to be sent for and comes at Elrond's request. Here we find that whilst in Rivendell he goes by the name of the Dúnadan, another alias, and that he is a friend of Bilbo's. This comes as quite a surprise and the fondness of the exchange between these two unlikely friends firmly establishes Aragorn as a man of worth and good character. In fact, it is Bilbo who first suggests an association between Aragorn and Arwen. He mentions that Arwen was present at the feast and wonders why Aragorn was not. However, any connection between these two characters is not elaborated further. Instead, Bilbo changes the subject and requests his friend's help with a song he is trying to finish, the lyrics of which reveal a further mystery. Bilbo later confides to Frodo that Aragorn's only contribution was to insist that he include mention of a green stone, although Bilbo had no idea why. Neither does the reader at this stage.

The final surprising event to occur that evening is observed by Frodo. As he leaves the gathering, he notices that Aragorn has a star shining on his breast and that under his cloak he is wearing elven-mail. Suddenly, we are treated to a very different vision of the previously nondescript ranger. The image now is of a warrior, noble and powerful, a lord even. Furthermore, Frodo notes that Aragorn is standing beside Arwen who sits next to her father, the lord of the house. By standing where he is, Aragorn is undeniably occupying a very privileged position. Although Frodo sees the couple speak to each other, the image is tantalisingly brief and he leaves the room before he can tell us anything further.

Aragorn's arrival at Rivendell has afforded an opportunity to observe the character in a very different setting from that of either the inn or the wilds. Our perception of him is gradually changing. He is no longer viewed as a homeless and sinister stranger, but as a man welcomed into the home of the Elves. He is obviously liked and respected, and, most importantly for determining our opinion of him, liked and respected by those characters already held in high regard by the reader.

~oo0oo~

The following day, Elrond holds a council to which many new characters attend and several have a story to tell. Aragorn is now dressed as he was in Bree and is once again sitting in a corner alone. The principal speaker is Elrond who recounts first the story of Elendil and his two sons, Isildur and Anárion. He talks of Númenor and the Last Alliance; we hear of Isildur's folly and of the shards of Narsil and of how those shards were returned to Rivendell after Isildur's death. We learn of the decline of the once great kingdoms of Arnor and Gondor and begin to appreciate that the story we are being drawn into has a very deep and complex history, Middle-earth suddenly being revealed as a much larger and richer place than simply the Wilderness beyond the Shire.

In response to Elrond's lengthy speech, Boromir, a newcomer who is introduced as the son of the lord of Minas Tirith, takes to the floor and tells of Gondor's on-going battles to keep the hostile hosts of Mordor at bay. It transpires that he has travelled to Rivendell specifically seeking an answer to a riddle concerning a broken sword. Boromir's request for information proves to be Aragorn's cue. Standing up, he produces the shards of the sword that he showed to the hobbits in Bree and announces that this is the very sword that Boromir is seeking. Not surprisingly, Boromir, a proud and lordly man, is amazed that this apparently insignificant traveller should make such a claim. But Elrond interjects firmly with this formal and revealing introduction.

'He is Aragorn son of Arathorn ... and he is descended through many fathers from Isildur Elendil's son of Minas Ithil. He is the Chief of the Dúnedain in the North, and few are now left of that folk'. [8]

For both the visitors to Rivendell and the reader, this emphatic statement of Elrond answers many vital questions about Strider. Frodo, certainly, makes the connection between all that has previously been said that morning and the title given to Aragorn now, and he is possibly ahead of the reader when he jumps up to offer him the Ring, an invitation which Aragorn declines. Although Aragorn explains to Boromir that the shards are those of the sword of Elendil about which Elrond has just been speaking and that they have long been treasured by Elendil's heirs, Boromir is still not convinced and his continued doubts inflame Bilbo to speak in his friend's defence. The hobbit stands up and recites the same riddle that Gandalf included in his letter to Butterbur. It transpires that it was Bilbo himself who wrote the poem for Aragorn, 'a long time ago when he first told me about himself' [9].

In light of the revelations about Aragorn's ancestry, the repeating of the riddle is a timely reminder and much can now be read with a fresh interpretation, especially when Aragorn goes on to talk movingly, and at considerable length, about his own hard life, his many journeys to distant lands and the long, sad decline of the once great people of whom he is the Chieftain. And now we know for certain what we may have already began to surmise; Strider is no ordinary traveller, but is actually the dispossessed heir of two kingdoms, a king in exile no less, but one reduced to living in the shadows, concealing his identity and enduring the scorn of those whom he protects. Without thanks or reward, he and his people have continued to maintain the peace in their homelands even though their days of glory have long since past. However, with the finding of the Ring, all that is about to change. Aragorn's hour is coming, and he knows it. The hidden hero has been exposed even if he is still far from being in a position to fulfil his undoubted potential.

Later in the discussion, Boromir returns to the question of Aragorn and his sword. He clearly desires all the aid he can find but he is still doubtful about the worth of the sword's owner: *'Mayhap the Sword-that-was-Broken may still stem the tide – if the hand that wields it has inherited not an heirloom only, but the sinews of the Kings of Men'* [10]. Aragorn takes no offence at Boromir's implied insult but he has, nonetheless, succeeded in working into the debate many details about himself that were not entirely relevant to the discussion at hand. Since he states quite unequivocally that he will come to Minas Tirith, his personal ambition is no longer in doubt. He is wise enough to know that much must still happen before he can make any move to claim the kingship, but he has skilfully opened the door on his claim. There will be no closing it now and the reader is left with the expectation of future tension between these two men.

The discussion progresses to the Ring itself and we discover more of Aragorn's relationship with Gandalf. We learn that they have spent many years searching for the creature, Gollum, whom Aragorn eventually caught and, at great personal pains, brought into the safe-keeping of the Mirkwood Elves. As he tells his tale of his arduous journey, we capture a glimpse of the difficult life that Aragorn has led, though he does not regale his adventures to garner sympathy. He glosses over his hardships and is dismissive of his perils. Unfortunately it turns out that his efforts to constrain the creature have been in vain and that Gollum has escaped from the Elves' care, a situation which Aragorn accepts with remarkable magnanimity given the long years he devoted to the search and the suffering he endured in the process.

The Council of Elrond is a chapter jammed full of information, much of it new to the reader and the revelations about Aragorn form only a small part of the astonishing facts revealed. Yet the chapter serves to raise the standing of Aragorn in our eyes quite dramatically. Far from being some dubious vagabond, Aragorn is now shown to have a long and noble lineage, the leader of a once greatly esteemed people. His race may have all but disappeared, but his own line, passing unbroken from father to son, has remained intact throughout the long years of their decline. He is revealed as a man with a hard and painful past, but also one with potentially a great destiny. He has not stated his intent to take the empty throne of Gondor although that is certainly implied by the resolute nature of his remarks to the heir of the man who stands in his way. He is undoubtedly a man with a mission, but through his unacknowledged labours protecting others, he is also revealed as a man possessing a deep sense of duty and a great nobility of heart. This is clearly a character who operates with an abundance of integrity and honour. Even at this stage in the tale, it is impossible to imagine Aragorn ruthlessly seizing even what is rightfully his by anything other than legitimate means and with due consideration for others. Gradually the pieces of the puzzle of just who is Strider are falling into place, but as they do so, his future looks increasingly fascinating and far from predicable.

~oo0oo~

The next day, Aragorn leaves Rivendell with the sons of Elrond to spend the next two months in the wilds searching for signs of the Black Riders. After his arduous journey from Bree, he might have been forgiven had he sought a restful sojourn in the comfort of Rivendell, but perhaps already we can appreciate that such passivity would be incompatible with what we have learned so far of his character.

When he returns, the first phase in the fulfilment of *The Riddle of Strider* is accomplished with the re-forging of the shards of Narsil. Aragorn gives the sword a new name, Andúril, the Flame of the West. Andúril is evidently a supreme weapon, a sword in the manner of other great mythical swords which are almost characters in its own right and essential prerequisites for any great warrior. The re-forging itself, however, is performed without any great ceremony, and quite what it must have meant to Aragorn to finally hold this magnificent heirloom in his hand, is left to our imagination. Now, though, he has the necessary implement to enable him become a hero on a par with any comparable swordsman from legend.

Suitably armed, and, to Frodo's evident delight, Aragorn is to accompany the Ringbearer on the Quest. But as the Company prepares to depart, Aragorn sits quietly with his head bowed to his knees. With the benefit of hindsight we can understand the enormity of what this moment meant to him, although at the time we are told, somewhat cryptically, that only Elrond fully understood its significance. We can at least discern from his sombre posture that Aragorn is greatly weighed by care and we can guess that, while he may fully intend to reach Minas Tirith, he has no illusions of the scale of the task ahead of him.

Soon the Company is on its way. Gandalf is the leader, but Aragorn consults with him often. Aragorn knows the land well, but before long he is restless. His concerns are justified when it becomes apparent that the Company is being watched. With the worsening weather compounded by the problem of spies, the question of an alternative route through Moria is raised when the companions fail to cross Caradhras. Aragorn is set against this course, although what dark tale he has to tell of his previous journey into the mines he does not say. The prospect of venturing underground clearly disturbs him greatly, but the decision is made for them when wolves attack in the night and their current situation becomes so perilous they have no option but to enter Moria.

We learn little more about Aragorn on the long march through the mountain other than that he knew the wizard better than any other in the Company. However, with Gandalf's shocking death, it falls to him to lead his companions forward. We can perhaps guess at how deeply Aragorn mourns his friend as he grapples with fulfilling his new responsibilities but he has little time to indulge in grief. He leads the Company onwards, successfully bringing his companions to safety in the land of Lothlórien, although, in his haste, he forgets that Frodo and Sam are injured. Distressed at this lapse, he tends them with great care and uses the last of the *athelas* leaves he gathered at Weathertop to bring them comfort.

Lothlórien, we soon learn, is a realm that Aragorn has visited before and one to which he is glad to return. He passionately chastises Boromir for speaking ill of it even though Boromir's remarks are made through ignorance. When the Company is met by the marchwardens, it seems that Aragorn is not only known here but has *'the favour of the Lady'* [11]. But, almost as if we are purposefully denied knowing anything of the significance of this place to him just yet, as he enters the realm we are only told that he sighed *'as if some memory stirred him'* [12]. Yet before the Company can proceed further, there is an obstacle to overcome: Gimli is not welcome. Nor will he submit to the proposed compromise of his being blindfolded. However, Aragorn diplomatically finds a solution and states that the whole Company should be treated similarly. Although this is not to the liking of Legolas, they all follow Aragorn's lead and a potentially explosive situation is averted. Aragorn may doubt that he is a leader of the calibre of Gandalf - as he later says to Éomer, *'when the great fall, the less must lead'* [13] - but he is, nonetheless, doing a more than adequate job.

On their way to Caras Galadhon, the Company rests at the hill of Cerin Amroth. As they prepare to continue their journey, Frodo observes Aragorn standing motionless at the foot of the hill. Aragorn is lost in memory, and Frodo's vision is not of his current travelling companion. Rather, he beholds Aragorn as he was in the past as a lord, young and fair, untroubled by his grim later years. As Aragorn returns out of his thoughts, he speaks the name of Arwen, smilingly telling Frodo that this is where his heart dwells and where it will remain, *'unless there be a light beyond the dark roads that we still must tread, you and I'* [14]. Aragorn was clearly reliving some cherished memory from the past, the reference to Arwen is an obvious clue, but, with the phrase in Elvish, no one could be expected to translate this on first reading. Like Frodo, we are left in the dark as to the nature of the events that Aragorn is remembering. Yet, even veiled as they are, with his recalling these memories there is a definite suggestion of future expectation. More baffling, however, is the statement that Aragorn does not return there as living man. If no longer alive, then by implication, he must return when he is dead, but we have to wait until the very end of *The Tale of Aragorn and Arwen* before we can guess at the circumstances when he might do this.

Later, a further riddle is supplied by Celeborn with his revelation that it has been thirty-eight years since Aragorn last came to Lothlórien. This comes as quite a surprise since some quick mental arithmetic places the ranger as being considerably older than we might have assumed from what we have learned so far. As yet, we know nothing of the exceptionally long lifespan of the heirs of Elros, and the only previous clue we had regarding Aragorn's age was his rather self-effacing comment to the hobbits when he first met them that he is older than he looks.

Safe now in Lothlórien, at last Aragorn is able to rest. In his own words, he is weary in body and in heart. Still grieving for Gandalf, we are given a rare insight into his thoughts and find that he is beset with doubts as he struggles to reconcile the conflicting demands placed upon him. He is undecided as to the best course to take for both the success of the Quest and the accomplishment of his own desires.With Gandalf gone, he knows he must lead the Company, but his commitment to do so potentially throws into doubt his own plan of going with Boromir to Minas Tirith to defend the city. Increasingly, he realises it is unlikely he could still do this if he is also to accompany Frodo to Mordor, which must surely be where his first duty lies. The lack of a concrete plan beyond Moria is proving a major headache. Furthermore, he is merely being pragmatic when he doubts that his presence would make much difference to the success of a mission so fraught with uncertainty. The sympathetic reader might pause to consider that even this most courageous of men might need to gird himself to once again to enter those lands of the Enemy where we know he has faced 'deadly perils' in the past. In the event, Celeborn's offer of boats allows Aragorn a most welcome breathing space to delay a decision upon this very difficult choice.

As the Fellowship prepares to leave Lothlórien, Galadriel gives Aragorn a gift of a sheath for his sword. When she asks him if there is anything more that he desires from her before they depart, he mysteriously replies: *'Lady, you know all my desire and long held in keeping the only treasure that I seek. Yet it is not yours to give me, even if you would; and only through darkness shall I come to it'* [15]. Galadriel responds by presenting him with an additional gift in the shape of a magnificent green stone. The 'treasure' Aragorn refers to is, of course, Arwen and not the jewel or any other secret desire, although, again, this is not necessarily inferred from the text. What is certain is that claiming the crown of Gondor is not in itself of paramount importance to Aragorn since his kingdom cannot be the sole desired treasure that Galadriel has long kept safe for him. When thanking Galadriel for his gifts, Aragorn addresses her as, *'Lady of Lórien of whom were sprung Celebrían and Arwen Evenstar'* [16] and it transpires that the stone had returned to Galadriel's keeping after she had previously passed it to her daughter, Celebrían, who, in turn, passed it to hers. From the few references made to Arwen prior to her arrival at Minas Tirith, this is another oblique indicator of her relationship with Aragorn yet one which is obscured by our not having previously heard of Celebrían.Yet, the passage is important because this is the sole mention in the main body of the book of the family connection between the lords of Lothlórien and Imladris.

The warmth of Aragorn's comments to Galadriel does, however, indicate the depth of the regard in which he holds the Lady of Lothlórien and confirms their previous association. As Galadriel gives Aragorn the stone, she also tells him to adopt the name of Elessar, a name said to have been foretold for him. Prior to this exchange, we have not heard of the name in which Aragorn will eventually rule his kingdom, and if we wonder where this prophecy came from, an answer will not be found within the pages of *The Lord of the Rings* or even in the Appendices. Bilbo's *Lay of Eärendil* is the only clue to the stone's origins, and from Aragorn's insistence that the hobbit include mention of a green stone, we can deduce that he was already aware of its existence and its significance.

The bestowing of the gift by such an esteemed figure as Galadriel causes Aragorn to perceptively appear taller and more kingly to those about him. Whether this is directly attributable to the present of the jewel or a result of the confidence boost the wearing of it must have engendered is unclear. Aragorn again transforms into a seemingly more regal figure as the Company passes through the Argonath and Frodo suddenly beholds Strider, not as a weather worn ranger, but as a king returning from exile. It is a magnificent snapshot of the emerging monarch, his hope swelled by the sight of his mighty ancestors immortalised in stone, and, henceforth, we see more of these moments as the part of Aragorn that is already Elessar steadily comes to the fore as he nears the time when he must embrace his destiny. Sadly for Aragorn, his joy is short-lived and the reality of his situation immediate returns to haunt him. Once again he frets over his choice of route and it is clear he is missing Gandalf desperately. The very fact that he reveals, if only to himself, how much he yearns to go to Minas Tirith, demonstrates the depth of the conflict taking place within him.

In the end, he rightly decides that the choice must lie with Frodo who is the appointed Ringbearer. Even so, as Frodo ponders his own direction and is subsequently challenged by Boromir, Aragorn pledges to remain at Frodo's side, in spite of his prospects of achieving his personal goal being greatly diminished by his choice. However, Boromir's attempt to take the Ring and Frodo's resultant flight makes his sacrifice unnecessary. As the Company scatters in disarray, Aragorn heads to Amon Hen seeking any sign that might aid him in his perplexities. Instead, he hears only the sound of battle as orcs overtake the Company. Racing to the aid of his companions, he arrives at the conflict too late to assist Boromir who is mortally wounded. In a scene laden with symbolism, Aragorn absolves the dying Boromir of his guilt and, in response to Boromir's plea for Aragorn to save his people, Aragorn promises to do what Boromir now can not. With the hobbits missing, Aragorn is convinced the Quest has failed utterly. Characteristically, he blames his own inadequacies and not the failings of others, and, by guarding Boromir's confession, he demonstrates his loyalty to his fallen comrade. Greatly moved by Boromir's death and distraught over the consequences of his own failure, he remains weeping beside him until he is joined by his remaining companions, Legolas and Gimli.

The scattering of the Fellowship represents one of the lowest points of the Quest for Aragorn and his dilemma precipitates a personal crisis of confidence in his abilities as a leader. But he does not buckle under the strain and his companions still have faith in him even if his own belief in himself is faltering. Together, the remaining members of the Company ponder the fate of the missing hobbits. Knowing it is vital that they now chose the correct course of action, when Aragorn finally reaches a decision, he does so emphatically, and in doing so a weight of care is lifted from him. His confidence returns quickly and, putting heart into his companions, he runs swiftly in pursuit of the orcs.

Throughout the lengthy chase that follows, we see the great tracker and hunter in action. Aragorn appears firmly in charge, seemingly resolute and determined. Yet when the question of whether or not to rest at night arises, he evidently still doubts his abilities to lead and has not forgiven himself for his earlier indecisions. Only once, when he sees dawn break over the White Mountains, does he give voice to his anguish at being unable to follow the path he yearns to take. We might sympathise with him even more once we have learned of the years he spent in Gondor in his youth and of the high regard in which he came to be held in that land.

On the Three Hunters run in their increasingly hopeless pursuit and Aragorn is on the verge of admitting they have failed in their search when they espy a large group of horsemen approaching down the orc-trail. As they await the riders, we discover that he knows something of these people and has been among them in the past. Greatly outnumbered, the three companions are surrounded by the Rohirrim, their spears perilously close and seemingly anything but friendly. But Aragorn handles this predicament with great tact and diplomacy, and successfully averts disaster when Éomer offends Gimli by insulting the Lady of the Wood. At first Aragorn is cautious in his dealings with Éomer, referring to himself as 'Strider', but, after establishing the loyalties of the riders, he publicly introduces himself by his right name and in quite spectacular fashion. Throwing back his cloak and grasping the elven sheath of his sword, he sweeps out Andúril, declaring:

'I am Aragorn son of Arathorn, and am called Elessar, the Elfstone, Dúnadan, the heir of Isildur, Elendil's son of Gondor. Here is the Sword that was Broken and is forged again! Will you aid me or thwart me? Choose swiftly!' [17]

Having a long name has its uses! This sudden and unexpected revelation proves timely, and Éomer is suitably impressed, if a little out of his depth once he learns the identity of his captive. Yet being an honest man, he does not doubt Aragorn's claim and, when Aragorn reveals that he has spoken with both Éomer's father and with Théoden in the past, Éomer is moved to act against the king's wishes. He lends horses on the understanding that the companions will return them eventually to Edoras and so justify his faith in them. It is a tangible measure of Éomer's instant recognition of Aragorn's worth that he is prepared to possibly gamble with the fate of his own life to assist him in this way.

Throughout this episode, Aragorn continues to grow in stature in the eyes of those around him. Éomer treats him with courtesy and respect, referring to him as 'lord,' as would be befitting for one with a claim to the throne of Gondor. If the reader has not already perceived Aragorn's potential role, Legolas's vision of a crown shining upon Aragorn's head should leave no one in any doubt that this is the returning king. This unexpected transformation in Aragorn is observed with amazement by his friends, yet we can only assume from Aragorn's speech that his personal confidence is growing in tandem with the new respect that he is being afforded by his companions. Finally being able to speak his true name to strangers after so many years adopting disguises must have been a momentous matter. And now that he is able to be himself in public, we begin to further witness the emergence of his true character. He is not, for instance, afraid to impart his own wisdom periodically, and in a manner that would be difficult to imagine of the despised ranger in Bree. His belief that it is better to begin a task than to refuse, even though there are no guarantees of success, is particularly applicable to both his own and Frodo's quests.

~oo0oo~

Throughout the first two chapters of *'The Two Towers'*, Aragorn is at the forefront of the story in a way that he has not been since *'The Council of Elrond'*. We see in his reactions to the events unfolding around him his compassion and grief for a fallen comrade as well as his steadfastness and loyalty to his friends. His decisions are balanced by his humility and self doubt, all of which are underpinned by the strength of his extraordinary personal determination. The pursuit through Rohan has allowed us to discover more about Aragorn's capabilities. This is a man who runs one hundred and thirty five miles in less than four days in an attempt to rescue two of his friends. Being such an experienced traveller, he possesses knowledge of the surrounding environment which is far in excess of that of his companions. He is familiar with both the people of Rohan and with the lie of the land where they dwell. He recognises the details of the emblems on the armour of their orc attackers and it is he who picks up the trail in the Emyn Muir and finds Pippin's brooch. Aragorn's worth as a tracker again comes to the fore when he solves the riddle of what became of Merry and Pippin.

However, the unexpected return of Gandalf comes as a surprise and a relief for all the remaining Company and for Aragorn in particular. He now has his guide and mentor to aid him in his perplexities and, furthermore, Gandalf absolves him of any blame over the difficult choices he has needed to make so far. Standing side by side as they prepare to depart for Edoras, they suddenly make an impressive pair of allies. Gandalf, in his new guise, no longer appears as a kindly, grandfatherly figure and Aragorn, now emerging from his own disguise, is no longer perceived as a humble travel-stained ranger. Both are revealed as lords of great might concealing hidden power beneath their drab raiment.

After Gandalf has recounted his own adventures, he gives Aragorn a message from Galadriel.

Where now are the Dúnedain, Elessar, Elessar?
Why to thy kinsfolk wander afar?
Near is the hour when the Lost should come forth,
And the Grey Company ride from the North,
But dark is the path appointed for thee:
The Dead watch the road that leads to the Sea. [18]

At this stage in the story, any talk of the Grey Company or of the Dead watching the road to the Sea is unfathomable to the reader and the message merely provides another riddle for the reader which, in this case, will not be solved for many chapters.

The reunited companions now ride to Edoras where Aragorn's usual diplomatic deftness deserts him as he demonstrates a very human reluctance to leave his treasured sword in the hands of another. Nowhere else in the story is he seen to be so stubborn or to behave so haughtily, and there is a hint of arrogance in his refusal to yield to the will of Théoden. While even the greatest among us have their off days, Aragorn's stance reveals a brief glimpse of the inner steel and self belief which, for all his modesty, sustained him throughout his long trials. Yet, at Gandalf's prompting, he submits to the wisdom of the wizard and does as required, although not before he places the doorwarden in fear of his life should he so much as touch his beloved Andúril. His good humour quickly returns though as he laughs at Gandalf's own reluctance to part with his staff.

For a time, Aragorn now occupies a subordinate role in the story, leaving Gandalf centre-stage to heal the ailing Théoden and spur him to the defence of his realm. It is, however, in Meduseld that Aragorn first meets the king's niece, Éowyn, and it is immediately apparent that sexual tension exists between these two characters. Tall and slender with her long golden hair, Éowyn inevitably catches Aragorn's eye. And she in turn is drawn to the stranger, immediately perceiving his power and his wisdom. There is undeniably great expectation for the reader in this first encounter. We could be forgiven for wondering if there is a romantic interlude brewing; is this fair maid to eventually become Aragorn's queen? Unlike the barely noticeable and riddled clues to Aragorn's relationship with Arwen, the reader is left in no doubt that something significant has taken place here. At their next exchange, Éowyn's interest is reinforced. Her eyes shine as she hands him a cup and he smiles as he looks upon her. But immediately there is a hitch. Aragorn's romantic past may be a mystery at this stage, but he is not so inexperienced he cannot detect sexual attraction. When he realises the effect he is having upon Éowyn, he is troubled and concerned. He clearly does not share her enthusiasm but there is no time for Éowyn or the reader to find out why as Aragorn leaves at once to ride to war. He does, however, spare a moment to glance back at her as he leaves, while she, in turn, stands watching until he is far over the plain. Éowyn, like the reader perhaps, has expectations of what might occur on his return and nurtures a hope that this introduction might prove to be merely an opening episode in their relationship.

Aragorn, meanwhile, although now fulfilling a subsidiary role, nonetheless rides to war at Éomer's right hand. He is treated with honour by the Rohirrim who all follow his lead when he salutes the White Rider, and at the battle of Helm's Deep we see Aragorn the warrior in action. His presence is an inspirational one as news of the return of the 'Blade that was Broken' spreads quickly among the men. He spends the night lending a hand wherever his sword is most needed and offering words of encouragement to the beleaguered troops. Aragorn is obviously a swordsman of considerable skill, competent in battle and familiar with taking command. The image we have of him wielding Andúril at Helm's Deep is now markedly different from that acquired of him in Bree. Since that inauspicious introduction we have become aware of at least a little of his past life as a warrior, a past which explains his possession of skill with a sword which could not have been acquired from the broken shards that he has carried around with him for so long. Furthermore, through his endeavours in battle, Aragorn's stature in the eyes of others also continues to grow. At one point, he even tries to parley with the enemy in what is presumably an act of mercy. Even to his foes, Aragorn is now revealed as a figure of great royalty and majesty. After so long in waiting, our ranger is suddenly hurtling at great speed towards his destiny.

Once the battle is over, Aragorn rides with Théoden and Gandalf to Isengard and is at last reunited with Merry and Pippin. While Gandalf and the king's company ride away to meet Treebeard, Aragorn remains behind to chat with his friends. And, where Gandalf once spared a kindly word to reassure him that his decisions had been wise, Aragorn now does the same for Pippin when the hobbit rues discarding his brooch on the trail. The interlude is a brief return to the simplicity of Strider for a man increasingly on the road to kingship, although his relaxed remark to Pippin, *'I am Strider and Dúnadan too, and I belong both to Gondor and the North'* [19] suggests he is perfectly at ease with this dichotomy and quite comfortable adopting his emerging persona.

Saruman takes no heed of Aragorn who remains silently in the background, seemingly no more than one of Théoden's men, but on the return journey to Helm's Deep, we meet some of Aragorn's own people, the Dúnedain of the North. His kinsman, Halbarad and a company of some thirty Rangers, including Elrond's own sons, have ridden to his aid. Aragorn's reunion with his men is a joyous one, Halbarad clearly a close friend, and it is he who carries Arwen's gift for his Chieftain.They have also brought messages, one from Elrond, reminding Aragorn of The Paths of the Dead, and which reinforces that sent by Galadriel via Gandalf; the other, from Arwen, delivered by Halbarad and more personal: *'The days now are short. Either our hope cometh, or all hopes end. Therefore I send thee what I have made for thee. Fare well, Elfstone!'* [20]

Receiving word from Arwen affects Aragorn profoundly and he falls silent for the remainder of the journey. With typical reserve, he keeps his thoughts and feelings from the reader, but, given the image of Éowyn hovering in the background, the reminder of Arwen is timely. The suggestion of their shared hopes and the use of the more familiar 'thee' rather that 'you' in Arwen's form of address suggests the matter of Aragorn's personal affairs is far from resolved. Interestingly, Arwen refers to Aragorn as 'Elfstone', confirming the earlier suggestion that Arwen had purposefully left the jewel in Galadriel's keeping in the hope that it might pass to him at some later opportunity.

The arrival of this small band of reinforcements serves to elevate Aragorn's status even further to that of a prince-in-waiting. He now has men of his own under his command, great knights to ride at his side, although our view of this fascinating people is glimpsed far too briefly, given that these are the only Dúnedain from the former kingdom of Arnor that we meet in the entire story. Later, as they prepare to leave the Hornburg, Gimli provides a description of the physical appearance of these dour men, but it is only in their great loyalty to Aragorn that we can truly discern their worth. And it seems Aragorn has other, more powerful, allies supporting him from behind the scenes. When the question of who sent the Dúnedain to Aragorn's aid is raised, Legolas and Gimli conclude that it was the Lady Galadriel who, in turn, sent word to Elrond. With the heavyweights of Middle-earth openly backing him, Strider has certainly come a long way from being a solitary ranger in Bree, coping with life's trials single-handedly.

Events are now moving very rapidly towards a conclusion and, as Aragorn himself says: *'An hour long prepared approaches'* [21]. Furthermore, when Gandalf asks him to take charge of the Palantír, we see Aragorn's growing willingness to trust in his own wisdom and indicators of his readiness to fulfil the role for which he has strived for so long. When Gandalf advises him against using the Palantír, Aragorn disagrees and reminds Gandalf that the Palantír is his by right. Gandalf unequivocally acknowledges this yet still advocates caution. There is a hint of bitterness in Aragorn's reply that he has never yet been hasty in his long years of waiting and, once Gandalf has departed, Aragorn goes against his advice and does indeed look in the Palantír. It is a mark of both his growing confidence and his accurate reading of the desperate situation in which those who oppose the Enemy find themselves that he is prepared to act against the council of the mentor and friend who has guided him for so long, although, of course, we do not yet know precisely how long. In the event, it proves to be the right decision, but what Aragorn sees in the Palantír is about to set him on the road to his most dangerous challenge to date.

At first, however, his decisions are deemed highly debatable and Aragorn is himself initially unsure of how to proceed. But when he learns from Théoden precisely how many days it will take the Rohirrim to come to the aid of Gondor, he resolutely decides his course and states that he is going to take the Paths of the Dead. This announcement is greeted with consternation and pleas to reconsider since legend has it that no one may pass that way and survive. However, Aragorn will not be gainsaid and, once the Rohirrim have departed, he tells Legolas and Gimli of the terrible battle of wills which ensued as he directly confronted the Dark Lord in the Palantir. Through Merry's eyes we have already witnessed how dramatically Aragorn appeared to have aged overnight and now we learn this encounter with Sauron has left him practically exhausted. Yet Aragorn apparently mastered the Stone eventually and revealed to Sauron that an heir of Isildur still lives; a bold move for one who has spent his life concealing this very fact from the Enemy. But, as he explains to his companions, Sauron is not yet above fear. And it seems it was precisely the planting of this seed of doubt which was Aragorn's prime motivation for taking this undeniably risky action. By confronting Sauron directly, Aragorn has laid down the gauntlet, but this is no vain challenge by an ambitious potential ruler to one who stands in his way. We now see the wisdom of his strategy. Aragorn's move is a calculated gamble designed to draw out Sauron's hosts before they are ready, hopefully rendering the assault on Gondor less effective. Crucially, by forcing Sauron to focus his efforts on the war at hand, Aragorn hopes to aid Frodo the only way he can.

The stakes for taking such a risk are extremely high, and Aragorn is gambling, not only with the fate of others, but also with his own personal future. By exposing his true identity in this way, he no longer has the luxury of anonymity, of being a mere foot soldier in the war against Sauron. He now becomes the prime target for the wrath of the Enemy and should he fall into the hands of his foes, his fate would be terrible. Furthermore, at this stage in the action, Aragorn, unlike the reader, does not even know if Frodo and Sam still live. By placing himself in this precarious position, he has once again demonstrated his readiness to jeopardise his own safety and ambition for the greater good.

However, Aragorn's use of the Palantír has also revealed an unexpected problem. An enemy fleet is approaching from the South which will overwhelm

Gondor before the Rohirrim can arrive. With the situation apparently hopeless, the reason for Aragorn's stubborn determination to take the feared road through the mountain now becomes clear. With his knowledge of lore, Aragorn has successfully unravelled the various riddles that have been brought to him and has arrived at a solution. Trapped within the mountain is a shadow host cursed by Isildur for failing to fight Sauron at the end of the Second Age. If Aragorn can pass through the mountain and secure the aid of these most unlikely allies, he might just have a chance of reaching the enemy fleet before it sails for Minas Tirith. But it is a most daunting task and one that only the heir of Isildur can attempt. Gone now is the need for stealth and secrecy for it is only in his true guise that Aragorn can hope to accomplish what he must, but, characteristically, he asks no one to come with him on this potentially suicidal mission. It says much for both his leadership and the faith of those who know him that not a single man dissents.

While journeying to the haunted mountain, Aragorn and the Grey Company pause to rest for the night at Dunharrow. Here, Aragorn again meets Éowyn who has lost none of her desire for him and, fuelled by tales of victory at Helm's Deep, desperately wants to accompany him to war. She is, however, distraught at hearing of his plan to take the Paths of the Dead, believing such a course to be reckless in the extreme and guaranteed to result only in his death. She allows the matter to drop when in company but waylays Aragorn on his way to his rest and begs him to reconsider. Aragorn tries to reassure her, denying that he seeks death, and stating that, given the liberty to do so, he would remain in Rivendell, *'where my heart dwells'* [22]. Here, the too few and too veiled previous references to Arwen can leave the reader entirely wrong-footed. For those who hold out hope of a union between Aragorn and Éowyn, Aragorn's polite intransigence can make him appear unmoved even to the point of indifference. With the benefit of hindsight, we can see that he is informing Éowyn in as proper a manner as he is able, and without bluntly acknowledging that he is aware of her infatuation, that his affections are given to another. Éowyn considers his words but she either does not understand or chooses not to. And when Aragorn reminds her of her sworn duty to the king which she seems to be abandoning fecklessly, he incurs her wrath for doing so. Spurned and hurt, she boldly leaves him in no doubt about her own feelings. She wishes to go with him into battle, not only as a soldier to win renown but also because of her love for him.

The next morning, when Éowyn finds Aragorn still set on his chosen course, she tries again to dissuade him but her efforts are to no avail. Finally, she falls to her knees, pleading with him not to leave her behind. This time Aragorn is more curt and forthright in his refusal. In his abruptness, Aragorn might be considered to be cold and heartless, foolish even to dismiss the attentions of so desirable a maiden. But Aragorn is a man in a great hurry and, furthermore he is not at liberty to permit Éowyn to come with him. Quite apart from the fact that his heart is given to another, his hands are tied. He would need the consent of Théoden or Éomer to condone this but neither is present. We, the reader, might infer from his distress as he rode away quite how much it has cost him to abandon her, but Éowyn is left feeling utterly wretched and desolate at his rejection.

The subsequent terrifying journey through the Paths of the Dead is a rite of passage for Aragorn. This is his moment when more is asked of him personally than at any time in all his years, and yet, we do not see this terrible route through Aragorn's eyes, but through Gimli's whose own fear serves to underscore Aragorn's implied courage. The dwarf is almost mad with terror, and it is hard to imagine that Aragorn would be less afraid himself, but if he is, we do not see it, and we are told that the Company only dares pass through this dreadful place because of the indomitable might of Aragorn's will.

The image we have of Aragorn now is of a great hero emerging to claim his destiny. Gone forever is the downtrodden, despised stranger sitting unloved in the corner of the inn; this is the returning king coming into his own, a great leader of men; men who are prepared to follow him to death, because, as Éowyn says, they love him. And at the Stone of Erech, itself a relic of his lost kingdom, Aragorn exudes might and majesty as he summons the Oathbreakers to him. It is a crucial moment and a watershed in Aragorn's journey to kingship. Only by acquiring the fealty of the Dead can Aragorn hope to play to the full his part in the coming war and simultaneously retain any hope of claiming the throne of Gondor. For the moment, at least, accomplishing these twin desires allows Aragorn to travel the same path.

His mind set, and bereft of the uncertainties over his route which have plagued him since Gandalf's fall, Aragorn is a stronger character, more resolute and lordly than we have previously seen him. The more archaic and formal nature of his speech reflects this change, Aragorn's dialogue with Éowyn being very different from that of Strider in Bree. Furthermore, his success in summoning the Oathbreakers is a substantial demonstration of the legitimacy of his claim to the throne. And when he emerges unscathed from the path beneath the mountain, Halbarad heralds the arrival of the king by unfurling Arwen's great standard, although in the deathly darkness of the Blackroot Vale we do not yet discover what emblems are displayed upon it. Having secured the aid of the Oathbreakers, there ensues a desperate race against time to reach Pelargir to intercept the enemy ships before they sail for Minas Tirith. Aragorn and his men show their mettle by riding with all speed on a journey the like of which, we are told, only Aragorn has endured before, the unearthly Shadow Host following in their wake. The king may have returned, but the war is far from won and Aragorn still has a mountain to scale before he can sit upon his throne.

~oo0oo~

As the story turns to the plight of Minas Tirith, we hear no more of Aragorn's adventures until his unexpected and triumphant arrival at the Battle of the Pelennor. Disembarking from the captured enemy ships in one of the most thrilling and heroic moments in the entire story, Aragorn, with Andúril a flame in his hand, the Star of Elendil on his brow, rides at the head of a now great army in time to change the course of the battle from one of anticipated defeat to one of unlooked for victory. Yet in spite of his triumph, Aragorn does not storm into the city to claim it as his own. We are now sufficiently familiar with his character not to be surprised that he chooses to wait outside the city walls so as not to cause dissent within while the Enemy is still undefeated, even though the Steward is dead and, as the victor in the battle, there would seem to be nothing to stand in his way.

He does, however, come to the Houses of Healing as the need for a healer who can cure the Black Breath is great. He is tired, tetchy and short of patience with the long-winded excuses of the staff for their inability to provide him with *athelas* leaves, but the extent of Aragorn's healing ability and the significance behind his possession of this skill is now revealed. By curing those afflicted, he is proven beyond doubt to be the true king since it turns out that only one from the bloodline of Elendil has the capacity to imbue *athelas* with the power to banish the Black Breath. First he successfully heals Faramir, although the effort of doing so appears to take Aragorn to the brink of death himself. By quite what means Aragorn imparts his skills, is not made clear, but some form of communication with his patient evidently takes place since, when Faramir awakes, introductions are unnecessary and the new Steward already knows and reveres his king.

Aragorn next turns to heal the stricken Éowyn. As he comes to her bedside, he talks most eloquently of his sorrow for what has befallen her, expressing his regret at his inability to return her love and his failure to help her: *'Few other griefs amid the ill chances of this world have more bitterness and shame for a man's heart than to behold the love of a lady so fair and brave that can not be returned'* [23]. Revealing depth of insight into the affairs of the heart, Aragorn tells Éomer that his sister does not really know or love him and that he represented nothing more than a means of escape from the thankless role of nursemaid, a chance to win renown, something for which her heart of a shieldmaiden yearned. Later, Éowyn is able to find true love with Faramir and her love for Aragorn remains more that of a young soldier for a great captain than of a woman for a potential lover. But Aragorn shows his understanding and empathy for others by his astute interpretation of Éowyn's feelings, and, amid so many other demands, his concern for her is a sign of his generosity of heart and the care that he has for all whom he encounters.

Merry is the furthest from death of the three characters we witness Aragorn attend and the hobbit quickly bounces back, asking for food and, in a delightful jest, Aragorn, teasingly rebukes him for being a poor soldier for having lost his pack in battle, his own love and affection for the hobbits demonstrably beyond doubt. Aragorn then labours long into the night healing all those in need, in spite of being weary from battle and barely having slept for days. On his cloak, he still wears the Elessar and so it is that his own people come to call him by the name of 'Elfstone'.

The following morning we learn of what befell the Grey Company between when we last saw them, racing from the stone at Erech, and their arrival at the Harlond in the morning of battle. Tolkien himself acknowledged that the solution to the difficultly of bringing Aragorn unexpectedly to the field of battle whilst simultaneously filling in the reader on the events which brought him to that point in the story were far from satisfactory. Consequently, we see the capture of the enemy fleet at Pelargir through the eyes of Legolas as he tells the tale to Merry and Pippin. We learn how Aragorn gathered to him a great host of men from the southern fiefs as the tumultuous news of the coming of an heir of Isildur was greeted with feverous excitement. We discover what a great and mighty lord Aragorn has became, although his sole concern throughout this entire mission was only that they would arrive too late to save the city of Minas Tirith. Against the main story of Frodo's and Sam's endeavours as the humble heroes of the tale, Aragorn is now undoubtedly fulfilling the role of the traditional epic hero, as we rather suspected he might. But the final outcome for any of the characters is still uncertain as it is by no means clear at this stage which, if either, of these parallel stories will ultimately triumph.

As the Captains debate their final stand, Aragorn fully endorses Gandalf's proposal that the remnant of their hosts should ride as decoys to the Black Gate. They themselves would have little hope of survival against the overwhelming might of Mordor yet, by supporting this plan, Aragorn further reveals the depth of his courage and his willingness to sacrifice his life for others. He rightly considers such an action to be merely a continuation of the course that he himself began by revealing his identity to Sauron in the Palantír. His stance also demonstrates unequivocally that Aragorn is no power-grasping adventurer; he will only claim the vacant throne when Sauron is defeated and the war finally over. He appoints Imrahil as ruler of the city and submits himself to Gandalf's lead, acknowledging that the success they have had so far has largely been due to the wizard's efforts. There is, however, no question that Aragorn desires to be king; his quick remark to Pippin that his House would be named Telcontar suggests that he has spent at least a little time indulging in the very human and very understandable activity of day-dreaming about his future role. Nonetheless, it is quite clear that his ambition is not one of personal vanity. He is the rightful heir and it is his duty to strive to fulfil the role for which he was born. It is one with divine implications although that aspect has yet to become apparent to the reader.

As Aragorn leads the host of the West towards the final battle at the Black Gate, some of the men under his command are overcome by fear of that dreadful place. Yet, instead of punishing them for their cowardice, Aragorn once again exhibits compassion and mercy by allowing them to retreat with honour, giving them a task to do that is within their capabilities. Aragorn may fight with medieval weaponry, but his is a very modern heart.

With the taunts of the Mouth of Sauron echoing in their ears, the final battle rages and all appears lost. But against all hope, the gamble pays off, the Ring is destroyed and the war is effectively over. The reign of Sauron is ended and Aragorn is made king. In a wonderful, joyful passage, we see Sam and Frodo finally reunited with Strider although at first they do not recognise him with his unfamiliar garb and his no longer grim face. This reunion is followed by Aragorn's glorious return to the city, where, at his coronation, we finally meet the king in all his majesty and splendour.Nonetheless, beneath the black armour and white robes, this is the same man that we met in Bree. With characteristic humility, Aragorn takes none of the credit for the victory of the West, instead acknowledging the efforts of others, principally Gandalf and Frodo whom he asks to assist with his crowning. Now, his journey is complete and the people of Gondor behold their king at last.

Aragorn slots into his role as monarch with remarkable ease for a man who has hitherto led such an apparently lowly existence. As yet, we know nothing of his upbringing in Rivendell or his education at the hands of the Elves which long ago prepared him for this role. Still, with demonstrable wisdom he competently sets about ordering his realm. He makes peace with his enemies, frees the slaves and grants provincial rule of those lands which are henceforth embraced under the benevolent umbrella of his vast domain. His dignified road to kingship has earned him the respect and gratitude of the leaders of the realms of Men now under his protection, as well as the leaders of the other races. Consequently, he is able to form strong alliances which secures the peace and allows the people of Middle-earth to prosper and thrive in the coming age. The return of the king is clearly a force for great good.

We see very little of Aragorn 'the king' in *The Lord of the Rings*. Throughout most of the story, we meet only Aragorn 'the ranger'. Here, he is arguably at his most human. Once he becomes king, it is as if a barrier surrounds him, and we rarely see the accessible face of Strider, only the distant figure of the monarch. This lack of approachability may have been a deliberate shift on Tolkien's behalf to reinforce the illusion of the distance between king and subjects, or it might merely be a consequence of the general compression of the story which occurs in *The Return of the King*. On occasion though, the mask is removed and we glimpse again the familiar character of the man we have come to know. When in Meduseld, perhaps significantly when not in his own realm, Aragorn jests in public with Éomer much as Strider might have done. In the company of the hobbits, he converses much as he always has, while he treats those whom he has long respected, particularly Galadriel and Celeborn, with the same deference he did in the past.

Only in one passage, as Gandalf takes him high up into Mindolluin to view his realm, do we see anything of Aragorn's inner thoughts as he embraces his new life. Now that he occupies the inevitably isolating position of king, Aragorn turns to the one person in whom he can confide his personal fears. For all that he is now the most powerful man in Middle-earth, he is still reluctant to lose his wisest councillor. Yet lose him he must and we learn that Aragorn is already troubled about the future of his realm. We could be forgiven for wondering if he is regretting spurning Éowyn, who is now healed and happy in the arms of Faramir. We do not yet understand the meaning of his comment that he will be old when the unborn babies in their mothers' wombs are also old, since we still do not know of his expected long life, though it is abundantly clear by now that he is no ordinary man. However, he takes the finding of the sapling of the White Tree as a symbol of hope and once this is in bloom in the Court of the Kings, Aragorn's secret is revealed. Arwen and her father, as well as all the lords and ladies of two Elven Realms, arrive in the city to see her wed to the king.

~oo0oo~

This then is the joyful conclusion to Aragorn's story, the traditional happy ending and few would begrudge him it. We now know that on all his long journeys and hard paths he travelled, Aragorn was nursing a love that he could not or would not claim. Quite how much this unfulfilled desire both tortured and comforted him in his loneliness, we can only guess, but it is clear that when Aragorn warned Merry that many hopes would wither in this bitter spring, he was not only fearful for Théoden's return to Edoras. Yet we do see something of the complexities extraneous to his relationship with Arwen in the grief of Elrond and his daughter at their parting. This was no diplomatic union between the lord of one realm and the king of another but a love match which came at a heavy personal cost to Arwen and her father.

Too quickly, it seems, we must leave Aragorn to rule his kingdom. As Galadriel tells us, he has now achieved everything he could possibly desire and has been given due reward for his labours. And this would be the end of Aragorn's story if it were not for the Appendices. Here, in these most fascinating bonus pages, something of the sheer scale of the history of Middle-earth is provided, if not in its entirety, then at least in far greater detail that we would possibly surmise from the text. Furthermore, much of this history deals with Aragorn and his ancestors, and between the various sections of *Appendix A* and *The Tale of Years* we can piece together a great deal. Integral to Aragorn's personality and motivation is the weight of his family history that he carries with him, and here we have the opportunity to read of the long, sad demise of the North Kingdom and the struggles of his forefathers. The combined influences of their many triumphs and failures inevitably played a part in shaping the values, principles and, ultimately, decisions of the man himself. Consequently, defending his people against his ancestral enemy has been his life's work. We discover that his dedication to this cause led him to venture abroad in his youth and we learn of the adventures of a young captain

Thorongil who served Rohan and Gondor so gallantly; a footnote in Gondor's history and yet one which provides an intriguing slant on our understanding of his relationship with Denethor. However, it is in the beautiful *The Tale of Aragorn and Arwen* that the mystery of Aragorn is unravelled further.

It is often remarked that Aragorn does not grow as a character within the story, but if his story is considered to start with *The Tale of Aragorn and Arwen* then his growth is considerable. In spite of all that we have learned so far, it still comes as quite a surprise to discover that Aragorn was raised at Rivendell as a foster son of Master Elrond, a revelation which belatedly lends another dimension to Aragorn's character entirely. So, the grim ranger was not always a lonely wanderer, he once had a secure and comfortable home with a loving and wise family. As a child he was given the name, 'Estel', meaning 'Hope' and actually grew up unaware of the identity of his true father or of the burden that he must take up on reaching adulthood. Discovering all this makes Aragorn's subsequent hard life and his long years in the wild all the more heart-breaking. He has clearly suffered considerably, but it is in his unattainable love for Arwen that he has endured the most. Now we have the chance to read of their first encounter and of how Aragorn loved her from that very first moment. We come to understand why, at Weathertop, he chose to recite that part of *The Tale of Tinúviel* which deals with the romance aspect of Beren's and Lúthien's story, a romance which, in many ways, mirrors his own.

His early infatuation was to remain unrequited for nearly thirty years yet, in all that time, he never sought comfort elsewhere. In Tolkien's world, once a heart is given to another, there is no breaking of that bond, even after death. Even so, knowing that he was the last of such a long, unbroken line of succession that would be doomed to extinction if he failed to win Arwen's love must have been a desperately hard burden for a young man to bear. Happily for Aragorn, Arwen, of course, eventually came to return his love, and it is only in the Appendices that we discover the part played by Galadriel in bringing this couple together. In her wisdom, Galadriel evidently recognised the worth of the tired young captain who came to her realm on his way home to her son-in-law's house and acted as matchmaker for her granddaughter. Dressing Aragorn as an elf-lord, she ensured that, on first meeting him again after so long, Arwen perceived only the great lord that Aragorn might yet become and not merely the weary traveller seeking rest. Now we can understand Frodo's vision at Cerin Amroth as he beheld Aragorn as he once was, young and fair, clothed in white and standing on the very spot that he and Arwen pledged their lives to each other nearly forty years previously. But by accepting Aragorn as her intended husband, we find that Arwen had to make an unenviable choice. To wed a mortal, she must renounce her own immortality, a fate which would sunder her eternally from her Elven kin. That she was prepared to endure this for the sake of a mortal man speaks volumes about both the strength of her love and the measure of the man for whom she was prepared to do this.

However, we now discover there was a further, and completely unexpected, twist in their tale. Aragorn might have secured Arwen's love, but he still had to gain the consent of her father. And it is here, at the very end of the book that we come to the crux of the riddle of Strider. Elrond refused to allow his daughter to marry Aragorn until he had claimed the kingship of both Gondor and Arnor. By permitting even this, Elrond was making an enormous sacrifice as he would still have to endure the eternal separation from his daughter that her choice demanded. However, Aragorn is now revealed as a distance descendant of Elrond's brother, Elros, and by denying Aragorn his desire until he had fulfilled this condition, Elrond would at least have the consolation of seeing his brother's line restored to the leadership of the fledgling dominion of Men. So Aragorn endured long years, and exactly how many we now discover, battling against a seemingly unconquerable enemy in the hope of one day attaining his prize. Yet somehow, and in this we are again reminded of the extraordinary strength of this unique character, he still retained hope that one day he would succeed, but it is little wonder that he became so grim to look upon. Furthermore, knowing exactly how much Aragorn has personally invested in achieving his goals, his willingness to sacrifice everything he desired when those goals were finally within his grasp, suddenly takes on a greater poignancy and raises our respect for him even further.

Finally, after so long apart, it is a joy to discover that Aragorn and Arwen still had so many years of happiness ahead of them and that their reign was a long and glorious one. In fact, throughout the Appendices, Tolkien heaps praise onto his king, almost as if he is compensating for having given him a less that auspicious introduction. We learn that Aragorn and Arwen successfully raised a family and produced an heir to continue the line of kings. In a tale so underpinned with a sense of loss, theirs is a story that points triumphantly to the future and is a beacon of hope for the ages yet to come. But even the best fairy-tales have to end somewhere and the final chapter in Aragorn's story is the remarkable manner of his death.

On first reading, it is in this that he probably surprises most of all. His decision to relinquish his life willingly might seem as if he simply abandons Arwen who is distraught at his passing. But Aragorn's comment that there is more than memory beyond the circles of the world implies that he has faith in what is yet to come, and, as his life slips away, Arwen calls him by his childhood name of 'Estel', or 'Hope.' We might assume that the name was given to the infant Aragorn purely in the expectation of what he would achieve in his lifetime, an expectation which he fulfilled admirably, and, without the benefit of later publications, it is doubtful we can fully appreciate the significance of the name at this particular moment. Even nurturing optimism in an existence beyond death, Aragorn's dignified passing, nonetheless, represents the very last of his many acts of courage. The following passage from *The Tale of Aragorn and Arwen* suggests that he departed serenely and at peace; these eloquent lines serving as a fitting epitaph for such a great man and they provide the most lyrical answer to the riddle of Strider.

'Then a great beauty was revealed in him, so that all who after came there looked on him in wonder; for they saw that the grace of his youth, and the valour of his manhood, and the wisdom and majesty of his age were blended together. And long there he lay, an image of the splendour of the Kings of Men in glory undimmed before the breaking of the world' [24].

Tolkien considered *The Tale of Aragorn and Arwen* to be the most important part of the Appendices precisely because of Aragorn's gracious acceptance of his approaching death. Furthermore, he added, *'it is a part of the essential story, and only placed so, because it could not be worked into the main narrative without destroying its structure'* [25]. That structure was, of course, the hobbit-centric nature of a story originally conceived as a sequel to *The Hobbit*. However, as Aragorn's original persona, the hobbit 'Trotter', evolved into the man 'Strider', and a man with a great destiny at that, the author was presented with the unenviable challenge of integrating his long back story into the main text. A full discussion of Aragorn's complex evolution is discussed in the next chapter, but Tolkien's solution of incorporating Aragorn's tale as a veiled sub-plot, which is only fully revealed after the completion of the main story, has undoubtedly been to the detriment of the level of appreciation felt for this most remarkable of characters. Far from being the bland personality he is sometimes perceived to be by the critics, Aragorn is a man whose heart beats with an unfulfilled passion and a driving ambition. He is without question a very heroic hero, possessing the most honourable of human qualities. As Gandalf tells Pippin, he is strong, stern, bold, determined and able to take his own counsel, taking risks at need. We might also add that he is courageous, wise, honourable, self-sacrificing, charismatic, gracious, loyal, generous, self-effacing, companionable, unpretentious, modest, inspiring and even possesses a sense of humour. And, although we see him in a variety of guises and roles, he consistently brings those same qualities to all of them. As the story unfolds, we have no trouble recognising his heroism; he is a character who easily earns our admiration. With thoughtful reading, there is no reason for him not to also earn our affection.

Chapter 2: Trotter

Of all the many and varied characters in *The Lord of the Rings*, the identity of no other would prove quite as elusive as that of Aragorn.Initially cast as a hobbit named Trotter, he eventually became established as a man towards the end of 1939, yet even then it would take nearly a decade before he would develop fully into the character of great stature that we find in *The Lord of the Rings*. During the early years of composition, the question of his true identity was an ongoing riddle, and only with the publication of *The History of Middle-earth* has it become possible to appreciate quite how difficult and protracted was that evolution. Throughout the first drafts, Tolkien repeatedly asked himself the question: who is Trotter? Even after completion of the very last chapter, amendments were still made; some were only added to the proof copy immediately prior to the publication of the first edition, while others did not enter the narrative until the second printing many years later. Of one thing we can be certain, Tolkien never set out with the intention that his hobbit ranger should become a great king descended from the heroes of his wider mythology. As he wrote to W.H. Auden in 1955: *'Strider sitting in the corner at the inn was a shock, and I had no more idea who he was than had Frodo'* [1].

Part of the problem appears to have been a lack of an obvious blueprint for Trotter's role even though a central feature of *The Hobbit* had been 'the returning king' in the shape of Thorin Oakenshield. While most of the other major players in the hobbit sequel, such as Gandalf, Bilbo, Gollum and Sauron, had either already appeared in the earlier work or, like the new generation of hobbits, could be incorporated within the emerging structure without too much difficulty, Trotter proved less amenable. Possibly, having already mentioned the existence of a king in the earlier work, Tolkien was not immediately drawn towards developing a character that would eventually emerge as a king returning from exile. This king from *The Hobbit*, of whom the wild and wicked things had not heard, might only be a vague and remote figure, but it would be quite reasonable to assume from the dwarves' chatter as they rode to Rivendell that a king was still ruling at that time. When revising the Prologue to *The Lord of the Rings* in 1948, Tolkien was able to exploit the vagueness of the dwarves' remarks by explaining that there had indeed *'once been a King at Fornost away North... But there had been no King for many ages'* [2]. The 'king' could then be dismissed as merely a generic reference to all the kings from the past to whom the law-abiding hobbits still deferred in memory, since it was the kings of old who had established the principles of governance to which they still adhered.

Perhaps it is fortunate that no mention was made in *The Hobbit* of any men dwelling in or around Bilbo's homeland. There are the men of Laketown and Dale, but these lived far away in lands that were of peripheral importance to the new story. Bard is clearly a forerunner of Aragorn, although he bears little resemblance to Strider's early persona of the hobbit, Trotter. Described as a tall, dark haired man, who, like Aragorn, is grim-faced, he too is the dispossessed heir to an ancient realm that no longer exists. Like Aragorn, he carries with him a great ancestral weapon with which he performs great deeds. Furthermore, in the early drafts of *The Lord of the Rings*, Bard's descendents initially appeared destined for a significant role in the sequel. Brand, the grandson of Bard is described as a strong king, his rule extending to *'much land to the south of the great falls'* [3] which would equate with the region that eventually became Gondor. The descendents of Bard, however, were soon to be displaced in importance by the descendents of Elendil.

The 'new hobbit' began in much the same vein as its prequel with Bilbo hosting a party and, on 19th December 1937, Tolkien wrote to his publisher, Stanley Unwin,to inform him that he had in the last three days written the first chapter. It was to be the first of many preliminary drafts composed throughout the long evolution of *The Lord of the Rings*, but noticeably absent from the original outline was any reference to a tall man sitting in the corner of the inn at Bree. At the outset, all that was planned for that stage of the hobbits' journey was that Bingo, the early name for Bilbo's nephew, and his companions, Odo, Frodo Took and Marmaduke, would spend the night at an inn where they would find a jolly landlord who would give them news of Gandalf. The journey to Rivendell, however, was to be passed over swiftly.

Progress on the story was initially rapid, but after a few months, and with the hobbits still not having left the Shire, work stopped for about half a year. Not surprisingly, the demands of Tolkien's day job often dictated the timetable, and the story would of necessity be written in fits and starts as the Oxford academic year permitted.When work resumed in the summer holiday of August 1938, and after only a few days of writing, the hobbits very quickly arrived in Bree. Here, they encountered the strange and wild hobbit known as Trotter sitting alone in a corner of the inn. In spite of Trotter being described as a *'queer-looking, brown-faced hobbit'* [4], he is dressed not unlike the later

Strider except that he wears wooden shoes rather than tall, well-fitting boots. Butterbur, who answers to the name of Barnabas and is himself a hobbit in this early conception, replies to Bingo's enquiry about this odd character much as his human counterpart does about Strider, although the presence of the wooden shoes serves to create a very different image.

'O! that is one of the wild folk - rangers we call 'em. He has been coming in now and again (in autumn and winter mostly) the last few years; but he seldom talks. Not but what he can tell some rare tales when he has a mind, you take my word. What his right name is I never heard, but he's known round here as Trotter. You can hear him coming along the road in those shoes: clitter-clap – when he he walks on a path which isn't often. Why he wears 'em? Well that I can't say' [5].

Nonetheless, given the huge transformation in Trotter's identity that had yet to take place, his introductory scene is remarkably similar in content and dialogue to the final narrative. Trotter calls Bingo over and throws back his hood to reveal a shaggy head of hair. In spite of some of it hanging over his forehead, Bingo is still aware of a pair of keen dark eyes which make him feel as uncomfortable as Strider's did Frodo. The ensuing conversation surrounding the incident with the Ring, as well as much of the substance of the conversation which occurs later in the parlour, changed very little. The matter of Gandalf's letter is present as well as the question of Trotter's reward. So, too, is his discomfort at the memory of the Black Riders although it is difficult to imagine his later incarnation saying, *'they give me the creeps!'* [6].

The episode as a whole, however, is noticeably less sinister and, in spite of the lurking menace of the Black Riders, lacks the gravity and the sense of impending doom of the final version. This is, in part, because Gandalf is not missing, the treachery of Saruman not yet having entered the story. Gandalf is, instead, merely waiting for the hobbits further along the road having visited Bree only a few days earlier. Also, Barnabas is less suspicious of Trotter than Barliman is of Strider. Consequently, for all the similarity with the final dialogue, there is no denying that 'Trotter the Hobbit' is unable to convey the same air of danger and mystery that surrounds 'Strider the Man'. In particular, the scene suffers from the absence of Aragorn's powerful physical presence. Unlike his later counterpart, Trotter is unable to tower over the hobbits as he reveals his broken sword, so the sense of how dangerous he could be if he chose never materializes.

However, in spite of the jollier atmosphere, the identity of this strange hobbit would nonetheless remain a mystery. During his summer holiday of August 1938 while staying at Sidmouth in Devon, Tolkien made notes on how the story was to proceed and among those notes appears the oft repeated question: who is Trotter? It would appear that Tolkien's own uncertainty over the identity of Trotter became an essential aspect of the character himself. Bingo suspects a disguise but, although the rangers were not considered quite trustworthy, he still finds something friendly, even familiar about Trotter's speech. Trotter is not who he appears to be, even if no one, not even the author, has any idea at this stage of his identity. Hardly surprisingly then, in this first draft, the letter confirming Trotter as a friend, which is initially produced by Trotter himself, lacks any revelation about his true name. With no other role envisaged, at first, Trotter's sole purpose seemed to be one comparable with that of Tom Bombadil - to be a guide for the unworldly hobbits in the absence of Gandalf, since, even in his hobbit persona, Trotter possessed knowledge and skills far in excess of those usually associated with his kind.

When embarking upon his hobbit sequel, Tolkien lamented to Stanley Unwin that he did not know what to do with hobbits except to make them comic, but that, *'their comedy is suburban unless it is set against things more elemental'* [7]. In making Trotter a different type of hobbit, one certainly less comic and one apparently harbouring some secret, be it only that he is someone other than who he appears to be, although that in itself inevitably begs the question of why a disguise should be necessary, Tolkien appears to be casting Trotter as a foil for the other hobbits' comic banter, perhaps in the hope that this darker character would introduce some of the balance he was seeking. Yet, in spite of his appearance of being a ruffian, and throughout all the various identities which were to emerge later, Trotter was invariably a benign figure and a force for good.

With both Trotter and Barnabas portrayed as hobbits, there is a noticeable lack of Men at this stage in the tale. Unsurprisingly, since the story began as a sequel to *The Hobbit*, the first men to appear are from the realm of Bard who, in the second draft of the opening chapter, arrived at Bag End bearing gifts for Bilbo to give to the children at his party Also mentioned in this draft are *'great lumbering tow-haired Men'* [8] who apparently drink all the beer in the inn in Hobbiton although these quickly disappeared without trace. By contrast, Bree, in its earliest conception, was inhabited solely by Men who were described very much as in *The Lord of the Rings* as *'brown-faced, dark haired, broad, shortish, cheerful and independent'* [9], an isolated community that no one could remember how it came into existence. Although this description remained unchanged, in the next conception, and for some time to come, all the people of Bree, including Bill Ferny, instead became hobbits rather than men. As a result, even The Prancing Pony had a round front door! While the concept of the rangers inevitably arises with the appearance of Trotter who, from the first, is introduced as one of their number, these, too, are also exclusively hobbits at first. Inevitably, there are no Dúnedain or their kingdoms of Arnor and Gondor, and so when Tom Bombadil takes a brooch for Goldberry from the hoard in the Barrow, he does not recall the lady who once wore it.

In fact, the description of Elrond in *The Hobbit* demonstrates the vagueness of Tolkien's initial view of Men in this later age of Middle-earth. Elrond, the son of Eärendil had existed in the legendarium since the earliest Silmarillion, *The Sketch of the Mythology* which was written in the late 1920's, yet this is not the Elrond we meet when Bilbo arrives at Rivendell.Devoid of his roots, Elrond is described as: *'an elf-friend – one of those people whose fathers came into the strange stories before the beginning of History, the wars of the evil goblins and the elves and the first men in the north. In those days of our tale there were still some people who had both elves and heroes of the North for ancestors, and Elrond the master of the house was their chief'* [10].

Years later, Tolkien himself described his use of the name Elrond in *The Hobbit* as a fortunate accident which, when he came to write the sequel, would provide a welcome link to the earlier ages. However, at the time of writing *The Hobbit* in the early 1930's, the means of linking his existing stories of his mythology with this later age of hobbits had yet to be devised. The necessary bridge would appear in the emerging story of Númenor which was only in an embryonic state at the time Tolkien began writing *The Lord of the Rings*. Its parallel development throughout the years Tolkien was also writing his hobbit sequel would increasingly to impact upon the story in general and upon the nature of Trotter in particular.

The consequences of the emergence of Númenor is the subject of the next chapter but it was not long before oblique references to those of Númenórean descent began appearing in the drafts of *The Lord of the Rings*. Before the story progressed even as far as the hobbits' arrival at Bree, amendments had been made to the scene on the Barrow Downs which introduced the very first mention of the men who dwelt in those parts long ago. When Tom now comments on the brooch, he says: *'Fair was she who long ago wore this* on her shoulder, and Goldberry shall wear it now, and we shall not forget them, the vanished folk, the old kings' [11]. And of the swords he found, he says they were, 'made many ages ago by men out of the West. They were foes of the Ring-lord' [12]. When the hobbits crossed a dyke, it was said to be the boundary of an old kingdom about which, 'Tom seemed to remember something unhappy and would not say much' [13]. It would still to be many years before the Witch-king of Angmar would enter the story so, here, Tom is referring to the fall of Elendil, and, on the journey to Weathertop, Trotter firmly anchors *The Lord of the Rings* within the larger mythology by telling of the importance of Weathertop as a fort and look-out post for the former king. The first of the Númenórean realms to emerge, however, was Gondor. Known originally as the land of Ond, it did not appear in the drafts until August 1939 so, when Trotter states there were big people away to the South, at that stage, he is most likely referring to the people in the south of the Shire who had been causing trouble. According to Trotter, the north and east were empty, a place where only adventurous rangers came occasionally.

With Trotter now accompanying the other hobbits, the action moves to Weathertop where the scene changed little from its early draft. Trotter recounts *The Tale of Tinúviel* with a 'queer eager face' [14] very much as Strider does and, later that night, he leaps out of the darkness with 'a flaming fire-brand in each hand' [15] to drive away the Black Riders. He even uses athelas to treat the injured Bingo although initially the plant is not associated with the Men of the West. Aid comes in the shape of Glorfindel and Trotter's connection with Rivendell is confirmed, as it is later, by this meeting. Glorfindel addresses Trotter as 'Rimbedir', the name by which he is known in Elrond's house. Just as his later counterpart is a man of many names, Trotter, too, has his aliases. Given the number of names that came to be associated with Aragorn, it comes as no surprise that 'Rimbedir' also underwent a series of changes. 'Padathir' was one of apparently several experimental names which were later superseded by 'Du-finnion' and 'Torfir' before eventually becoming the 'Dúnadan'.

By the time the company arrives at Rivendell, Bingo's view of Trotter is very like Frodo's is of Strider in that he admits he was suspicious of him at first but has grown fond of him. In conversation with Gandalf, Bingo raises the question of Trotter's identity and tells Gandalf that he believes he has seen Trotter somewhere before. All Bingo receives by way of an answer from Gandalf is that all hobbits 'seem to remind me of one another' [16]. Yet Bingo's question prompts Tolkien to leave another note in the margin asking: who is Trotter? Nonetheless, Trotter would remain a hobbit for at least another year.

This phase of writing ended with Bingo chatting to Gloin at the feast, but when work resumed, Tolkien returned to the very beginning of the story and started all over again. At this point, he decided that the Bree-folk should not to be hobbits and that rangers were best not as hobbits either. This appears to be the very first emergence of the possibility that Trotter might not be a hobbit at all. Alternatively, if Trotter was to remain a hobbit, Tolkien reasoned that he ought to be someone very well known, and for the time being he experimented with this option. His initial thought was that Trotter could be Bilbo in disguise which would be compatible with Bingo's feeling on first meeting him that he really knew Trotter's identity all along. This scenario, however, would prove limited because of the 'happy ever after' ending to Bilbo's story already published in *The Hobbit*. The next thought was that Trotter should be Fosco Took, Bilbo's first cousin who disappeared when a young lad and for whose disappearance Gandalf was blamed. Here Tolkien was capitalizing upon a suggestion in the first chapter of *The Hobbit* that Gandalf was believed to have been responsible for the disappearance of several young hobbits who went off *'into the Blue for mad adventures'* [17]. This idea never materialized, but the possibility that Trotter was actually a character in disguise, a notion implied right from the beginning by Butterbur's mysterious introduction, had now firmly taken root.

This second phase of writing came to a halt before the hobbits even reached Bree, while the third phase involved another complete rewrite of the entire story as it stood at that time.   Christopher Tolkien dates this phase to after October 1938 but before August 1939, and when complete, there would then be six versions of the opening chapter in existence. Frodo now replaces Bingo as Bilbo's nephew and the nature of the people at Bree is altered once more to become the familiar mix of men and hobbits which was retained into *The Lord of the Rings*. Tolkien clearly had difficulty settling on the origins of the Bree men since there are apparently numerous uncompleted drafts on this matter. They were variously described as *'descendants of the sons of Bëor'* [18] or, alternatively, *'the return of the Kings of Men over the Great Seas'* [19], a Númenórean ancestry they would eventually lose. For a time, the rangers also became a mix of both hobbits and men, and, although the North Kingdom as a separate entity had yet to be devised, the ranger men were finally given their Númenórean roots. Now consistently described as: *'the last remnant of the kingly people from beyond the Seas'*

[20], these rangers were said to be few in number and seldom seen, although, unlike their mistrusted counterparts from both the earlier and later drafts, they were welcome in Bree as *'bringers of news and tellers of strange tales'* [21]. Aragorn's rangers, therefore, became established before he did.

In spite of this increased presence of men in the story and those with Númenórean ancestry at that, Trotter stubbornly remained a hobbit, although the possibility that he is not what he appears continues. Butterbur now replies to Frodo's inquiry about the mysterious figure in the corner of the inn: *'I don't rightly know. He is one of the wandering folk – Rangers, we call them. Not that he really is a Ranger, if you understand me, though he behaves like one. He seems to be a hobbit of some kind'* [22].

Yet, possibly by the end of 1938 and most certainly well before August 1939, the story was again at a halt and with the action ceased in the exact same place as the first phase - in Rivendell.Christopher Tolkien believes that little was written between February 1939 and the summer of that year when a new set of notes appeared which were unequivocally dated as August 1939. Tolkien was apparently unhappy with the current structure, although it seems there is no specific evidence to suggest why. However, in mid-September, and in spite of the recent outbreak of war, he still wrote to Stanley Unwin expressing a determination to complete the work. His solution to this current impasse was to attempt another rewrite, this time with Bilbo as the hero, although, again, this was inevitably doomed to failure because of the boundaries to Bilbo's tale imposed by the ending of *The Hobbit*.

Trotter was becoming something of a stumbling block with further evidence in the drafts of Tolkien continuing to ponder the question of his identity: *'Who is Trotter? A Ranger or a Hobbit?'* [23] The next thought was that the plot would work better if Trotter was a hobbit under Gandalf's influence and so Trotter became Peregrin Boffin in disguise. This change primarily arose because Tolkien decided that Gandalf had never instructed Frodo to leave Hobbiton and was terribly upset to discover that he had done just that. Peregrin would be another favourite nephew of Bilbo's, so, at this stage of development, Tolkien envisaged Bilbo having two nephews: Frodo Baggins and Peregrin Boffin, with Peregrin being the elder of the two. Peregrin was a grandson of Donnamira Took, Bilbo's mother's second sister. A young lad of five years when Bilbo returned from his adventures, dark haired and lanky, he dreamed of mountains and far away places, encouraged, or so his father believed, by his Uncle Bilbo's tales. As a result of this unwelcome influence,

Peregrin was banned from visiting Bilbo. However, determined to have adventures of his own, Peregrin eventually ran away from home. The first time he did so, he was found still within the Shire, if half starved, but after that initial adventure, he disappeared for good and it was Bilbo who got the blame. In this new guise of Peregrin Boffin, Trotter now acquired a proper name along with his pseudonym and a true identity which he kept concealed behind his ranger disguise. Although that identity remained a hobbit one for the time being, this transformation still represented another small step in Trotter's progress towards becoming Aragorn.

In the next draft of the scenes at Rivendell, Peregrin, like Strider, missed the feast, but only because his help was required in the kitchens; none of Elrond's children, including Arwen, having yet entered the story. When Trotter appears in the Hall of Fire, Bilbo greets him very much as he does Strider, and Frodo is similarly surprised that his uncle and travelling companion know each other. Bilbo requires Peregrin's help with a song he is writing, just as he does Strider's, and Elrond says that Bilbo's friend, here called 'Ethelion', shall be found. However, before Trotter can be brought to the Hall of Fire, and apparently right in the middle of writing the script, Tolkien evidently had a complete, and very sudden, change of heart about Trotter's identity and wrote, *'Trotter had better not be a hobbit – but a Ranger, remainder of Western men, as originally planned'* [24].

This very first suggestion that Trotter should be connected with the men of Númenor was a watershed moment in the development of the character, even though the abruptness with which the change was introduced suggests that the thought had been brewing for a while even if it had not actually been committed to paper. As Christopher Tolkien points out, Tolkien's assertion that the idea was one 'originally planned' can not possibly refer to the very first drafts of *The Lord of the Rings* as there is no doubt Trotter was at first intended to be a hobbit.

Yet even now, with the question of Trotter's identity being raised once again and a possible answer emerging, Trotter was still to remain a hobbit for a while longer. And before the hobbit character was dispensed with for good, he was provided with an opportunity to recount how he came to be wearing wooden shoes. Trotter's role in the hunt for Gollum now enters the story and, at the Council of Elrond, he tells how he tracked the creature through Fangorn Forest to the Dead Marshes. Trotter seems as reluctant as Aragorn to elaborate upon the 'deadly perils' he encountered during that search, although he does reveal that he was captured and taken to Mordor where he was only saved from death by Gandalf himself. It is left to Frodo to guess from his story that Trotter had been tortured and that his feet hurt, hence the need for wooden shoes, items that were inevitably dispensed with once he became a Man. Then, Trotter was instead said to have been captured in Moria, and, while all suggestion of Aragorn being a captive of the Dark Lord was removed from *The Lord of the Rings*, an echo of Trotter's experiences remained in Aragorn's evil memories of Moria, his perils on the Morgul Vale and his dread of the Black Riders. As noted earlier, Trotter's discomfiture at the mention of the Black Riders was present even from the very first draft of his conversation in the palour in the Prancing Pony and is one of those pieces which survived his transformation into a Man even though the original reason for Trotter's fell memories did not.

Trotter was not, however, the first named character in *The Lord of the Rings* to be awarded a Númenórean ancestry. Boromir now enters the narrative and, although he would temporarily lose this status, he is said to be a man from the land of Ond, the first of the two Númenórean kingdoms to emerge. Not that his ancestry impresses Frodo, the merits of whose potential companions are discussed after the Council of Elrond. Frodo concludes that Trotter, here still a hobbit, will be the brains of the party since Boromir is *'only one of the big folk, and they are not as wise as hobbits'* [25]. At this point, Gandalf speaks in Boromir's defense and reminds Frodo that the man is of an ancient race which the hobbits have not met before. Even so, Tolkien himself had doubts about including Boromir in the Company. Having such physically diverse characters would inevitably affect their very disparate capabilities and, by the time the Company reached Caradhras, the problem of having the thus far very resourceful Trotter reduced to sitting helpless on a pony, while Boromir rescued all the hobbits single-handedly, was enough to finally tip the balance and Trotter's days as a hobbit were numbered. Subsequently, Tolkien changed his mind about Boromir's ancestry and amended the above statement about his origins with a note: *'Correct this. Only Trotter is of ancient race'* [26].

Eventually, in spite of a fleeting idea that Trotter might have been an elf from Elrond's household, possibly one of the Rivendell scouts and someone only pretending to be a ranger, the question of 'Who is Trotter' is answered at last. On an undated scrap of paper, Trotter's true name and identity at last emerges, and as a Man called 'Aragorn'. The name had, in fact, already arisen as a suggestion for Gandalf's horse and it clearly was not decided upon without much deliberation. According to John D. Rateliff, there is still in existence a piece of paper containing some thirty crossed out names from where Tolkien experimented with finding the right name for Trotter. Tantalizingly, at the beginning of *The Treason of Isengard* a few incomplete, single syllable examples are given, namely Bara, Rho, Dam, before, finally, the name of Aragorn son of Aramir appears.

The precise meaning of the name 'Aragorn' remains unclear. One definition is found in the Foreword of *The Peoples of Middle-earth* where Christopher Tolkien recounts how an interpretation of the name was brought to his attention by Christopher Gilson. Spotted among Tolkien's papers at Marquette University and 'roughly written', on a piece of paper from a torn manuscript, the rest of which dealt with the choice of the Half-elven, the meaning of the name is given as 'Kingly Valour', a suitably appropriate definition which is provided by Aragorn's grandmother, Ivorwen, at his naming. This definition cannot, however, be considered definitive since the presence of a large 'X' on the page indicates that Tolkien had changed his mind about something, although what precisely is uncertain. What can be determined, however, is that Tolkien did eventually alter the other matter found in the manuscript, that of the choices of the Peredhil. The original choice before the children of Elrond that they could either depart with him when he left Middle-earth or, if they chose to wed a mortal, they would become mortal themselves and die, differs from that in *The Lord of the Rings* whereby Elrond's children would automatically become mortal if they choose to remain behind. It may well have been, therefore, the earlier version of this choice that Tolkien was rejecting here. If so, then we have a stronger case for considering 'Kingly Valour' to be the meaning of Aragorn's name.

The worth of this assertion is rather muddied, however, by the fact that Tolkien did not mention this definition when he replied to a suggestion made by Mr Richard Jeffrey that Aragorn might mean 'Tree-king'. Writing near the end of his life on 17th December 1972, Tolkien maintained that Tree-king could not be correct as it had *'no special fitness for him'* [27], a curious denial given the importance of the White Tree to the Númenóreans and that 'Tree-Day' was the fourth day of the Dúnedain week. However, in this letter, Tolkien does concede that many of the names of the line of Arthedain are not *'readily interpretable'*, and he confirms that the 'ara' part of Aragorn's name derives from the Sindarin 'aran' meaning 'king'. Our understanding is further complicated by the definition given in Tolkien's commentary, *Words, Phrases and Passages in various tongues in The Lord Of The Rings*, which Gilson has now published in *Parma Eldalamberon XVII*. Here the meaning of 'ara' is the same as that cited in the above mentioned letter, but the 'gorn' part of the name is instead said to be from the same root which also gave us 'Gorgoroth', meaning 'dread', although in Aragorn's case the 'dread' is of the kind which engenders respect and is interpreted rather as 'reverence' or 'awe'. Along with 'Kingly Valour', we therefore have another possible meaning of 'Aragorn', that of 'revered king'.

With the appearance of a new name, there is also is a huge leap forward in the matter of Trotter's identity. Not only is Trotter now a man, he is also said to be a man of Elrond's race, described as a descendant of the ancient men of the North, a hunter and a wanderer who only pretends to be a ranger. Although he hangs about Bree, he is a member of Elrond's household and a friend of Bilbo. This description of Elrond's race as the ancient men of the North is very reminiscent of that given in *The Hobbit*, and when, much later, Aragorn enters the Houses of Healing, he too refers to Elrond as the eldest of his race. Yet Aragorn undoubtedly meant that Elrond is the eldest of the extant descendants of Eärendil, all of whom, except for Elrond and his three children, were descendants of Elros. However, the line of descent of the half-even was by no means clear at this stage. Elrond's children had still not appeared and, although Elros existed, the matter of his descendants was far from formalized.

The story progressed as far as Balin's tomb with Trotter still in his hobbit guise and Tolkien, even now, was toying with retaining the Peregrin Boffin idea. However, the passage ends mid-sentence and that does seem to be the last of Peregrin Boffin, although he survives for a time as a hobbit without his alter ego and was eventually partially incorporated into the character of Peregrin Took. Finally, on a page listing five points headed 'Final Decisions' and dated Oct. 8th 1939, number five on the list reads: *'Trotter is not a hobbit but a real ranger who has gone to live in Rivendell after much wandering. Cut out shoes'* [28]. After *'real ranger'* was added, *'descendant of Elendil. Tarkil'*.

At last Aragorn becomes a descendant of Elendil and, as he does so, his potential is inevitably vastly extended, although what this actually meant for the development of the character was still far from clear. Certainly, now he has not only become a Man but a Man from a very noble bloodline at that, the character we meet in the remainder of Trotter's story must inevitably be perceived very differently from that found so far. Yet what is most striking about Aragorn's tale up to this point is the sheer volume of dialogue spoken by 'Trotter the Hobbit' which either remained completely unchanged in the final narrative or which changed very little when Trotter became a Man. As Christopher Tolkien comments, *'when my father decided that Trotter was Aragorn and was not Peregrin Boffin his stature and his history were totally changed, but a great deal of the 'indivisible' Trotter remained in Aragorn and determined his nature'* [29].

This is perhaps less surprising if we remember that, while on the face of it, there is a huge gulf between the nature of a hobbit ranger and that of a great Númenórean king, for the most part, we only meet 'Trotter the Hobbit' in situations where, when we meet Strider in those same situations later, Aragorn too is in his ranger guise. At such times, he is purposely concealing his true nature, both in the content and in the manner of his speech. As a result, even the hobbits are largely unaware of his potential. Also Aragorn reveals very little of his history until his speaks at the Council of Elrond. For the most part, it is only then, when he tells of his life and the role of his people, that his words become unmistakably those of Aragorn and not of Trotter. These particular passages did not exist in the early drafts so there is no comparison to be made and, by the time Trotter is required to lead the Company and assume Gandalf's role, 'Trotter the Hobbit' has already been dispensed with. Consequently we are never placed in a position where the disparity between the characters is too large to be reconciled.

More remarkable, however, is the number of incidents prior to this transformation where Trotter utters words which appear to have no particular relevance to 'Trotter the Hobbit' but which could have been specifically written for 'Strider the Man'. For instance, on first meeting the hobbits in Bree, Trotter remarks that he is older than he looks. There is no apparent reason for him to say this. 'Trotter the Hobbit' does not possess the longevity of 'Strider the Númenórean'. Even in the guise of Peregrin Boffin, who would have been 81 years old when he met Frodo in Bree, a respectable age even for a Hobbit, it hardly explains why Trotter should claim to be older than he appeared.

'Trotter the Hobbit' appears as well versed in Middle-earth history as Strider and this knowledge is in evidence on the journey to Rivendell. Although the legend of Elendil and Gil-galad has no specific affiliation to Trotter in his hobbit guise, the legend is nonetheless freely available to all and, as a well travelled ranger, it is reasonable that Trotter should be familiar with both the site of Weathertop and the legend. Sam, in comparison, is completely ignorant of the name of Weathertop. More surprising is that 'Trotter the Hobbit' chooses to recount *The Tale of Tinúviel*. Strider's rich voice as he tells the story which has so great a parallel to his own romantic aspirations is to be expected, but why Trotter, with his queer and eager face, should be especially moved by the story is a mystery. Knowing, as we now do the importance of this story for Tolkien personally, Trotter's account may have been of no greater significance than the fulfillment of a wish to include the tale somewhere within the narrative and it just happened that it was Trotter who was given the job.

Another curious occurrence at Weathertop is Trotter's use of athelas to treat Bingo. At this stage, the plant has no special significance for Trotter and yet its use is apparently as effective as when Strider uses it to treat Frodo. Trotter simply states that it is a healing plant known only to Elves and some of those who wander in the wild. His success as a healer is entirely due to the properties of the plant rather than to any inherent skill of his own beyond the practical abilities expected of a competent ranger. The appearance of athelas in this context may owe more to it having first appeared in the *Lay of Leithian* where Huan brings a leaf to Lúthien so she might heal Beren. However, the name 'athelas' was apparently only added to the Lay at a later date and possibly Tolkien only decided it was the same leaf once the connection between Lúthien's descendants and Aragorn had been established.

Trotter's ties with Rivendell and his unexpected integration into Elrond's household are also surprising given that he lacks Strider's family connections. On the journey from Weathertop, Trotter reveals that he has been to Rivendell many times and remarks that it is not his *'fate to sit quiet, even in the fair house of Elrond'* [30]. Even allowing for his friendships with Gandalf and Bilbo which provide him with reason to be a regular visitor, in his hobbit guise, Trotter clearly lacks the long association with Elrond and his household that Aragorn enjoyed and, of course, Arwen is completely absent from the story at this stage. Trotter's words are, therefore, another example of how seamlessly at times the one persona of Trotter could replace the other even though the meaning behind the words spoken might change entirely. This is particularly so in the scene where the Company prepares to depart from Rivendell. As Trotter sits with his head bowed to his knees, only Elrond fully understands what the moment means to him. Applied to Trotter, it is impossible to do more than guess at the meaning here. Even when applied to Aragorn, the full implication of this is not initially clear, although, once we have read of the condition that Elrond placed upon his marriage, a great deal can be deduced with the benefit of hindsight and the identical scene takes on a far greater significance than it ever could for Trotter.

~oo0oo~

According to the *Foreword* of the second edition of *The Lord of the Rings*, the Company reached Balin's tomb towards the end of 1940, but Christopher Tolkien believes his father erred in this recollection and this episode was instead written nearer the end of 1939, an assertion which would certainly be compatible with Trotter's development at this stage. During this next phase of writing, there was extensive revision of the existing chapters, in part, to explain Gandalf's disappearance, but also to accommodate the change in Trotter's identity. These dual considerations resulted in Tolkien developing more background information regarding the movements of both characters prior to Trotter's appearance at the inn in Bree. The beginnings of the rangers' long labour watching the Shire now appears with Trotter undertaking this task on his return from the hunt for Gollum. Having decided that Gandalf and Trotter are allies, they meet later at Sarn Ford where, Gandalf 'begs' Trotter to watch the East Road while he travels East. In this conception, Gandalf gives Frodo's letter to Aragorn and, in what might have been an intriguing encounter, Aragorn warns Tom Bombadil of the approaching Black Riders.

With the change in Trotter's identity, it is inevitably a very different ranger that the hobbits find sitting in the corner of *The Prancing Pony* although, with the exception of the loss of the wooden shoes, Trotter is described much as in his earlier hobbit incarnation as queer-looking and brown-faced. The sense of mystery surrounding the stranger is maintained by Frodo observing Trotter's dark look whilst simultaneously finding something strangely attractive in his face. An early version of the *'Riddle of Strider'* also adds to the sense that Trotter is not all he seems.

> *All that is gold does not glitter,*
> *all that is long does not last;*
> *All that is old does not with;,*
> *not all that is over is past.* [31]

Beneath the rhyme, Trotter's true name is given as 'Aragorn', but 'Celegorn' now replaces 'Aramir' as the name of his father. With Tolkien inclined to offer more sureties over Trotter's trustworthiness than he eventually did for Strider, the letter also includes the first reference to Aragorn being of the line of Isildur, a revelation which prompts Frodo to exclaim that the Ring belongs to him. However, Tolkien evidently thought better of having Frodo prepared to surrender the Ring to a complete stranger, regardless of any encouraging ancestry or glowing testimony of Gandalf's, and this sudden moment of comprehension on Frodo's part, together with all mention of Isildur, was instead delayed until they had arrived in Rivendell, the scene eventually finding a slot at the Council of Elrond. The later placing also had the additional advantage of enabling the suspense and uncertainty over Aragorn's trustworthiness to be maintained throughout the journey to Rivendell.

Tolkien also removed other early proffered sureties of the identities of both the hobbits and Aragorn. Originally, Trotter carried with him a letter of his own which contained an identical verse, a sort of reference of good character which he kept about his person. And in a further passage removed later, Trotter comments that he has no doubts about Frodo's worth after overhearing him sing a song that he recognized as having being written by Bilbo. In *The Lord of the Rings*, Strider's friendship with Bilbo is something he conspicuously neglects to mention until he and Bilbo appear together in the Hall of Fire. Had the hobbits known of the friendship, this revelation might have confirmedStrider as a friend in Frodo's eyes more firmly than any character reference provided in a letter, although, once again, the sense of mystery surrounding the ranger would undoubtedly have been reduced had their acquaintance been acknowledged sooner.

Aspects of the Prancing Pony episode which do enter at this stage include Trotter's lamentation that his looks are against his being taken on trust and his vow to save the hobbits with his life or death. That Trotter makes this vow standing up with a light gleaming in his face, *'keen and commanding'* [32], is a measure of how differently Tolkien already envisaged the character following his transformation into a Man. Significantly absent from the scene, however, are the shards of Narsil. In the next amendment to this draft, dated by Christopher Tolkien as no earlier that August 1940 since it was written on exam scripts Tolkien only received at this time, several more versions of the riddle appear, all of which refer to either the brandishing or re-forging of a broken blade. Elendil's sword subsequently evolved out of this one line in the verse.

With much of Trotter's hobbit dialogue remaining unchanged when he became a Man, there were few alterations of note in the chapters between Bree and Rivendell. Rather, it is at Rivendell that the transformation in Trotter impacts further. There is still no Arwen, but Trotter is now addressed as 'Tarkil' by Bilbo as a sign of honour and respect for the men of Númenor. Meaning 'mortal man', Tarkil was to remain an alternative name for Aragorn for some time and partially survived into *The Lord of the Rings* as 'Tark', the orcs term of abuse for the men of Gondor.Like Peregrin or 'Perry' earlier, Tarkil aids Bilbo with his poem, but, unlike in *The Lord of the Rings* where the Dúnadan's sole contribution was the inclusion of the emerald, Tarkil initially composed most of the work. The evolution of Eärendil's Lay was apparently a complex one with Tolkien penning fifteen different versions. Adapted from the poem *Errantry*, emerald was originally the material used to make the merry messenger's sword. Then, as Tolkien steadily adapted the lay to tell Eärendil's story, the mariner acquired a helm with a shining emerald upon it which was later moved to the mariner's breast, the very place Aragorn wore the Elessar. Post-*The Lord of the Rings*, Tolkien provided alternative origins for the jewel but, with Aragorn's role in the composition of the Lay eventually reduced to just that one line which connects the emerald with Eärendil, this does seem to lend weight to the provenance of the Elessar that Galadriel gave Aragorn being that of Eärendil.

The Council of Elrond progressed substantially at this time and, reflecting the growing importance of Númenor, the coming of Elendil to Middle-earth is expanded further. Elendil is now a survivor of the fall of Númenor rather than his earlier conception as the king of Beleriand. However, instead of arriving at the Lhûn, he, and his two sons, Anárion and Isildur, came South, sailing up the Sirvinya, the early name for the Anduin, where he established the chief city of Osgiliath as well as Minas Anor and Minas Ithil.At this point in the recounting of this history, it seems the narrative jumps abruptly to Boromir's explanation of how he sought Imladris, suggesting that some original text is missing. As Christopher Tolkien notes, this is unfortunate because the lost pages may well have contained a verse similar to *Seek for the sword that is broken* since the text resumes with Trotter placing the broken sword on the table in the familiar scene. At Boromir's ensuing amazement, Elrond introduces Trotter as: *'Aragorn son of Celegorn, descended in right line [added: through many fathers] from Isildur of Minas Ithil, son of Elendil'* [33]. With such an introduction, Aragorn's ancestry is now unequivocal.

Intriguingly, at this stage Tolkien proposed an altogether different history for Elendil's descendants. Although Trotter is again confirmed as a descendant of the Men of the West and of the kings of the city of Ond, here those of Elendil's line had long ago been banished from Ond by the ancestors of Boromir. This scenario itself evolved from an earlier outline where it was the Chief of the Nine who drove out the Númenóreans, in which can be seen the beginnings of the War with Angmar in the North. When the Men of the West returned from the war against Sauron, the people of Minas Tirith, murmuring against those of Númenórean descent, refused them entry to the city. Faced with this treachery, Valandur, who is presumably the son of Isildur, broke his sword against the city gate, and the Men of the West retreated to the North to dwell at Osfored *'in slowly waning glory and darkening days'* [34]. With an ancestral background such as this, Aragorn, not surprisingly, is bitter towards Boromir and asks: *'What do the men of Minas Tirith want with me – to return to aid [them] in the war and then reject me at the gates again?'* [35].

Consequently, it seems the North kingdom was originally of no more importance than a refuge for those displaced from what would later become Gondor. By implication, those of Númenórean descent subsequently dwelt nowhere but the North, which would be compatible with the position at that time that the Men of Bree were of Númenórean origin and Tolkien's own note to himself from earlier that only Trotter and not Boromir is of ancient race. Confusingly, this situation was contradicted almost immediately by a further suggestion that the blood of Westernesse was said to remain *only* in Minas Anor. This radically different history of Minas Tirith was struck through soon after and rejected completely, but it nonetheless represented an important step in Aragorn's evolution. In this outline, Aragorn is undoubtedly a man of high lineage, one displaced from an ancestral kingdom and on a mission to reclaim what is rightly his.

In these successive drafts of the Council of Elrond more elements of the final story continue to appear. The breaking of Elendil's sword beneath him is now included along with the arrival of Valandil and his safe-keeping among the Elves. Valandil is said to have then dwelt with the remnant of his father's people in the North and Aragorn speaks of his heirs much as he does in *The Lord of the Rings*. He also provides the first hint of his long journeys by mentioning that he has been to Minas Tirith and beyond. By the time the fifth version of the Council of Elrond is reached, the familiar story of Elendil arriving in the North is in place with his sons coming South to the land of 'Ondor'. The North Kingdom now becomes a distinct realm with its own capital city, although the name of that city went through several changes before Annúminas finally emerged. It was at this point that the earlier suggestion that the Men of the West only remained in Minas Anor was removed.

Bilbo's recital of *All that is Gold* is introduced here as a response to Boromir's continued doubts about Bilbo's friend, Tarkil. So too is more detail of Aragorn's capture of Gollum, although the creature neither bit him, nor would Aragorn touch him. Here Aragorn's reaction to the news of Gollum's escape is centered more on ruing his own wasted efforts than his concern for the effect Gollum might have on their plans. *'What!' cried Aragorn [Elfstone] in angry surprise, 'Then all my pains are brought to nothing!'* [36] A particularly important inclusion at this time was the matter of the re-forging of the sword, an act which now became dependent upon the finding of Isildur's bane, although Tolkien only gave it a name, 'Branding', much later when the Company departed from Lothlórien and Galadriel presented it with a sheath.

Tolkien continued to revise the early chapters until the point where the story had previously been abandoned in the Mines of Moria, although some anomalies still remained such as Boromir being the tallest of the Company. Consequently, he alone ploughed through the snows during the aborted attempt on Caradhras, leaving Trotter to help carry the hobbits. And Tolkien seemed set to retain the existing view that it was Gandalf who feared to enter the mines, not Aragorn, the conversation at this time being almost identical to that in *The Lord of the Rings* except that each character spoke the other's lines. However, a typing error in continuity evidently triggered a rethink and the speakers were permanently reversed.

With Gandalf's fall in Moria, Trotter leads his companions safely to Lothlórien, much as he does in *The Lord of the Rings*, stopping to tend the injured Frodo and Sam with athelas. The jest about the mithril coat is present and the first line of the *Bye, bye, Bunting* parody, *'This is a pretty hobbit-skin'* [37] appears. Aragorn's earlier sojourn in Lothlórien is not yet envisaged so, when the company approaches the realm, it is Aragorn, not Gimli, who expresses a hope that Elves still dwell there, and while Cerin Amroth is present, Aragorn standing at the bottom of the hill lost in distant memories of Arwen is not. Aragorn is introduced by Legolas as *'elf-friend, beloved of Elrond'* [38], although he obviously does not yet have the favour of the Lady who says on meeting him, *'Your name is known to me, though never in all your wanderings have you sought my house'* [39]. Conversely, Galadriel is unknown to Aragorn who later remarks that she was a friend of Gandalf's, *'one of his secrets that he did not tell me'* [40]. He nonetheless still sleeps without fear for the first time since leaving Rivendell.

At around this time, Aragorn's name underwent several changes, progressing through an astonishing cycle from Trotter to Aragorn to Elfstone to Ingold to Elfstone before eventually returning to Aragorn again. Tolkien reasoned that, being a Man, Trotter should not have a 'Gnome-elvish' name like Aragorn, so, after also considering Elf-friend, Elfspear and Elfmere as alternatives, every reference to Aragorn from the first appearance of the name in Gandalf's letter was retrospectively changed to Elfstone son of Elfhelm. Although the distinction between Noldorin and Sindarin had not yet arisen, Tolkien's discounting of an Elvish name is clearly at odds with the statement in *Appendix F* that the Dúnedain alone of the races of Men spoke Sindarin and that most of their names, such as Aragorn, Denethor and Gilraen, were derived from that language. However, when the Company arrived at Lothlórien, Tolkien decided to change Trotter's name again, this time to Ingold son of Ingrim. He considered the 'Ing' element of Ingold was more appropriate for Aragorn as it was said to represent the 'West', and this was the form of address used by Galadriel on first meeting him.

However, when Galadriel unclasped an emerald brooch described as deep green set in gold and gave it to Gimli, who then named himself 'Elfstone', the incongruity of the name when applied to a dwarf but the fitness of the name for Trotter must have immediately become apparent since the passage halts abruptly and the use of Ingold is abandoned. Trotter's name then reverts back to Elfstone, although not before other names such as Elfstan, Eledon, Eldakar, Eldamir and Qendemir have all been considered. The name of 'Elessar' also appears at this time, although the gift itself is not a brooch but a gem set in silver and hung on a chain around Galadriel's neck. The choice of an emerald was an appropriate one given Aragorn's future role as a healer. Emeralds have long been considered to have healing powers and the Egyptians in particular prized the jewels as symbols of renewal and rebirth. Although the healing power of the Elessar was later superseded by that of the Silmarils, this feature of the jewel was not entirely lost and was responsible for the years of toil falling from Aragorn's shoulders as the brooch was pinned upon him.

~oo0oo~

The passage of the Great River was written during the winter of 1941 and progressed in almost its final form at first writing, but it is clear that in the first draft Tolkien had yet to clarify precisely how much time had passed since

Elendil's day or how distant was Aragorn's relationship to his ancestor. As the Company speeds through the Pillars of the Kings and Aragorn announces his arrival in his ancestral homeland, the number of generations he cites between himself and Isildur is at first very few. Naming himself Eldamir the son of Eldakar son of Valandil, he is initially the great-grandson of Isildur and not the thirty-ninth generation he eventually became. Yet contradicting this, and in the same draft, the Pillars of the Kings were said to have been made '*many ages ago*', wardens of a '*long-vanished*' kingdom [41]. This short time span also conflicts with the fall of Gil-galad being described by Elrond as '*very long ago*' [42] in an earlier, if undated, passage where he recounts the event to Frodo. Neither is it consistent with Gandalf's revised explanation to Frodo on awaking in Rivendell that Aragorn son of Kelegorn is '*descended through many fathers from Isildur the son of Elendil*' [43]. The situation changed little in the next copy which, as it was made by Christopher Tolkien himself, can be confidently dated as August 1942. By then, Aragorn's name had been restored throughout the revisions, but curiously not in the passage through the Pillars where Aragorn instead named himself, Eldamir son of Valatar son of Eldakar son of Valandil. Christopher Tolkien confirms that Valandil can be none other than the son of Isildur, yet, amended as it was with the inclusion of just one additional generation, it cannot be assumed that the retention of so few generations between Isildur and Aragorn was an error. Clearly a great deal of ancestry and expanse of time still needed to be introduced to reconcile these positions.

While writing the Great River episode, Tolkien formulated his first outline for the remainder of the story. What was originally proposed was considerably simpler than the eventual plot, although with much envisaged that was nonetheless very different. Frodo and Sam were still to set off on their own in response to Boromir's attempt to take the Ring, and Merry and Pippin would encounter Treebeard, although they would not yet be captured by orcs. Aragorn would become separated from Legolas and Gimli, and, instead of searching for Merry and Pippin, would go with Boromir to Minas Tirith. The lure of the Ring would make Boromir an unpleasant character, jealous of Aragorn so that, when the Lord of Minas Tirith, presumably Boromir's father, is slain and Aragorn chosen to succeed him, Boromir would seek the aid of Saruman to oust his rival. Legolas and Gimli were to wander north, Legolas heading for Lothlórien and Gimli going home. In one scenario, they would be captured by Saruman but, in another, they would be reunited with Gandalf, his return being an event foreseen by Tolkien from very early on. Aid for the besieged Minas Tirith would then come in the guise of Gandalf and Treebeard. There would be a further battle at Gorgoroth and, after the fall of Mordor in which Sam would die, Aragorn, who had earlier suspected Boromir's treachery, would remain as lord of Minas Ithril and slay Boromir who would not, in this conception, repent.

Even though very little of this abandoned plotline materialized, it is quite clear that by this stage Tolkien had come to view Aragorn as the epic hero in his story, a great hero and warrior who would become lord of his people. However, if his slaying of Boromir was not to be a stain on Aragorn's heroism, Boromir needed to be a much changed character from the one we came to know. Certainly, in these proposed plotlines, Boromir is not accorded the respect he later receives. By making him the undisputed villain, he becomes dispensable, an inconvenience who can easily be removed to make way for Elendil's heir. In the final text, it is inconceivable that Aragorn should slay Boromir and his repentance is one of the most conspicuously religious moments in the book.

Also in evidence at this stage is Aragorn's own ambition. Although divided in mind and acutely aware of having taken on Gandalf's role, he still desires to go to Ondor where he would become *'a great lord, and maybe would set up again the throne of Elendil's line'* [44].Yet in another abandoned plotline, we also see the beginnings of his willingness to sacrifice his personal goals. Here, Legolas would accompany Boromir to Minas Tirith, but Trotter would wander alone searching for the missing hobbits. Overwhelmed with grief, and believing he has failed as Gandalf's successor, he would be tempted to pursue his own desires, but nonetheless, forsakes his ambition. Even so, at this stage, Tolkien does not view Aragorn with the regard that is so evident in *The Return of the King*. Aragorn's great functions within the legendarium have not yet emerged, and the full impact of Aragorn's lineage and what this meant for his potential had yet to become apparent. It may be significant that at this time, Isildur was the younger son of Elendil so Aragorn's ancestry failed to distinguish him as markedly as it did later. When Arvedui tried to claim the throne of Gondor on the death of Ondoher, he used the fact that Elendil stood at the head of the line of kings, and that he himself was a descendant of Isildur, the *elder* son of Elendil, as the main tenet of his argument to support his claim. Trotter's case was, therefore, more obscure and his lesser descent would have weakened any claim he might make to the lordship of Minas Tirith. Here, Trotter is one to be chosen as a lord, not one who could claim his inheritance by right, and there are seemingly minor differences to the final text which betray Trotter as being a lesser character.

For instance, at first Aragorn did not keep Boromir's confession a secret. Apparently this was rectified almost immediately and Tolkien even made a note of his intent, *'Don't let Trotter tell of Boromir's misdeed'* [45], but the incident does demonstrate how the character revealed his nature to the author even as the words made contact with the paper.

With the abandonment of most of this early synopsis, Aragorn, Legolas and Gimli set off in pursuit of the captured Merry and Pippin. In an early form of his verse lamenting his not yet being able to go to Minas Tirith, Aragorn introduces some of the symbols of kingship. In particular, the first reference to the Silver Tree appears here which is swiftly followed by the *'wingéd crown and throne of gold'* [46]. The pursuit continues in much the same vein as in the final narrative, culminating with the Three Hunters encountering the 'Rohiroth'. Originally, Tolkien proposed that Aragorn and Éomer would already be acquainted prior to their meeting, although this is not reflected in the first draft. However, Aragorn did know Éomer's father so his time in the service of the Horsemen is already envisaged, and this is confirmed in the next version. In this original encounter, it is Aragorn who demands that Éomer give his name first to which Éomer complies immediately. When, in response, Aragorn declares himself to be Aragorn son of Arathorn, this was the very first use of 'Arathorn' in the narrative other than in amendment. The name of 'Aragorn' had not long reappeared in the text either. Boromir's parting words of 'farewell Aragorn' were its first use since Tolkien restored it after abandoning his many experiments with other titles. The use of 'Aran' or 'Ar[a]' as the prefix of the kings of Arthedain was settled upon early in the composition of the Appendices so it is tempting to speculate that the reappearance of 'Aragorn' and the emergence of 'Arathorn' was as a result of this decision, although there are no dates available to confirm this. The hobbits, however, continued to use the name of 'Trotter' throughout, just as they did 'Strider'.

As Aragorn whips out his sword, which is still called 'Branding', the Riders' wonderment at the speed of the companions' passage causes Éomer to remark that *'the name of Trotter was not so ill given'* [47], changed eventually of course to *'Strider is too poor a name, son of Arathorn... 'Wingfoot' I name you'* [48]. The three companions are lent horses much as they are in *The Lord of the Rings*, enabling them to reach Fangorn where they are reunited with Gandalf. Although not remarked upon in the text, this happy event occurs on 1st March, a date which is also Aragorn's birthday. The day is well known in the UK as that of Saint David, the patron saint of Wales who, like Aragorn, also died on the same date as his date of birth. However, the date of the reunion was set long before it became Aragorn's date of birth, its inclusion in *The Tale of Years* still being several years away. It might be of greater significance for such a remarkable event as Gandalf's return that St Aubin or Albinus, a Catholic saint renowned for his miracles, is also remembered on that day were it not for the original date of Gandalf's return being 30th January. There may, therefore, be no significance whatsoever in the date of 1st March. Concerned that too much of his story was taking place in the depths of winter, Tolkien decided to put back the date of theCompany's departure from Rivendell by a month, changing it from 24th November to December 25th. This had the knock-on effect of deferring the reunion with Gandalf by a similar period of time. That Gandalf returned on the same day that later became Aragorn's birthday was probably no more than another happy and fortunate coincidence enabling Tolkien to provide his troubled ranger with a rather superb birthday gift.

With the companions reunited, Gandalf and Gimli were to ride on ahead to Edoras where they would gain entry to Meduseld without any of the hostility and laying aside of arms that occurs in the final scene. Although their arrival is famously reminiscent of Beowulf's arrival at Heorot, the similarities may only have occurred to Tolkien during the course of composition since the challenge of the doorwarden was not present initially. In a revised draft, however, the influence of Beowulf is evident with the doorwarden speaking Old English, words which Aragorn could understand, and it was in this phase of writing that Tolkien also introduced Aragorn's verse, *Where now the horse and the rider*, another addition inspired by an Old English poem, this time, *The Wanderer*.

The story is then further revised so that the four companions all arrive together, and as they come before Théoden, Éowyn stands behind him. From the beginning, she is Théoden's niece and the sister of Éomer, although at first she is accompanied by another woman, Idis, who makes a very brief appearance as Théoden's daughter. At this stage of composition, Tolkien envisaged a mortal wife for Aragorn, and Éowyn was his intended bride. Her attraction to him is immediately apparent and Aragorn's interest, too, is unmistakable. After she leaves the hall, he is said to have, *'stood still, looking at the dark doors and taking little heed of other things'* [49]. Although in *The Two Towers*, Aragorn appears concerned, even distressed, by Éowyn's attention, in this scenario, there is no doubting that he reciprocates her interest, *'Long she looked upon Aragorn, and long he looked upon her'* [50]. When talking of the coming battle, his remarks that, if he lives, he hopes to ride with her, a sure sign that he wishes to see her again. However, throughout the writing of this episode much was struck through not long after composition, and this potential love match was soon rejected on the grounds that Tolkien considered Aragorn to be *'too old and lordly and grim'* [51]. As he notes in a draft letter, *'He was old, and that is not only a physical quality'* [52]. Tolkien instead proposed that Éowyn should die, either avenging Théoden or saving him, and that Aragorn, in his grief, would never wed another. Aragorn's future role as the founder of a great dynasty, a matter of primary importance to the function of the entire mythology was obviously not envisaged by Tolkien at this time.

Surprisingly perhaps, Galadriel still had a role as matchmaker even in this brief affair. Gandalf, on his return, brings a message to Aragorn from Galadriel, just as he does later, but, with Aragorn's ride of the Paths of the Dead not yet conceived, the meaning is quite different.

Elfstone, Elfstone, bearer of my green stone,
In the south under snow a green stone thou shalt see.
Look well, Elfstone! In the shadow of the dark throne
Then the hour is at hand that long hath awaited thee. [53]

In the last line of the verse, there is a hint of Aragorn's long labour in preparing for his role of king, and, as Christopher Tolkien explains, the green stone is on Théoden's brow above his graying hair while it is Éowyn who stands behind his throne in the shadows. Galadriel has no specific reason to take such an interest in Aragorn's affairs beyond a general altruism towards the good folk of Middle-earth, but this must be the germ of her later, pivotal role in bringing together Arwen and the travel weary Thorongil. Wisely perhaps, Tolkien subsequently removed all mention of a green stone in connection with Théoden, leaving the Elessar as the sole green gem of note.

~oo0oo~

The narrative now moves to war with the first draft of the battle at Helm's Deep. Aragorn's emerging role as both warrior and captain is now in evidence and he is endowed with the same prowess as a warrior that he demonstrates later, leading an onslaught that apparently *'none could withstand'* [54]. But neither is he invincible. At one point he is saved by Legolas with a well shot arrow, and, in a further incident, he is hit on the head by a stone, causing him to stumble to his knee. In these drafts, Aragorn plays an, if anything, even more commanding role than in *The Lord of the Rings*, although in his original parley with the enemy, there is no mention of his majesty. Aragorn's healing skills are also in demand. He not only tends both Éomer and Gimli, but also the injured Snowmane who has been shot in the shoulder by an arrow. In a scene which was regrettably removed from the final narrative, there is a rare glimpse of Aragorn's thoughts at this stage of the Quest. While treating the horse with athelas, the fragrance draws his mind back to Weathertop and the escape from Moria, causing him to wonder what has become of Frodo and to regret that he was not with them still.

Absent from any of the proposed plotlines is Aragorn's journey through the Paths of the Dead, a crucial episode in Aragorn's story but one which only gradually evolved out of the emerging tale. The concept of the Oathbreakers has its origins in the current conception that the men from Dunland lost their land to the Rohiroth for failing to fight for Elendil and Isildur, a battle which, at this stage of development, occurred only five hundred years previously. However, a watershed moment in the evolution of the Paths of the Dead episode occurs with the sudden appearance of the Palantír. In his 1955 letter to W.H. Auden mentioned earlier, Tolkien includes the Palantíri among those revelations about which he knew nothing until they manifested themselves on paper. Yet as soon as they made their appearance, Tolkien immediately recognised them as a part of the rhyme of lore that had been running through his mind, and realised that they represented the stone element of the seven stars and seven stones and one white tree.

Although in the original draft the Palantír shattered into fragments, it quickly became the means of seeing events taking place elsewhere. At first their range was deliberately limited to some hundred leagues because Tolkien had no wish for the stones, unlike the rings, to be too closely associated with Mordor. Initially, there were five of these stones, placed strategically between Isengard and Minas Morgul, and in origin they were said to be associated with the same old seers from Gondor who made Amon Hen and Amon Lhaw. The original idea that anyone could freely use these objects rapidly changed so that they instead become the means of trapping the unwary, and any who attempted to look in them, except one with a *'will of adamant'* [55], would find their thoughts and minds brought swiftly to Mordor, exactly as happened with Pippin. Their association with Aragorn, however, was much slower to materialise. When Gandalf handed the Palantír to him, it was only for him to take care of it, not because it had any special association for him personally since they had no connection with either the North or Elendil at this time. In the next rewrite, the stones became potentially even more dangerous, and, having identified a very useful plot mechanism for his story, Tolkien sketched out a history for them whereby they were said to have belonged to the Men of Old, and the possibility that they may have been made by Fëanor appears. As their number increased to seven, they also became located in the North, although the chief stone was said to have been at Osgiliath before its ruin, suggesting that at least some of Gondor's history was already mapped out at this time.

In spite of this promising breakthrough, not long after the appearance of the Palantíri, work on *The Lord of the Rings* halted and did not resume until 1944, a break of over a year. In the *Foreword* of the second edition, Tolkien states that the beginnings of Chapters 1 and 3 of *Book Five* had been written at this time, and this assertion is repeated in a 1957 letter to Caroline Everett. *The Passing of the Grey Company*, however, did not exist and the question of how to bring Aragorn unexpectedly to the Pelennor, yet still inform the reader how he came to be there, was, in Tolkien's own words *'the chief problem'* [56]. So, when work resumed in April 1944, Tolkien instead tackled the journey of Sam and Frodo to Mordor. The break, however, seemed to have done some good. By May of that year, Faramir had appeared, and he brought with him more of Gondor's history, including the line of kings which at this stage ended, not with King Earnur, but with a King Elessar. The era of the Stewards now follows, and Christopher Tolkien notes that Denethor, who was introduced as Boromir's father at the breaking of the Fellowship, had, in fact, never been referred to as a king even though Boromir was originally named as the son of the King of Ond. With that plot line abandoned, Tolkien appears to have never wavered from the possibility of Aragorn occupying the vacant throne.

Throughout the summer of 1944, Tolkien continued to concentrate on the story of Frodo and Sam, and, on 12th October of that year, he wrote to Christopher to say he had just begun *Book Five*. This clearly contradicts the above statement from the *Foreword*, but Christopher Tolkien argues that his father was mistaken in his published recollection and that he did indeed begin those chapters at this later time. Faramir's inclusion in the preceding outlines, which could not have been written prior to 1944, was apparently the principal factor which persuaded him that his father was, in fact, confusing this break from writing with the subsequent hiatus which lasted from October 1944 to the summer of 1946. Before this next long break in writing, however, the first steps were taken with the chapter that would eventually become *The Passing of the Grey Company*.

Originally, much of the action that would eventually take place at the Hornburg instead occurred at Dunharrow. Here there were said to be caves, possibly a 'holy' place, the exact word is apparently illegible, made by the *'forgotten men in the Dark Years'* [57] who dwelt in that region from before the time of Gondor. Possibly recognising an opening to develop some useful ancient legend, Tolkien continued to ponder what became of these people, and, in the next version, these men were said to have made a temple in that place out of fear of the Shadow. They did not hold to the lord of Gondor, and, approaching now the final story, when the Eorlingas first came to those parts, they met one old man in a cave who wished to tell them something but died before he could do so.

Slowly, other elements for the Paths of the Dead episode also began to emerge. Among the assembled host at Dunharrow, there are now Rangers of the North who have come seeking Aragorn. They numbered only seven at first yet Aragorn remarked, *'Last and fewest, but to me not least'* [58]. Halbarad, too, suddenly appears, although neither as Aragorn's friend and fellow Dúnadan, nor in his original incarnation as Gandalf's horse whose coming from Rivendell at Gandalf's call may well have inspired the idea of his human persona riding to Rohan. Rather, Halbarad is here Denethor's sister son who arrives from Gondor seeking aid from Théoden in a role that was later given to Hirgon.

The idea of Aragorn going off on a mission of his own also arises at this point. He is to supersede Éomer as the commander of a separate force which would pass over the mountain with the intention of coming upon the enemy from the rear. Another element which arose at this time, but again in a slightly different context, a detachment from Rohan was to ride south to intercept the enemy fleet coming up the river. Again, it was Éomer who initially would lead this attack and the rangers were instead to come directly to Minas Tirith. Aragorn would, nonetheless, have a commanding role in the battle as all were to flee before the sword of Elendil. In a third outline for the chapter, Aragorn was to ride over the mountains with his rangers and drive off the Southrons before entering the city and meeting Denethor. By the fifth outline, Aragorn had acquired new information which guided his actions, although this came via the messengers from Gondor, not from his use of the Palantír. As a result, Aragorn would still take his rangers over the mountain, while the Southrons would sail up the river and, in this conception, Gondor would be defeated.

This idea was, however, short-lived. Instead, rumour of a king who had been entombed in the mountains would inflame the people of South Gondor to defeat the Southrons, bringing the story of Aragorn's arrival to Minas Tirith nearer to that of *The Return of the King*, and to Tolkien's own surprise, *'The fleet sailing up the River is an ally!'* [59]. As Aragorn disembarks from the enemy ships, he emerges *'like a great king of old'* [60], a worthy successor to Elendil, and in a scene which prompted Tolkien to make a note reminding him of *'Frodo's vision'* [61]. Subsequently the coming of the ships and the banner displaying the White Tree featured among the images Frodo sees in Galadriel's mirror.

At this point, Tolkien took his second long break from writing *The Lord of the Rings,* a period of eighteen months which lasted until the summer of 1946. During this time he turned instead to his Númenor legend where his further work ensured Aragorn's hitherto under-appreciated potential could not fail to become apparent. *The Notion Club Papers* were particularly important and the significance of this work is discussed in detail in Chapter Four. Prior to this time, it did seem that Tolkien had yet to give voice, if not thought, to what being an heir of Elendil could actually mean for the character. Noticeably, it was only when Tolkien returned to *The Lord of the Rings* after this last long break that Aragorn acquired his elven bride. Yet even at this stage Arwen did not appear immediately. So, when the Grey Company sets out in response to Galadriel's message and overtakes Théoden on the plains, Halbarad does not yet bring her message.

At the Hornburg, Aragorn looks in the Palantír, if initially without Halbarad accompanying him to the tower, his later inclusion being purely to provide the weary and grim-faced Aragorn with someone to lean upon. Aragorn subsequently reveals to Legolas and Gimli that he has looked in the stone, and, in reply to Gimli's surprised consternation, Aragorn originally remarks that he told Sauron he had a *'rascal of a rebel dwarf here that I would exchange for a couple of good orcs, thank you!'* [62]

A variation of this remark was famously retained in the first edition. *'You forget to whom you speak,' said Aragorn sternly, and his eyes glinted. 'What do you fear that I should say: that I had a rascal of a rebel dwarf here that I would gladly exchange for a serviceable orc?'* [63]

In 1963, the sharpness of Aragorn's retort to Gimli was criticised by Eileen

Elgar, but in an unpublished reply, Tolkien defended his remark, noting that *'Gimli should have known better than to question the action and judgement of the greatest Captain of Men and a superior strategist. Gimli's remark was silly and impertinent; but although Aragorn at this point in the story was under great stress, his original reply was more grim humour than serious rebuke'* [64].

In spite of this defence, the remark was still removed from the second edition; an action which Tom Shippey suggests is a shame as he believes it demonstrated an underlying tension between the man and the dwarf. At this stage, however, the dwarf is an essential element in the fulfilment of the early version of Malbeth's prophecy which predicts that an elf, a dwarf and a man would all take the Paths of the Dead, making Aragorn's remark all the more strange, unless, as suggested, it was indeed merely a jest.

With Aragorn's use of the Palantír, Sauron's ignorance of Aragorn's existence and his sudden revelation being a blow of him enters the story, while, in a further rewrite, Aragorn's role as decoy becomes clear as he tells Legolas and Gimli he hopes Sauron will think Isildur's heir possess that which Isildur took from him, and so might his plans go awry. When Aragorn departs from the Hornburg, he leaps onto Hasufel who, in the absence of Roheryn, is his only horse throughout.

As already mentioned, a particular difficulty was how to bring Aragorn unexpectedly to the Pelennor whilst also explaining how he came to be there, although it seems the only solution ever considered was to recount the journey subsequently as part of *The Last Debate*. At this stage, Aragorn's entire journey, beginning with his leaving the Hornburg, was to be included in that particular narrative so Aragorn's parting from Éowyn forms part of that same episode. Éowyn was at first less restrained and dignified than she is in *The Return of the King*. Weeping and throwing her arms about him, she implores Aragorn not to go, her distressed behaviour causing Gimli to later remark that Aragorn was so moved that *'he went through all perils after like a man that can feel little more'* [65]. It is impossible to know exactly what to make of Aragorn's rejection of Éowyn at this time. The difficulties posed by allowing her to accompany him still held sway. Possibly, Tolkien had already decided that Aragorn's bride must be an altogether different person.

Isildur's curse of the Oathbreakers now enters the story, while the Stone of Erech had an interesting evolution. In the final narrative, the stone is a great globe that was brought out of Númenor at its ruin but originally it was one of the Palantíri that had been housed in a tower set within a stone ring and, on coming to Erech, Aragorn would find it buried in a vault. On reaching Erech, the banner, which is here Isildur's, is unfurled and at first Elendil's badge could be seen in the dark. Later, the location of Erech shifted to the south coast and when Aragorn rode forth, men believed he was *'as a king risen from the dead'* [66] and, as he gathered all men to war, the terror of *'the black king'* [67] was said to precede him as he went. Neither of these phrases is used in connection with Aragorn in *The Return of the King*, and instead, the 'King of the Dead' became the leader of the Shadow Host. The subsequent omission of these phrases does illustrate the usefulness of these drafts in determining Tolkien's early train of thought. Aragorn's passage through the Paths of the Dead has been taken as a form of symbolic death and rebirth, and the presence of these early titles suggests the thought may also have been in Tolkien's mind. What is less easy to determine is whether their eventual removal represents a change of heart or a desire to undermine any possible allegorical interpretation.

At this point, a unique conception for Aragorn emerged. As he rode through Lebennin, the people were to cry *'the Lord of the Ring has risen'* [68]. This was later changed to *'the Lord of the Rings'* [69] which Christopher Tolkien suggests might have been for no other purpose than to illustrate the confusion on the part of the men of Gondor over this unexpected appearance of Isildur's heir. Merry then lays the foundations for the motives behind the ride to the Black Gate when he wonders if this was some device on Aragorn's part to draw the eyes of Mordor away from Frodo, although Gimli refutes this. He instead asserts that Aragorn would not spread a falsehood himself and he therefore concludes that either there was truth in the rumour and Aragorn did indeed have a ring, or the people were mistaken. Tolkien did toy with the idea of giving Aragorn a ring as a gift from Galadriel and as an explanation for his sudden increased power. However, he decided this would leave Lórien defenceless and the only ring given to Aragorn remained the ring of Barahir, an ancestral heirloom which already existed in the mythology but not one with any inherent power. This was to prove a wise decision. Much of Aragorn's appeal stems from the fact that, competent and capable though he is, he is nonetheless still just a man and what strength he possesses he has to find from within himself. Endowing him with a ring of power would have stripped him of much of his heroism.

In the outline for the battle of the Pelennor, Aragorn is still wielding

'Branding' which is not named Andúril until the first typescript, although the name of Narsil, rather surprisingly perhaps, only enters here. Tolkien did, however, use a pre-existing smith as the sword's maker. The dwarf, Telchar, had been named as the forger of both the dragon helm of Túrin and the knife, Angrist, since *The Lay of the Children of Hurin*, while, in the *Quenta Silmarillion*, the last version of *The Silmarillion* written prior of *The Lord of the Rings*, Thingol had an armoury of *'swords and axes, shields and helms, wrought by Telchar himself or by his master Zirak the old'* [70]. By giving Narsil a dwarvish origin, Tolkien sticks to a tradition found throughout the early northern Sagas which credits dwarves as the most skilled in the making of arms. 'Tyrfling' was a dwarf sword that appears in *The Poetic Edda* as well as the Icelandic *Saga of King Heidrek the Wise*, while in *The Prose Edda*, King Högni's sword, 'Dáinsleif', was an heirloom of the dwarf, Dáin. According to legend, it was Icelandic dwarf smiths who taught the craft to the legendary smith, Wayland, the possible maker of Charlemagne's sword, 'Joyeuse', and of 'Gram', the sword of Odin.

Aragorn now unfurls his banner as the Black fleet approaches the city, although the gems on the standard were not yet made by Arwen. However, Aragorn's marriage finally enters the story, and 'Finduilas', the early name for Elrond's daughter, becomes a late addition to the manuscript. Finduilas eventually became the name of Denethor's wife and its use here may be no more than another example of Tolkien recycling names; 'Barahir', for example, was an early choice for 'Hirgon', as 'Beren' was for 'Beregond'. However, that Finduilas, daughter of Orodreth, loved Túrin, a mortal Man, might have influenced Tolkien's early choice of name for Aragorn's bride, as well as also being the reason he later rejected it. The acquisition of such a bride inevitably alters Aragorn's motives. His remark to Galadriel that she knows *'all my desire and long held in keeping the only treasure that I seek'* [71] tells us something of the importance of his potential bride to him. So it is quite extraordinary that a character who would exert an enormous influence upon Aragorn throughout his entire story, affecting his every action and underscoring his choices, an influence that would surely resonate in every line of dialogue he uttered, only actually appeared once his role in the story was almost complete. Yet, by belatedly bequeathing Aragorn an elven wife, and one of the High Elves at that, Tolkien finally elevated Aragorn from being a great chieftain among Men to being one of a very elite group of mortals whom Tolkien considered deserving of such a treasure. That this group previously consisted of just two other characters, the First Age heavyweights, Beren and Tuor, demonstrates perhaps more vividly than any descriptive accolade the esteem in which Tolkien came to view his king. Aragorn's marriage was also to prove the means for Tolkien to implement one of the core requirements of his legendarium, the entering of the divine into mankind, yet Tolkien himself only discovered Aragorn's potential to fulfil this role remarkably late in the day.

Aragorn's story now moves rapidly towards its conclusion. Victory is secured with his arrival, but his coming indirectly causes the death of the Steward. Denethor's despair at the arrival of the black ships probably has its roots in the Greek myth of Theseus who promised his father that if he succeeded in defeating Minotaur he would change the black sails for white ones on his homecoming. But he forgot, and his father, believing his son to be dead and all hope lost, threw himself off a cliff. The choice of sail colour might also reflect Aragorn's own symbolic death and be a consequence of his being hailed as the King of the Dead. Furthermore, in the earliest tales of the mythology, it was the black ship, Mornië, that ferried the dead to their final fates, and at around this time, Tolkien also proposed black sails for the ships of the Númenórean survivors whose coming to Middle-earth struck terror into the hearts of those who witnessed their arrival.

However, in this early conception, Denethor is fully aware that the Black Fleet is under Aragorn's command because of his use of the Palantír. Nonetheless, he still despairs and, as he prepares to burn, he says to Gandalf that he has seen, *'ships coming up Anduin: I will no more yield to an upstart - and even if his claim be true of the younger line: I am Steward for the sons on Anárion not Isildur   than [to] my dark foe'* [72].

At this stage, the prospect of deferring to Aragorn was clearly as much a factor in Denethor's suicide as his expectation of defeat. Yet it is no more apparent here than in the final narrative whether Denethor's residual suspicion and jealousy of Aragorn from his earlier service to Gondor in the guise of Thorongil was a factor in his belligerent stance. What is clear from Denethor's remark, however, is that Aragorn's being of the younger line of Isildur was definitely a potential constitutional obstacle to his claiming the crown.

Originally, Tolkien intended that Denethor should welcome Aragorn to the city, although he would refuse to yield the Stewardship until the battle was won and proofs given, something to which Aragorn would agree. Denethor would be cold and only feign courtesy but, believing Faramir to be near death and the tenure of the Stewards about to end anyway, he remarks that the city can take what lord it chooses, to which Aragorn would reply that *'he will not be 'taken', he will take'* [73]. Why Tolkien abandoned this exchange in favour of Denethor committing suicide probably owes more to the symbolism evoked by comparing his death with that of Théoden, but it cannot be denied that the lack of confrontation which eventually greeted Aragorn at his coronation, and in particular Faramir's unequivocal acceptance, undoubtedly made for a more joyful and less controversial occasion than if there had been a scowling Denethor lurking off scene.

At first, Halbarad would survive the battle on the Pelennor and it was he who would furl the standard at day's end. Aragorn is as reluctant to enter the city as he is in *The Return of the King*, but comes to heal the injured as the *'Lord of the Rangers of Forod'* [74].He wears Galadriel's green jewel, but 'Elfstone' was initially a name of his own choosing rather than one foretold at his birth.Inside the Houses of Healing, he is reunited with Pippin, who addressed him as 'Trotter', just as he later calls him 'Strider', and to the same ensuing amazement of Imrahil. Aragorn then asserts that the name of his house shall be 'Tarakil', which was changed in the next draft to 'Tarakon' before becoming 'Tarantar,' a name which remained in the first typescript, 'Telcontar' only appearing in the first proof. The title of 'Envinyatar', the renewer, did not appear until the second edition, its belated addition pointing to Tolkien continuing to ponder Aragorn's role even after first publication.

From the first draft of *The Houses of Healing*, the healing ability of the Kings of Gondor is present and so too is the prophecy that in this way the true king may be known, although originally Aragorn enters the city ahead of Gandalf who seems to take little note of Ioreth's words. When Aragorn asks for athelas, its use by Lúthien to heal Beren now becomes another fortunate accident as the ability to utilise its powers becomes an inherited feature of Lúthien's descendants. When Aragorn tends to Faramir, the scene lacks the out-of-body experience, but the same telepathic communication exists that occurred later. Éowyn, of course, now lives, although Gandalf's explanation of her frustration at being confined to the role of nursemaid was originally spoken by Aragorn. The jest with Merry is present, but Aragorn says *'may the Shire for ever live unwithered and unchanged'* [75]. The 'unchanged', perhaps too reminiscent of Denethor's plea, was later struck out.

~oo0oo~

The remainder of Aragorn's story was mostly committed to paper in its final form. The original synopsis had been written long before and this included the ride to the Black Gate, although one persistent difference was that Gandalf would dismiss the fainthearted, not Aragorn. Aragorn's coronation initially lacked its later detail, and Faramir and Imrahil placed the crown upon his head, not Frodo and Gandalf. Aragorn did not return the white rod of the Steward's office, suggesting that originally this role was not to continue. Even when he did so, Faramir initially broke it in dramatic and symbolic fashion as he cried *'Behold the King!'* [76]. In the first edition, Faramir hailed Aragorn as Chieftain of the Dúnedain of the North; the term 'Dúnedain' first appearing in the drafts of Aragorn's arrival at the Pelennor, while the phrases 'Dúnedain of Arnor' and 'bearer of the Star of the North', were not introduced until the second edition.

According to a 1958 letter to Rhona Beare, the unusual style of the white crown of Gondor was fashioned on the high head gear of the Egyptians, with Osiris in particular usually depicted in such a way. With his crown flanked by ostrich feathers, it only takes a small leap of imagination to envisage Aragorn's lofty crown with its seabird wings on either side. In the same letter, Tolkien also states that the use of a diadem in the North Kingdom rather than a crown reflected a similar difference in the use of royal symbols found in the north and south kingdoms of ancient Egypt. Originally, however, Aragorn was already wearing his crown when he disembarked from the Black Ships, and this was only changed to the Star of Elendil when the book was in proof. Furthermore, at his coronation, Aragorn's head was initially bare as he came forward to receive his crown and this heirloom of Elendil only appeared in this particular scene in the second edition. Yet the conferring of the Star upon Aragorn was of greater significance than its small size might suggest. The original wearer of a Star on the brow was Eärendil whose use of the Silmaril in this fashion enabled him to come to the Blessed Realm, and a star worn in this manner was also a passport to the realm of Faery in *Smith of Wootton Major*. The bequeathing of such a jewel, even if belatedly, is another indicator of Aragorn's transformation from ordinary man into returning king.

Later, Tolkien expanded the history of the Elendilmir so that it became an heirloom of the line of Silmariën, but this jewel was said to have been lost with Isildur at the Gladden Fields, so the Star worn by Aragorn became a replacement made at Rivendell for Valandil, Isildur's son. In a late account published in *Unfinished Tales*, Aragorn would find the original in Saruman's hoard in Orthanc with the aid of Gimli. Surprisingly, given its importance, in

The Tale of Years, Aragorn appears to give the Elendilmir to Sam, but in *The War of the Ring* Christopher Tolkien confirms that the Star of the Dúnedain referred to here was not, in fact, either of the two Elendilmirs, but Aragorn's ranger cloak brooch which was shaped as a rayed star.

Following the coronation, a small, but telling amendment occurs between the first and second editions where Aragorn's rather hesitant comment upon Mindolluin that, *'I may have life far longer than other men'* [77], was changed in the second edition to a more certain, *'I shall'* [78]. Also, in the original scene of the finding of the White Tree, Gandalf and Aragorn need to dig to uproot the sapling whereas the ease with which Aragorn removes it from the soil in *The Return of the King* might be taken as an indicator of its willingness to be borne back to the city by the rightful king. Another very late addition is the sceptre of Annúminas which Elrond only brings with him in the final proof. His daughter is still Finduilas at this stage and is named now as the grand-daughter of Galadriel and Celeborn. At the parting of Elrond and Finduilas, no mention is made of their sorrow, this scene at first being included in the Appendices. Aragorn finally takes his leave at Dol Baran, just as he does in *The Return of the King*, and it is only here that the name of Arwen finally appears. And not even in the first draft of *Many Partings* but in the second! She was immediately named 'Undómiel', while 'Evenstar' arose with the introduction of the gift to Frodo. There were a few rejected names; first 'Ellonel' before 'Amareth' and then 'Emrahil', the latter prompting an experimental change to 'Ildramir' for the similar sounding 'Imrahil'.

Another important change that occurred very late in the course of composition was the introduction of the name 'Strider'. Remarkably, 'Trotter' persisted right up until the third draft of the chapter *Homeward Bound* in spite of it clearly being a totally unsuitable name for what had become a very tall, long-legged, man. As Verilyn Flieger notes, the change of name was essential to convey the more serious tone the story had developed. *'Trotter'*, she says, with its animal associations cannot be taken seriously. *'One thinks at best of horses, and at worst of pigs'* [79]. British readers are perhaps more likely to think of yellow Reliant Robins!

Although Aragorn's part in the narrative was now over, his prolonged evolution which resulted in his becoming a very different character from that originally penned, meant there was now much information that Tolkien wanted to include about his ancestry, his past life and his death, which could not be satisfactorily inserted retrospectively. Tolkien did manage to introduce a few references to Aragorn's romance with Arwen within the actual body of the story, but, as with so much else, he found that the Appendices were the place to include information that could not otherwise be worked into the main text. So, when the king parted from the company at sunset near Dol Baran, it was not quite the end of Aragorn's tale.

~oo0oo~

The last chapter of *The Lord of the Rings* was written in 1948 and Christopher Tolkien believes that work on the Appendices was already well underway by this time. All the fundamental structure of *The Realms in Exile* was in place although there are apparently few external dates to verify the timing of much of the composition. The development of *The Tale of Years* proved crucial for finalising the chronology of the Third and Fourth Ages and it seems probable that elements of this and of *Appendix A* were developed together. Notable features of the North kingdom which were established early in this phase of writing were the story of Isildur's death, Valandil remaining at Rivendell, the splitting of the realm into three kingdoms, the rejection of the claim to overlord ship from Arthedain and the subsequent use of the prefix, Aran or ar[a] to identify the High King. The name of 'Arthedain' only arose during the writing of *The Tale of Years* and was at first the name for the whole of the North Kingdom, only being replaced by 'Arnor' in the fourth version. The Southern line of kings was devised first, not surprisingly since Gondor, in its original conception as the land of Ond, entered the story long before the northern realm. Gondor, of course, also featured more prominently in the tale itself and it must surely have been this greater prominence which at first placed Anárion as the elder of Elendil's two sons. Yet, remarkably, it was not until the fourth text of *The Tale of Years*, that Isildur became the elder of the two brothers. While this change was also significant for Arvedui's tale, it seems unconceivable that Aragorn's ancestry was not at the root of this rethink.

Much of Aragorn's story which was eventually incorporated into *The Tale of Aragorn and Arwen* was at first part of *The Tale of Years*. The revealing of his ancestry, his first meeting with Arwen, the subsequent meeting in Lothlórien, although not yet Elrond's condition on the marriage, all appeared in the very first version as part of the history of Eriador. Originally, however, this chronology only included events up to the departure of the Ringbearers so later aspects of Aragorn's story, in particular the account of his death, were covered in a summary at the end. However, the sheer volume of information about Aragorn's life made this arrangement unsatisfactory. A similar problem had arisen with the history of Númenor which was at first also confined to *The Tale of Years* before being afforded a more substantial slot of its own. Aragorn's story, too, evolved into a separate entity and *The Tale of Aragorn and Arwen* was begun.

Apparently there is no evidence of an actual date of composition, although Christopher Tolkien suggests it was written at the same time as *The Realms in Exile*. Even then, Tolkien was still unsure about where to position the text and, at one point, the familiar opening line of *'Arador was the grandfather of the king'* [80] was awkwardly placed following an account of the journeys of King Elessar to the Brandywine Bridge, which itself followed the story of Arvedui.

The early draft is worth reading if only for the many gems of information which failed to make it into the published version. For instance, here 'Evorwen' is said to be the daughter of Gilbarad and she and 'Dirhoel' live in a *'hidden fastness in the wilds of Eriador'* [81]. Both Evorwen and Dirhoel are of the blood of Isildur, although neither is from the same line as the heirs. Both are foresighted, although it is still Evorwen who predicts a great role for the child of Arathorn and their daughter, 'Gilrain', who is described as a fair maid, and, like all the Dúnedain women, is fearless and strong. The heirs of Isildur apparently, *'journeyed much and went often into great perils'* [82] so Aragorn's long journeys are less of a peculiarity to him, even if he is the most travelled of his line. His much delayed marriage is not exceptional either as it is not usual for the heirs to marry *'until they had laboured long in the world'* [83]. The deaths of Arador and Arathorn remained unchanged, as does Aragorn's fostering in Rivendell. Here he grew straight and tall, and, with Elrond being as a father to him, his sons played a role in his education, teaching him of hunting and war, and *'many secrets of the wild'* [84].

Christopher Tolkien chose to publish this version only to the point where Aragorn returns to Imladris at the age of twenty, resuming with the scene on Cerin Amroth which lacks any of the later conversation. Elrond's requirement that Aragorn should reclaim the dual crowns before his marriage is present, although he also stipulates that Aragorn must first attain his full stature. In the Tale, Aragorn's 'stature' referred to his mental and physical strength and this he had already achieved when he arrived in Lothlórien. However, the most striking difference between the early version and that in print is the inclusion of a detailed summary of Aragorn's role in the War of the Ring. Its subsequent deletion possibly explains why *The Tale of Aragorn and Arwen* is preceded by the words 'a part'. This resume was rewritten several times, eventually ending up twice its original length and some of it is reproduced in *The Peoples of Middle Earth*. It is a glowing testimonial commending Aragorn's strength in refusing to wield the Ring of Power, his wisdom and humility in surrendering to the judgement of Elrond and his heroism in daring to take the Paths of the Dead. The summary concludes with Aragorn's death, although Arwen does not call him 'Estel' as that name, even in its original form of 'Amin', was one of the last aspects to be introduced, as was Aragorn's final parting from his mother.

Apparently, the earliest complete draft of *The Tale of Aragorn and Arwen* still exists, a rough, much corrected manuscript with a portion of it typed. Of the original handwritten scripts, Christopher Tolkien notes that they were written *'so fast that without the later text scarcely a word would be interpretable'* [85]. There was clearly a great deal that Tolkien wanted to say and Christopher Tolkien comments that his father *'took great pains with the story of Aragorn'* [86]. He also remarks that the tale was ended with *'great finality'* [87] and wonders if his father might even have considered that *'it should stand as the final element of The Lord of the Rings'* [88]

Certainly, it was only in the writing of these final passages that Tolkien illustrated Aragorn's exceptional qualities and achievements, although the scale of his greatest achievements is perhaps, even here, not fully illuminated. Without doubt, Tolkien's own appreciation of the character had been long and slow in realisation. The very late introduction of the trappings of kingship and the many revisions ironing out any irregularities or inappropriate comments in Aragorn's speech, particularly any of Trotter's anger and bitterness, all point to a very belated defining of the character. The care Tolkien invested in Aragorn is apparent from the extraordinary number of names that he experimented with throughout his evolution and in the repeated expressions of praise he finally bestows upon the character in the Appendices. Even so, some aspects, such as the 'rascal of a dwarf' remark, escaped revision until the second edition and were not amended until 1965.

In part, this difficult evolution can inevitably be traced back to Trotter's hobbit roots and the early conception of the hobbit sequel as an entity independent of the larger mythology. Trotter undoubtedly first appeared in the guise of a hobbit because the story set out as a sequel to *The Hobbit* and it was, therefore, a tale about hobbits which was demanded. Yet Tolkien himself professed his own personal preference for his invented mythology over *The Hobbit*, referring disparagingly to *'newfangled hobbits'* and *'this rabble of Eddaic-named dwarves'* [89]. Aragorn's transformation into a man would, therefore, come to provide a significant, and for the author a no doubt welcome, link to the larger mythology. Certainly, the potential of *The Lord of the Rings* to reach the epic proportions it finally did would have been greatly diminished had Aragorn not become the returning king. As Glorianna St. Clair notes, *'to add another hobbit would be superfluous. To introduce the King of Númenor in a tavern near the Shire was brilliant'* [90]. Aragorn, in effect, came to provide a living intermediary between the higher tone of *The Silmarillion* and the very prosaic tone of *The Hobbit.*

Yet, if Aragorn's story was to successfully and realistically support the weightier demands of the emerging character and, importantly, link *The Lord of the Rings* to the more serious matter of the existing legends, Aragorn needed to find his roots. It was the evolving story of Númenor which came to provide them and the continuing development of this aspect of the mythology throughout the years that Tolkien was simultaneously writing *The Lord of the Rings* had a profound effect upon Aragorn's own development. However, while Númenor would, on the one hand, provide a solution for Aragorn's ancestry and endow him with an appropriately elevated status, the inclusion of Númenor within the mythology also exposed an unexpected problem.

Chapter 3: The Númenor Dilemma

At the Council of Elrond, Aragorn talks eloquently about his kin and their long trials, but from his words we can piece together little about his people from the fleeting glimpse we are granted of the Northern Dúnedain. They prove to be an elusive race throughout *The Lord of the Rings* yet the image we gain is of a race of people living in poverty, sleeping rough in the wilds; nomads with no proper homes; men whose hard lives have shaped them into taciturn, if distinctly loyal, companions. Elendil's people have long suffered from the enduring malice of Sauron and never recovered from the combined losses of the Last Alliance and the Disaster at the Gladden Fields; losses compounded in the ensuing years by the endless barrage of assaults launched against them by the Witch-king of Angmar. Their cities had long been abandoned, Annúminas in ruins. Even the names of their former settlements conjure images of death and decay. Fornost is known in the Shire as Dead Man's Dike, hardly an alluring sounding place in which to live. The Northern Dúnedain have become the poor relations of the Men of the West, enjoying none of the relative affluence of their distant cousins in Gondor, a realm which, even in its decline, still boasts a great city, several harbours and ports, all supported by a demonstrable agronomic economy.

There appears to be nothing comparable in the North Kingdom at the end of the Third Age and quite how these people live their day-to-day lives can only be imagined from the vaguest of outlines provided. We can be sure that scratching a living would be hard; those few coins the rangers spend in The Prancing Pony not easily come by. The upland nature of the region suggests the soil would not lend itself to the productive agriculture of the rich, fertile lowlands of the Vale of Anduin or the Garden of Ithilien, although sheep in all probability grazed upon the Evendim Hills; coniferous timber was surely abundant and Lake Neniual would have provided good fishing. With the Men away providing what was in effect an unofficial police force for Eriador, the work of raising and feeding families would have fallen to the women. We do not know if the wives and children of the Dúnedain were also reduced to living a hunter and gatherer existence like their men, or if they still had homesteads and farms after the fashion of the Edain. Túrin, we know, grew up in a substantial house with cattle grazing in the fields around it, part of a settled community producing its own food. Post- *Lord of the Rings*, his father, Húrin, was said to be so inured to the comforts of a domicile lifestyle that when he was finally released by Morgoth he needed aid to survive in the wild as he had never needed to fend for himself in that way before.

The 'hidden fastness in the wilds of Eriador' mentioned in the draft of *The Tale of Aragorn and Arwen*, provides a clue to how the Northern Dúnedain lived, and this remote-sounding place may even have been where Aragorn was born. That Ivorwen was present at Aragorn's 'naming' suggests that she lived near to her daughter, if not in the same dwelling. It is possible the families of the Dúnedain lived in something like the stockades of the people of Brethil and, post-*Lord of the Rings*, Tolkien provided details of the social organisation of the forest-dwelling Haladin. These people were said to be free men who owned their own land and homesteads, but their chieftain lived in a defensive stockade with a bare-earth dike in front, a structure which sounds similar to many a British Iron Age hillfort.

In the days of the kings, the Dúnedain no doubt traded freely with all the peoples of Eriador, but contact with other communities declined as the need for secrecy increased. Certainly, at the time of the War of the Ring, there is little suggestion of there being any liaisons with the Shire folk. Rangers were sometimes spotted on their borders and perhaps there was limited trade with the less suspicious of the peripheral communities, but, by and large, hobbits and rangers kept to themselves. The Dúnedain only maintained minimal intercourse with the people of the Breeland who were conspicuously distrusting, while the Dunlendings were said to be unfriendly. The rangers did, however, benefit from ongoing aid from Elrond, and it is more than likely they traded with the Elves at Lindon and even the Dwarves in the Blue Mountains who may well have provided ore for weapons. That Aragorn was able to enter the service of Thengel suggests that some communication with Rohan was also probable.

Even so, the impression we have is of a once great people now in decline, enduring an existence that is a far cry from that enjoyed by the ancestors of these Kings of Men during the early days of the North Kingdom. When Elendil swept up the River Lhûn in the wake of the destruction of Númenor three thousand years earlier and established the realm of Arnor in the North, his seat at Annúminas was built in memory of the Dúnedain's glorious dwellings on Númenor, and, as the residence of the High King, his palace would have been every bit the equal in magnificence of anything found in Gondor at the height of its power. We can be sure those of Elendil's direct bloodline would not have sat in the corner of inns as vagabonds, despised and distrusted.However, with numbers dwindling, two chieftains slain before their time, and with Aragorn unwed and without an heir, these people showed great fortitude and strength of character to persevere with their thankless task of protecting those who, in return, treated them with such scorn. As Tom Bombadil told the hobbits on the way to Bree, these are the *'sons of forgotten kings walking in loneliness, guarding from evil things folk that are heedless'* [1].

So successfully does Tolkien blend the history of the Dúnedain and their long sad decline into the fabric of his story, it can come as a surprise to discover that when he began writing *The Lord of the Rings* the Dúnedain of the Third Age did not exist and even their ancestors, the Númenóreans, were only a very recent addition to the mythology. Certainly, on reading the published *Silmarillion*, the progression through the Ages seems obvious and seamless, the Second Age, *Akallabêth*, picking up the saga at the end of the First Age with the legend of the fall of Númenor while *The Rings of Power* brings the story to the end of the Third Age and the Dominion of Men, where, as Tolkien said in a 1954 letter to Hugo Brogan, eventually ordinary history began [2]. Furthermore, the two main works which record the bulk of the mythology, *The Silmarillion* and *The Lord of the Rings*, were to become so interrelated in Tolkien's mind that, prior to the publication of *The Lord of the Rings*, it was very much his desire that they should be presented as one entity. Yet at the end of 1937 when Tolkien began writing *The Lord of the Rings* in earnest, the legends, although said to be in coherent form, were still nowhere near completion. There was no Galadriel; Finrod was the name of his father, Finarfin and even Eärendil, one of Tolkien's earliest conceptions, only acquired his role of plea-bringer to the Valar in that very year. Most importantly, there was no Second Age.

Initially, the state of the legendarium was of little consequence for the new book since *The Lord of the Rings* was planned as a sequel to *The Hobbit*, not *The Silmarillion*, and so only the most tenuous links with the greater mythology were required. Hobbits, after all, were entirely absent from the earlier legends and Bilbo's adventure had taken place in a completely different part of Middle-earth from where the Elves of the First Age did battle with Morgoth. Even the presence of the Necromancer in *The Hobbit* was initially of no greater significance than an excuse to separate Gandalf from the dwarves. Tolkien was therefore free to largely ignore awkward matters such as the compatibility of the landscapes and unresolved questions about how his later characters connected with those of the earlier tales. But as the story became increasingly epic, it inevitably became drawn into the world of the larger legendarium. As Tolkien noted in the Foreword of *The Lord of the Rings*: *'As the story grew it put down roots (into the past) and threw out unexpected branches'* [3] and as it did so, he increasingly found that the hobbit sequel could no longer be treated so lightly. Bridges were required which would span the void between these two worlds. As Trotter shed his hobbit skin and came to need roots that would stretch far back into the created mythical past of the earlier ages, the bridge to hand was the legend of Númenor.

This story was one which drew Tolkien back time and again throughout the years he was writing *The Lord of the Rings*. It was a legend that was to evolve into a crucial chapter in the history of Aragorn's ancestors. While Aragorn and his kin may not take centre stage in *The Lord of the Rings*, the Númenóreans became an essential part of Tolkien's larger legendarium, providing the link which would connect the Edain of the First Age with the Rangers of the Third. The Númenóreans emerged out of the remnants of those three Houses of the Edain which survived the Great Battle at the end of the First Age. Their loyalty to the Eldar was rewarded with the Gift of Númenor, and here they dwelt in glory for most of the Second Age. They were the Kings of Men, unrivalled by any race before or since, superior in skill, wisdom and stature. They were granted long life and the grace to depart at will when old age finally overtook them. Númenor was a land under the guardianship of the gods, the seasons were kind, the land plentiful, the nearest to a paradise for Men anywhere on earth.

For Aragorn especially, the inclusion of Númenor within the legendarium would have far-reaching implications. As Tolkien confirmed in 1964, Númenor was an ingredient in the mythology which *'came into operation in my need to provide a great function for Strider-Aragorn'* [4]. The legend not only linked him to the early Men of the mythology, but also to the High Eldar and the Divine, a matter of vital importance both in providing the high bloodline required by the returning king, but also for the wider functions Aragorn would yet be required to fulfil. However, the inclusion of Númenor within the legendarium also created problems for the wider mythology on such a scale that they were never entirely resolved and were even a contributory factor in *The Silmarillion* remaining unpublished in Tolkien's lifetime.

~oo0oo~

Arguably, Aragorn owes his Númenórean descent to an experiment conducted by Tolkien and CS Lewis in the mid-1930's. Famously, both men were frustrated by the dearth of stories capturing their imaginations and so decided to have a go at writing their own. Having *'tossed up'* [5], it was decided that Tolkien would write a story about time-travel, while Lewis would write about travelling through space. As a result, Tolkien began work on a completely new project, *The Lost Road.* Set initially in contempory England, *The Lost Road* would chronicle the adventures of a series of fathers and sons from different historical periods, all with connections to the sea and, in particular, the Western shores of the Old World. Each pair would have names that could be interpreted as variations of Bliss-friend and Elf-friend, the final father and son being that of Amandil and Elendil whose story would include a reworking of the legend of the drowning of Atlantis.

This particular myth of a land drowned by the sea and of a civilisation lost forever was one which had great personal significance for Tolkien. Since childhood he had repeatedly dreamed of this phenomenon, what he described as his *'Atlantis haunting'* [6] and, in 1965, he wrote of Númenor:

'N. is my personal alteration of the Atlantis myth and /or tradition, and accommodation of it to my general mythology. Of all the mythical or 'archetypal' images this is the one most deeply seated in my imagination, and for many years I had a recurrent Atlantis dream: the stupendous and ineluctable wave advancing from the Sea or over the land, sometimes dark, sometimes green and sunlit.' [7]

In *The Lord of the Rings,* he gives this dream to Faramir who speaks of, *'the great dark wave climbing over the green lands and above the hills, and coming on, darkness unescapable. I often dream of it'* [8]. Tolkien had evidently been very troubled by this dream, and, writing in 1964, he noted: *'It still occurs occasionally, though now exorcized by writing about it. It always ends in surrender, and I awake gasping out of deep water'* [9].

With such personal images firing his imagination, and with numerous tales of great floods to be found in legend, it was perhaps inevitable that a story featuring this phenomenon would eventually appear somewhere in his mythology. Of all the myths of lands drowned by the sea, we are probably most familiar with the biblical story of the flood, and Snorri Sturluson's summary of this event at the beginning of *The Prose Edda* foreshadows Tolkien's tale perfectly. *'But as time passed, people became dissimilar from one another.*

Some were good and held to the right beliefs, but the large majority turned to the desires of the world and neglected God's commandments. For this reason God drowned the world and all living things in a flood, except for those in the ark with Noah' [10].

In fact, there is an element of divine punishment in most drowning legends including Plato's Atlantis, and Tolkien too chose to turn his version into one of morality whereby it was the shortcomings of mankind which evoked the wrath of the Gods and so precipitated their downfall. The drowning of Númenor would also provide Tolkien with a plausible explanation for two major events within his mythology, the reshaping of the world from the flat earth of his earlier legends and the physical removal of Valinor from that world.

Tolkien's legend mirrors Plato's in that the people of both civilisations enjoyed their earthly paradises only by divine grace and, while they remained true to the laws of their gods, theirs was a life of great bliss. Inevitably, however, the less desirable traits of human nature eventually came to the fore. The Men of Atlantis began to conquer lands and enslave peoples with whom they had previously co-existed peacefully, while the Númenoreans turned from benign teachers of the Men of Middle-earth into domineering tyrants. The downfall of both Atlantis and Númenor was triggered by an act of aggression towards another civilisation and by the turning away from the teachings of their gods. In the case of Atlantis, it was their pursuit of imperial ambitions, while the Númenóreans desired immortality. So, while the Men of Atlantis sought to master Europe and Asia, the Men of Númenor planned to seize control of Valinor. The gods, in their wrath, destroyed Atlantis in floods and earthquakes in a single day and night, just as Eru cast down Númenor when Ar-Pharazôn broke the ban on sailing West and bought his armada to the shores of the Blessed Realm.

As with so much of Tolkien's work, the roots of his story occupy that elusive place just beyond the reach of certifiable records where legend and history almost converge but tantalisingly don't quite. Plato's story was probably based on the demise of the Bronze-age Minoans of Crete who flourished between the 27th and 15th centuries BC before being decimated by the Thera volcanic eruption, the largest of its kind ever recorded in history. The Minoans had an unusually advanced civilisation. Like the Men of Númenor, they were skilled with metals and ores; they built great palaces and were considered a peaceful people, although there were indications of human sacrifice, a practice adopted by the Númenóreans in the later days of their realm.

However, Plato's story is just one of many ancient tales featuring drowned lands, and myths of prosperous and developed civilisations which are one day completely lost occur throughout the world. One of the earliest is found in *The Epic of Gilgamesh* which is notable because Gilgamesh desires immortality, although his seeking eternal life is incidental to the flooding of the world. The Breton legend of *Y's*, like those of Atlantis and Númenor, tells of a land that was once an earthly paradise but the sins of its people, here of a sexual nature, evoked the wrath of the Gods and the city was drowned as a punishment. According to Irish legend, the island of Hy Brasil once existed off the west coast of Ireland where there also dwelt an advanced civilisation which one day disappeared beneath the Atlantic. Tolkien mentions Hy Brasil in his lecture, *On Fairy-Stories*, and rumours of an island shrouded in cloud were documented on numerous occasions until late in the nineteenth century. Cornwall, too, has its own legend of a sunken land in the form of Lyonesse, a mythical place associated with Arthurian legend. Alfred, Lord Tennyson in his *Idylls of the King* is one Arthurian writer who names Lyonesse as the site of the battle between Arthur and Mordred. In Wales, Cantref y Gwaelod was a realm said to have existed in what is now Cardigan Bay and where, incidentally, the last king, Gwyddno Garanhir, went by the name of Longshanks, Bill Ferny's name for Strider. While in this instance it was the drunken negligence of one of the princes charged with minding the flood-gates which allowed the sea to burst through and submerge the land, echoes of many of these stories can be found in Tolkien's own legend. Like Hy Brasil, Lyonesse, and Cantref y Gwaelod, Númenor is a land to the west of the known lands, and Tolkien gave a nod to all these tales by including Ireland, Cornwall and Wales in his Númenor-related time travelling stories of both *The Lost Road* and the later *Notion Club Papers*.

The very first germ of Tolkien's own Númenor legend appeared in about 1930 when Fionwë, the forerunner of Eonwë, permits the men of Bëor and Hador to depart with the Elves from the war-stricken Beleriand. However, a decade earlier Tolkien created an island race of seafaring mariners in the unfinished piece, *Ælfwine of England*. Here, he describes the land of Eneadur, which was said to be on the outer borders of the lands of men where there lived the Ythlings, the Shipmen of the West. Far inland, in what must surely be an early conception of the Meneltarma, these mariners had a *'high place of the Gods, sacred to Ulmo Lord of the Sea'* [11]. Like the Númenoreans, these people delighted in the building of ships, and a remnant of this skill persisted into the Realms in Exile of the Third Age as witnessed by the great navies of Gondor, one of whose captains was none other than Aragorn himself.

However, the giving of an island dwelling to the Edain as a reward for their valour in the fight against Morgoth is first introduced in the unfinished novel, *The Lost Road*, and the accompanying drafts of *The Fall of Númenor*. The precise relationship between these two works is a complex matter, and a perusal of the early drafts of the legend demonstrates quite how embryonic the story was at the time Tolkien turned to writing his hobbit sequel. But there can be no doubt that the concept of Númenor was already in existence before work commenced on *The Lord of the Rings*. Tolkien sent a manuscript of *The Lost Road* to his publisher in 1937 which was returned to him at the end of that year, and it was only then he began writing *The Lord of the Rings* in earnest.

Which work, *The Lost Road* or *The Fall of Númenor*, was written first is only really of academic interest. As with so many of the early drafts provided in *The History of Middle-earth*, there are few external dates to enable the compilation of a comprehensive chronology, but much can be gleaned from when certain terms and characters first appear in the various drafts of each work. Elendil, for instance, features strongly in *The Lost Road* but is absent from the first draft of *The Fall of Númenor* where the king who survives the Downfall is instead named 'Amroth'. Yet by the second draft of *The Fall of Númenor*, Amroth has been replaced by Elendil, suggesting that at least one version of this work predates *The Lost Road*. That *The Lost Road* contains the names 'Sauron' and 'Tar-Kalion', rather than the earlier forms of 'Súr' and 'Angor' found in *The Fall of Númenor* would seem to confirm this. Humphrey Carpenter even claims in *Biography* that the initial drafts of *The Fall of Númenor* date from the late twenties and early thirties, and Tolkien himself, in his 1964 letter to Christopher Bretherton, also implies that *The Lost Road* incorporated existing work on the legend [12].However, Christopher Tolkien concludes that, in all probability, the concept of Númenor only arose during the course of Tolkien's discussions with C.S. Lewis on their respective projects. It appears fairly safe to claim, therefore, that *The Lost Road* provided the catalyst which significantly moved the legend forward, while the evolving world of *The Lord of the Rings* made Númenor's continued development an absolute necessity. Given the importance of the Númenórean legend to Aragorn's story, it was, perhaps, a fortuitous fall of the coin that determined which of the two stories, time or space, Tolkien would write.

The Lost Road is of particular interest since it provides us with a unique and very human glimpse of Elendil, one of Aragorn's most renowned and influential ancestors. Aragorn himself proudly declared his descent from Elendil on numerous occasions; he adopted the name as his war-cry as he lunged into battle and he also repeated Elendil's vow at his coronation. However, unlike *The Fall of Númenor* which evolved into a vital phase of the mythology, *The Lost Road* was never finished. As Tolkien himself later wrote, *'it was too long a way round to what I really wanted to make, a new version of the Atlantis legend'* [13]. The story was abandoned without any of the separate tales being completed and, by the end of 1937, only four chapters existed. The first two featured the present day character, Alboin, whom we meet initially as a child in the company of his father, Errol. As a young boy, Alboin is clearly an autobiographical character. He possesses a love of created languages and 'discovers' ancient legends very much in the manner that Tolkien described his own discoveries which arose in his mind as 'given' things [14]. Later, as a grown man, Alboin receives a visitation from a ghostly Elendil who offers him the opportunity to travel back in time and experience fully the visions he has been experiencing; a journey we never actually see.

In the final two chapters of *The Lost Road,* we meet Elendil properly. These passages are particularly memorable for breathing life into this Noah-like character whose human face remains elusive in spite of his being a pivotal character in the history of Middle-earth. As Elendil outlines to his son the choice facing the Númenóreans in the darkening days of the realm, we are treated to homely glimpses of his life on that island, such as his white–walled house with its golden roof and the garden hedge that he planted at his wedding. This day-to-day normality is a stark contrast to the very vivid picture otherwise provided of how Tolkien perceived life in Númenor in its latter days when the king was aging and the teachings of Sauron dominated the minds of the people. For those Númenóreans who remained true to the Valar, life was one of constant fear of arrest and subsequent torture and death. Men were now afraid of the night as the woods were *'filled now with horror'* [15]. The image Tolkien paints is of a land defiled with ugliness as preparations are made for war. Under Sauron's tutelage, the Númenórean ships no longer need the wind to traverse the seas and men build towers even taller than before but, as in all things implemented by Sauron, beauty has given way to functionality. The land has begun to feel crowded and bland, and, as the fear of death among the Númenóreans grows, Númenor is described as, *'only a cage gilded to look like Paradise.'* [16] The Second Age is born but it is not a happy one for Men.

At this time, Elendil has none of his later importance, but he is still a commanding figure. He is said to be of the blood of kings and yet, indicating the difficulties faced by those who remained true to the teachings of the Eldar, his son, here named Herendil, is apparently teased for seeming to possess Eressëan blood, both because of his physical appearance - he is dark haired and shorter than his peers – and because of his 'Godfearing' ways. Elendil's connection with the line of kings, however, is not emphasized, so that when Herendil asks his father from whom the king, Tarkalion, is descended, Elendil replies, *'From Eärendel the mariner, son of Tuor the mighty who was lost in these seas'* [17] but makes no mention of any descent of their own.

Tolkien apparently wrote notes on how Elendil's story was to proceed and, in a scenario which clearly did not envisage any future role for the character, Elendil was to drown rescuing his son from one of the ships that sailed for Valinor. Nonetheless, being 'of the blood of kings', theElendil of *The Lost Road* was well placed to become the ancestor of the kings of Middle-earth when that role eventually emerged, and he was the obvious candidate to become the illustrious forefather from whom Trotter could become the heir. Elendil's coming to Middle-earth therefore became an essential element in the creation of a complete genealogy for Aragorn, enabling him to subsequently trace his ancestry through the kings of Arthedain and Arnor to Elendil and from Elendil to the descendants of Elros in Númenor through to the great heroes of the First Age and, importantly, to Lúthien, the daughter of the divine Melian.

~ooOoo~

In contrast to the contempory novelist style of *The Lost Road,* the drafts of *The Fall of Númenor* merely provide summaries of the basic plot, although each draft is more detailed than the last and all are immediately recognisable as the legend which eventually appears in *The Silmarillion.* In all these early versions, and in spite of some substantial differences, the basic premise of the story remained the same: the Men of Númenor, gifted with an earthly paradise, eventually grew discontented with their lot, desiring the immortality they felt was denied them and, goaded by Sauron, they made war on the Valar and so initiated their doom. Importantly, it is here that the unique features of the Dúnedain - their height, their wisdom and their longevity; features which would also become characteristics of Aragorn - began to emerge.

Inevitably, while certain aspects of the legend remained consistent throughout the many rewrites, Tolkien rejected a number of ideas before settling on his final themes. For example, in a complete turn about from the account found in the *Akallabêth*, initially the Númenóreans were allowed to sail west as far as Tol Eressëa and their kings were even permitted to visit Valinor once in their lifetimes. Indeed, in this conception, it was these visits to Tol Eressëa and the physical proximity of that island to the radiance of Valinor which endowed the Númenóreans with their longevity. By the second version, however, the Númenóreans' long lifespan had become a gift given by Fionwë, the son of Manwë, and their long spans were instead a reward from *'the Lords'* [18]. This change in the method of attainment of longevity occurred quite incidentally to the later requirement that the longevity of those of Númenórean descent should persist, if to an ever dwindling degree, beyond the destruction of Númenor, but it was a necessary alteration if an exceptionally long life span was still to be a feature of the Dúnedain in Aragorn's day.

However, proximity to Valinor remained an element in determining this characteristic of the Númenóreans. As Scull and Hammond point out, the dwindling of the features of the Dúnedain, *'was not a normal tendency, shared by peoples whose proper home was Middle-earth; but due to the loss of their ancient land far in the West, nearest of all mortal lands to "The Undying Realm"'* [19]. Decline in lifespan was less rapid in the descendants of Elros who, at five hundred years, had the longest span of any of the Númenóreans. In the late Third Age, Aragorn's two hundred and ten year span was, therefore, exceptional, even for the Dúnedain, and, in fact, Aragorn lived to a greater age than any of his predecessors since Celebrindor, the fifth king of Arthedain. Originally, the reason for Aragorn's greater lifespan was included in *The Heirs of Elendil* as part of *Appendix A*: *'in Aragorn the dignity of the kings of old was renewed, and he received in some measure their former gifts'* [20]. Although the final phrase was eventually omitted, Aragorn on in his deathbed confirms that his long years were 'given', undoubtedly as an acknowledgement of his past sacrifices and exemplary life.

The possession of greater wisdom was another characteristic of the Númenóreans which emerged at this time and which is shared by Aragorn. Elven-wise, his wisdom can partly be attributed to his upbringing by Elrond, his friendship with Gandalf and his own endeavours, but it was also an inherent feature of his race. The Edain of the First Age were already superior in this regard to their 'lesser' peers, but Fionwë enhanced their capabilities even further so that the Kings of Men became unrivalled among the Secondborn. Certainly, the Númenóreans were better educated than any of their predecessors, learning of the Valar and of the creation myths from the Eldar who, in the early days of Númenor, were regular visitors to the island. However, wisdom is more than just a possession of knowledge; it is also a measure of understanding and a perception of truth, both of which provide the basis for making sound judgments. Tolkien generally gave his Elves greater 'wit' than his Men, yet, according to his 1951 letter to Milton Waldeman, the Dúnedain on Númenor had become *'in appearance, and even in powers of mind, hardly distinguishable from the Elves'* [21] So, if the minds of the Dúnedain were to be considered comparable with those of the Firstborn, their greater 'wisdom' must also refer to an enhanced mental capacity. Yet this wisdom was not sufficient to save them from themselves, and, as the later Númenóreans turned from the teaching of the Eldar, their judgment was found to be wanting and with disastrous results.

Tolkien undoubtedly intended the Númenóreans, whom he describes as *'the better and nobler sort of Men'* [22], to represent the best of the human race. At first, they fulfilled this criterion admirably by using their wisdom for the benefit of those in Middle-earth, who, rudderless and abandoned by the gods, were living in a dark age by comparison. However, as their fear of death grew, the Númenóreans were to prove just as capable of committing atrocities as any other race of Men. They not only imposed themselves upon the Men of Middle-earth, looting rather than teaching, but once Sauron had come among them on Númenor, even their own kin were not spared and those who held to the old beliefs were subject to slaughter and sacrifice. The last king, Ar-Pharazôn, who was said to possess courage and strength of will rather than wisdom, became the greatest tyrant of them all. Tolkien might have created the Dúnedain as examples of mankind at its best, but they always remained Men and, as such, were subject to the same flaws. Indeed, it was the succumbing to these flaws which was, after all, the crux of the legend. As Tolkien noted to Milton Waldman, *'Reward on earth is more dangerous for men than punishment'* [23], and it was the desire of the Númenóreans for even more time in which to prolong their enjoyment of all the pleasures Númenor had to offer that made them susceptible to the wiles of Sauron. The potential to become the very worst of mankind was, therefore, always present within them. And this potential existed in spite of these Númenórean kings, even the later ones, being every bit as much the descendants of Lúthien as was Aragorn. Her divine bloodline evidently did not confer upon her descendants any immunity against performing evil. And quite how far the Dúnedain were able to fall from the grace granted them is demonstrated by the emergence of the Black Númenóreans. Not only were these a thorn in the flesh of the Gondorians for centuries, the most extremely perverted examples, the Mouth of Sauron and some of the Nazgûl, were still to be found in Middle-earth at the time of the Ring War.

As the Númenoreans began to lose faith, the mortuary culture of embalming their dead and building great tombs began to arise. This is in evidence in these early drafts, although here greater numbers of Númenóreans would survive the drowning than the few of the Faithful who escaped in Elendil's nine ships in the final account. As a result, this culture arose instead among the survivors in Middle-earth whose great towers were built in an attempt to reach the Straight Road. At one stage, they even succeeded in devising aircraft in the hope of reaching that lost pathway. This desire of the survivors remained, if to a lesser degree, even in the descendants of the Faithful and is seen in the building of the Barrows on the North Downs and in the great tombs of Rath Dínen in Minas Tirith.

Although there was no outward display of religion at the time of the War of the Ring, religious practice was still alluded to in rituals such as the Standing Silence before meals, a vestige of former thanksgiving observed by those aware of earlier traditions. Religion had been important to the Dúnedain; in fact, the dual roles of king and priest were indivisible, and their kings, at least in the early years of that realm, routinely gave thanks to Eru on Meneltarma at certain times of year. This single, outdoor pillar was the nearest the Númenóreans came to temple building until the arrival of Sauron whose vast golden monstrosity became the site of the worst atrocities and was where his many victims were sacrificed. However, the legacy of this sorry episode in Númenórean history had a profound affect upon how their descendants handled religion in the Third Age. The lack of organized thanksgiving stemmed from a desire to avoid false worship which, in turn, led them to largely avoid worship of any kind whatsoever. Yet, as Aragorn discovered, a Hallow had once existed in Mindolluin where the kings of Gondor had given thanks in the past and Tolkien suggests that the worship of God was renewed by Aragorn in the Fourth Age. Something similar to this Hallow must have existed at Annúminas and provision for thanksgiving would inevitably have featured in the rebuilding of the city.

The Númenórean king was not only a priest, he was the ultimate power within the realm and, therefore, of paramount importance to his people. Tolkien describes the Númenóreans as living in *'a simple 'Homeric' state of patriarchal and tribal life'* [24] and this example set the blueprint for how Aragorn implemented his rule in his two realms. Yet Aragorn was no dictator. He granted autonomy to the lands under the benign umbrella of the law of the King of the West, and, as Tolkien explained, even though the power of a Númenórean king was unquestioned, he still had to rule within the *'frame of ancient law'* [25]. Tolkien wrote on more than one occasion that he was not a democrat, but he explained that his dislike of democracy stemmed from the inevitable corruption of the principle of equality which occurs with formalization. A king as possessed of the humility and wisdom demonstrated by Aragorn would, therefore, fulfil his ideal of the hereditary leader who genuinely rules for the good of all. Aragorn re-established the Great Council of Gondor and retained the services of his Steward who acted as his deputy. His dealing with Beregond's case suggests that the dispensing of justice was his domain but, in so vast a realm, the Lords of the Fiefs would undoubtedly have handled all but the most difficult of cases. Democracy was not alien to the Dúnedain and the adoption of some sort of communal system of decision making would be entirely compatible with Aragorn's profound sense of fair play and justice. Later, Tolkien illustrated the extremely democratic way in which the Haladin had arrived at their decisions in the First Age. Even though they had a heredity chieftain, in a small population such as theirs most of the people were able to gather in one place for a 'Folkmoot'. Here, each of those assembled was given two stones, one black and one white, with which to indicate their verdict. Different practices may have been utilised by the other Houses of the Edain and these would have been refined in Númenor, but it is more than probable that the Dúnedain of Arnor also operated a system of debate that allowed the people a voice.

~oo0oo~

Of the attributes bestowed upon the Dúnedain in tandem with the Land of Gift, great stature is one of the more tangible characteristics utilized by Tolkien as a means of illustrating the superiority of the Númenóreans over 'lesser' Men. This feature was in evidence from the very first draft of *The Fall of Númenor* where the Númenóreans were said to be greater in body than even the Firstborn and, again in the third version, they were also said to be *'exceedingly tall, taller than the tallest of the sons of men in Middle-earth'* [26]. This description was retained in *The Silmarillion* where they were also said to be more like the Firstborn than any other Men, which is compatible with Tolkien's statement to Milton Waldeman. It was, therefore, no accident that Aragorn was the tallest of any in his day.

Quite why Tolkien chose this particular feature is unclear and there are few historical or literary examples of tall men of worth who might be considered inspirations for this trait. The Norse hero, Sigurd, was a massive man, both broad and tall, while Beorhtnoth, whose death at the battle of Maldon in 991AD was the subject of Tolkien's 1953 alliterative poem, is described as exceedingly tall with one estimate of his height made from the size of his boots suggesting he stood as much as 6'9" high. Yet recounting possible examples very quickly begins to feel no more credible than merely citing the coincidental. Take Beowulf, a man who was remarkably strong, indeed the mightiest man on earth, but he was not said to be especially tall.By contrast, height in Middle-earth is an important and complex matter, although any attempts at correlating this physical feature with more sublime characteristics such as power or worth or humility will inevitably be doomed to failure by the multitude of exceptions which immediately spring to mind. As a general rule, those individuals or races which exhibit particularly desirable characteristics such as courage, loyalty or wisdom are also endowed with greater stature. Leaders and rulers, especially, are usually taller than those whom they lead, while the most humble, as exemplified by the hobbits, would inevitably be the shortest. At this point, the generalizations obviously fail, although the hobbits were not completely untouched by these correlations.Merry and Pippin, thanks to drinking Treebeard's draught, were granted a few extra inches in height which undoubtedly reflected the increased regard in which they came to be held.

This great stature of the Númenóreans, greater than that of any other race of Men before or since, does, however, hark back to a theme that was in evidence even from the earliest stories of the mythology. Mentioned frequently, the relative height of Elves and Men was a matter which clearly interested Tolkien with stature becoming his means of reflecting the dominance of each of these kindreds in Middle-earth at any particular time. Consequently, the Elves encountered in *The Cottage of Lost Play*, which is set in a much later era, were tiny, although, in keeping with the greater prominence of Elves in the past, in this same work, Elves and Men were said to have been *"of a size' in former days'* [27]. That 'former days' equates with the First Age is clear from the parity of height given to Men and Elves in the *Quenta Silmarillion*, the last draft of *The Silmarillion* to be written prior to the commencement of *The Lord of the Rings*. Here it states: *'In those days Elves and Men were of like stature and strength of body'* [28]; the height of the people of the House of Bëor, for example, being *'no greater than that of the Elves of that day'* [29].

However, the greatest men were always exceptional, and Tuor as he came before Turgon, even in his earliest tale, *The Fall of Gondolin*, was said to be a man of such stature that he was, *'taller than any that stood there'*, [30] although this description replaced an earlier text suggesting that Tuor's height was not exceptional among Men who, by their nature, were taller than the Elves of Gondolin. This is compatible with the statement in the *Quenta Silmarillion* that those of the House of Hador were actually *'of greater strength and stature in body than the Elves'* [31]. Similarly, in the first version of Túrin's story, *Turambar and the Foalókë*, Men were again said to be mightier than the Elves who were *'of slighter build and stature than Men'* [32]. Beleg, for instance, was tall for an elf, but he was not of the stature of Túrin. Indeed, Túrin was such a mighty man that in the *Quenta Silmarillion* it was said that, even as a boy, *'his stature was great among men, and surpassed that of the Elves of Doriath'* [33]. Generally, however, the Edain were of comparable height to the Eldar, so the Dúnedain of Númenor, with their enhanced stature, would inevitably have been taller which is consistent with the 'elf-like' Herendil, Elendil's son from *The Lost Road*, being teased because he was shorter than his peers.

Notably, Tolkien qualifies many of his statements on height with phrases such as *'in those days'* or *'of that day'*, indicating that these descriptions were pertinent only *at that time*. Right from the earliest tales, it was always Tolkien's intention that the Elves should diminish in stature as their power waned while Men should increase in stature as their power waxed. Indeed, the fading of the Elves was to be a direct consequence of the increasing dominion of Men. The great stature of the Númenóreans in the Second Age therefore reflects an expected progression of increasing height among Men, fulfilling criteria which Tolkien established early on in *The Book of Lost Tales*, where the Men in *Gilfanon's Tale* were said to be *'almost of a stature at first with Elves, the fairies being far greater and the Men smaller than now'* [34].

The height of the Dúnedain, however, like longevity, was a gift and their lofty stature slowly declined following the Downfall, mirroring a similar reduction in the span of their years as both these gifts were gradually withdrawn. This erosion in height over time is illustrated by a note written by Tolkien in 1969 which gives an indication of the rate of this decline. Here, Elendil and Isildur were both said to be seven feet tall, while Aragorn, who lived three thousand years later, was *'probably at least 6ft. 6; and Boromir, of high Numenorean lineage, not much shorter (say 6 ft. 4)'* [35]. Aragorn was, therefore, still unusually tall by today's standards. On first meeting him, we are soon aware that he is tall but, with the story told from the perspective of hobbits unfamiliar generally with the Big Folk, it is only later when compared with other men that we really appreciate that his stature is exceptional. Taller than the rest of the Fellowship, his height is mentioned frequently, but specifically at moments when he appears most kingly. These descriptions culminate at his coronation, where, as the king, he is naturally the tallest of any present, and this in an elite assembly which included all the great knights and lords of Gondor, fellow Dúnedain of Arnor as well as the half-elven sons of Elrond, who, although no indication of their height is given in *The Lord of the Rings*, were elsewhere said to be of men's stature [36]. In fact, Aragorn would have been the tallest of any among Elves or Men alive in his time, which, given his position as the king of most of Middle-earth, is entirely consistent. He would even have surpassed Galadriel who, like the half-elven, and according to a note in *Unfinished Tales*, stood at *'man-height'* [37]. Here it is confirmed that 'man-height' equates with the Dúnedain measurement of two rangar, a ranga being 38 inches, the length of a Dúnedain man's stride.

Other physical features of the Númenóreans are not described in detail, but we do know that successive generations were fairer than those that had gone before and Tolkien's statement to W.H. Auden that the Dúnedain became in appearance indistinguishable from the Eldar does suggest that they possessed something approaching the beauty of the Elves. Tolkien had already devised different characteristics for the distinct Houses of the Edain and, again, Aragorn can be seen to have inherited pre-existing features of his race. However, on occasion, characteristics given to him appear to have also influenced the later descriptions of his ancestors when amended after completion of *The Lord of the Rings*. Aragorn's dark hair streaked with grey is one of the first details we learn about him, as are his 'keen' grey eyes, his colouring being typical of the Dúnedain that we meet in the late Third Age. These features are also typical of their ancestors from the House of Bëor, and, noticeably, the word 'keen' was a post-*The Lord of the Rings* addition to the existing description of these people. Also said to be *'lithe and lean in body'* [38], a later inclusion possibly inspired by Gandalf's description of Aragorn in his letter to Frodo, they were *'hardy and long-enduring'* [39], the fairest of their race. Of Men, they were most like the Noldor and, of all the Edain, they were also the most beloved by them, although this was a turn around from the position prior to *The Lord of the Rings* where those of the House of Hador were thus favoured. When we meet Aragorn in *The Prancing Pony*, he is a weather-beaten eighty-eight year-old, albeit with, according to a note written at the time of the creation of the Second Age, the appearance of a *'hardened man of say 45'* [40]. Yet he was described as 'fair' in his youth, and this is how Frodo sees him in his vision at Cerin Amroth. With so many features in common with the Noldor, no wonder Arwen could be convinced that Aragorn was an elf-lord!

Nor were the similarities between the Noldor and the Men of Bëor only physical. These men were also the bravest of the three Houses of Edain, *'Eager of mind, cunning handed, swift in understanding, long in memory; and they were moved sooner to pity than to mirth, for the sorrow of Middle-earth was in their hearts'* [41], a description which could readily apply to Aragorn. Again, this was amended post-*The Lord of the Rings* with the latter part previously stating that these people were, *'short-lived, and their fates were unhappy, and their joy was blended with sorrow'* [42]. The shorter lifespan might have been dropped, but Aragorn, with his stern countenance and his sad face, undoubtedly possesses the more thoughtful outlook of the House of Bëor and his reflective wistfulness is unmistakable throughout his story.

While Aragorn is clearly a descendent of the House of Bëor, of the original refugees from Beleriand who evacuated to Númenor in the early years of the realm, those of the House of Hador were actually by far the most numerous. These people typically were yellow-haired and blue-eyed, although we encounter none of their descendants fitting this description in *The Lord of the Rings*. Temperamentally, they were very different from those of the House of Bëor and were originally described as *'quick to wrath and laughter, fierce in battle, generous to friends, swift in resolve, fast in loyalty, young in heart'* [43].Aragorn was also a descendant of this House and, although he did not inherit the colouring of ancestors such as Tuor and Huor, he did inherit some of the character traits typical of these people. Remembering his indecision at Parth Galen and at the Hornburg, perhaps he could not be described as swift in resolve, and his wrath he largely kept in check, but he was undoubtedly fierce in battle, loyal and generous to friends and when, post- *The Lord of the Rings*, this generosity *'to friends'* was extended to include *'foe'* [44], Aragorn's qualities can once again be seen exerting an influence.

~oo0oo~

The emergence of the Dúnedain on Númenor therefore, not only provided the means by which Aragorn's ancestry could be extended far back into Tolkien's mythical past, their emergence also became the means by which he could be set apart from other Men, and by which Tolkien could bequeath him characteristics which underlined this distinction. However, none of this would have been possible without the arrival of Elros. As the brother of Elrond, Elros' existence enabled the elvish and mannish lines of descent of Eärendil and Elwing to be segregated and to remain so until they were finally reunited with the marriage of Aragorn and Arwen. Elrond had long been the only son of Eärendil ever since his introduction in the very earliest *Silmarillion, The Sketch of the Mythology,* and he is also mentioned in the first version of *The Fall of Númenor* as having taken council with Amroth, the king of Beleriand who preceded Elendil. However, by the second version of *The Fall of Númenor*, and in the absence of his brother, Elrond is actually named as the first king of Númenor. It was he who built the capital city and he is, therefore, quite definitely a mortal at this stage. The Alliance of Gil-galad and Elendil is also included in this account which is notable for Gil-galad being named as a descendant of Fëanor. Furthermore, this account is, in essence, almost identical to that which, according to a note Tolkien made whilst on holiday in Sidmouth in 1938, Elrond was to recount to Bingo in the early drafts of *The Lord of the Ring.*

What is surprising is that Tolkien chose to use this version of the Númenor legend as the basis for his draft in *The Lord of the Rings*, since Elros had, in fact, already appeared in the mythology at this time and he is present in the *Conclusion* to the *Quenta Silmarillion* which Christopher Tolkien can confirm was written immediately prior to the commencement of work on *The Lord of the Rings*. He further states that Elros' inclusion here was not, unlike a seemingly earlier reference to him found in *The Sketch of the Mythology*, a later amendment. Elros, therefore, undoubtedly existed prior to work on *The Lord of the* Rings and it must further be concluded that even though his creation was essential for the development of Aragorn's ancestry, Aragorn was not the driving force behind his creation.

However, Aragorn's increasing importance to *The Lord of the Rings* does appear to have influenced the role of the emerging Númenor legend. Although Elros appears in the *Conclusion,* no mention is made in that work of Númenor. Rather the fate of men following the overthrow of Morgoth was simply that they fled far away. The most obvious conclusion to be drawn from this omission is that Tolkien intended to write differing traditions for the later histories of Men and Elves, but Christopher Tolkien refutes this as unlikely. It does, though, raise the question of what precisely Tolkien intended to do with his Númenor legend at this time, if not to include it in *The Silmarillion.*

That the story eventually became completely integrated into the mythology to the extent it was is perhaps precisely the matter Tolkien was referring to in the statement mentioned earlier that Númenor *'came into operation in my need to provide a great function for Strider/Aragorn'* [45].

Indeed, by the third version of *The Fall of Númenor*, Elros has replaced his brother as the first king of Númenor, although one peculiarity worth noting at this stage is the choice of the half-elven. The element of choice had been associated with Elrond from his earliest conception, while that of both brothers is included in the *Conclusion* to the *Quenta Silmarillion*, where Elros chooses to *'abide with Men'* and Elrond chooses *'to be among the Elf-kindred'* [46]. The choice offered to them in the third *Fall of Númenor*, however, allowed the brothers to alter their decision at a later time, a situation which of necessity needed to be amended with the arrival of Arwen and her decision to choose differently from her father.

With two major new stories developing almost simultaneously, it was inevitable that references to people and events associated with the Númenor legend began creeping into the text of *The Lord of the Rings* as Tolkien consciously weaved together the threads binding these two tales. Tom Bombadil's comments have already been noted, and Trotter, too, even though not yet possessed of a Númenórean ancestry himself, mentions Elendil on the journey to Rivendell. Present in the very first draft were Trotter remarks that the Men of the West had not lived at Weathertop, but that Gilgalad and Valandil, who is briefly Elendil's brother, had made a fort there. And as the hobbits passed through what would become Rhudaur, Trotter told how Elendil had overthrown the evil inhabitants of that land on his way to make *'war on the Dark Lord'* [47]. Although that particular piece of history was later altered, the passage nonetheless demonstrates the deliberate integration of the legend into *The Lord of the Rings*. Another early incidence occurs when the hobbits have a discussion about the three elf-towers to the west of the Shire on their way to Farmer Maggot's farm. These towers must surely have their roots in the towers built by the surviving Númenóreans who longed to reach the Straight Road. Later, it became Gil-galad who built these towers for Elendil, and this desire to look westward survived in the form of Elendil's use of the Palantír.

The story of Elendil's coming to Middle-earth found in *The Fall of Númenor*, however, was not always compatible with that found in *The Lord of the Rings*. In an amendment to the second version of *The Fall of Númenor*, again added during the course of the development of *The Lord of the Rings*, Elendil is named as a survivor from Númenor who, as we might expect, sailed up the Lhûn to establish a realm in the North of Middle-earth. In this account, though, it was his brother, Valandil, who sailed up the Anduin to establish the southern realm. However, as has been noted previously, the third and fourth versions of the Council of Elrond provide a different scenario entirely. Here, Elendil, together with his sons, who are named as Anárion and Isildur, sail up the Sirvinya and establish the one realm, Ond, in the South, from which Elendil's descendants were later ousted and driven into the North by the ancestors of Boromir. That this account from *The Fall of Númenor* contains the name of 'Anduin' for the Great River rather than that of the earlier, 'Sirvinya' found in the versions of the Council of Elrond, must inevitably place this work as later, so it is strange that Valandil is still present and that it is he, rather than Isildur and Anárion, who establishes the southern realm.

Furthermore, in spite of the very late naming of the kingdom of Arnor, it would appear that Tolkien intended from very early on that there should be a North Kingdom, or that at the very least, Men of the West should dwell in the North. From a note found among *The Lost Road* papers which refers to the *'Stone-Men'* [48], the origins of the South kingdom can be dated to August 1939, about the time Boromir entered the story and while Aragorn was still a hobbit. Much later, Tolkien confirmed that the whole idea of Gondor arose from that one particular reference and yet, in the very early drafts of *The Lord of the Rings*, before either Boromir from the land of Ond or Aragorn as the heir of Elendil had appeared, Tom Bombadil mentions a lost kingdom of Men from the West. Coupled with Trotter's early references placing Elendil in the North, Elendil's temporary diversion to the South is particularly hard to explain especially when one considers that this version only arose after Aragorn, who was, after all, based in the North himself, had been named as his descendant. The presence of Boromir would seem to be the most likely explanation. Although Boromir would briefly lose his Númenórean ancestry, he was originally introduced as a man of that race and from a named realm at that. Trotter, on the other hand, was still a hobbit at the time of Boromir's introduction and without any Númenórean connections of his own. Neither was there anything comparable with the land of Ond established in the North at that stage. Nonetheless, it does seem, at least at times, as if the story in *The Lord of the Rings* was progressing independently of the corresponding development of the Númenor legend since, as Christopher Tolkien notes, an accurate chronology which accounts for all the irregularities does not seem possible.

Elendil's coming to Middle-earth was not only important for Aragorn's family history, his son, Isildur, had his own role to play in anchoring the Númenor legend to the embryonic hobbit sequel. During the second phase of the development of *The Lord of the Rings*, and with Trotter still a hobbit, Isildur's claiming of the Ring enters the story. Initially, there was no connection between the Ring and Númenor, and, in the earliest account of this episode, the Ring was just said to have been lost from the hand of an elf as he swam across a river to escape his enemies. Here, the beginnings of Isildur's flight from the Gladden Fields can be seen, although the job of cutting the Ring from Sauron's hand was first given to Gil-galad who then handed the Ring to Isildur. With Isildur himself eventually given this role, Elendil's coming to Middle-earth and the story of the Ring are bound irrevocably. This important link between the main crux of the plot of the hobbit sequel and the heirs of Elendil inevitably drew the Númenor legend right to the heart of the new story. Once this link was established, it was only a matter of time before Aragorn's true identity would finally emerge.

~oo0oo~

As noted in the previous chapter, between the end of 1944 and the middle of 1946, a period of some eighteen months, Tolkien took a break from writing *The Lord of the Rings* and turned once again to work on the Númenor legend. In part, this lengthy return to Númenor was merely a distraction at a time when Tolkien was mulling over how to proceed with the larger tale. Tolkien did mention the difficulty of writing the last chapters in his letters, and as we have seen, it was only when he returned to *The Lord of the Rings* after this long sojourn among the Kings of Men that Aragorn's full development was finally achieved. This return to Númenor has, therefore, to be considered important, especially when we consider that Tolkien's publisher was clamouring for copy at this time. Certainly, one of the pieces Tolkien worked on during this break, *The Notion Club Papers,* appears to have had a profound affected upon how Tolkien came to view Elendil's descendants far into the future and this matter will be explored in the next chapter.

However, Tolkien had another problem he was grappling with, and it was one which arose directly as a result of the inclusion of Númenor within the mythology. While the development of the Númenor story provided the solution to the overriding problem of creating a suitable background for Aragorn, perhaps less expected were the repercussions felt by the mythology itself. When searching for clues on how the inclusion of Númenor affected other aspects of the legendarium, it soon becomes apparent that the greater prominence of the legend threw quite a spanner in the works. Previously well-established ideas were derailed leaving some issues still unresolved in Tolkien's lifetime. It was not only inevitable questions of continuity which came to trouble Tolkien; he appeared to suffer a loss of confidence in his own creation to the extent that he set about purposefully de-mystifying major aspects of his cosmology. That he would consider revising the origin of the Sun or the role of as central a concept as the Two Trees indicates quite how radically he was thinking.

The predominant factor fuelling this uncertainty was the increasing importance of Men in the legendarium, since it was Men who would inevitably inherit the mythology of the Elves and the Valar. The question of who precisely recorded these ancient stories, and perhaps even more importantly, the question of when, needed to be resolved since the emerging answers to these questions were proving to have implications for the nature of the stories themselves. Númenor may have solved the problem of Trotter, but any uncertainty Tolkien already felt about the validity of the existing framework for his mythology was only exasperated by its inclusion. Nor were the emerging problems swiftly resolved. Possible reasons *The Silmarillion* was never completed are many; the lessening of Tolkien's friendship with C.S Lewis who had been such a driving and inspirational force, has been cited as one, while the sheer scale of the task for an increasingly aging and tired man is another. Later too, Tolkien appears to have become detached from the legends with his interests moving more to the metaphysical aspects where the difficulties of devising a consistent eschatology undoubtedly hindered completion of the work. It could, and with some legitimacy, be further argued that the dual transformations of Trotter into a man, and of Aragorn into a Númenorean, were also factors which prevented *The Silmarillion* being completed in Tolkien's lifetime.

To fully appreciate the problem, we first need to look at the structure of Tolkien's mythology prior to the inclusion of Númenor. His legendarium was undoubtedly the closest to his heart of all his works and even as a young man, Tolkien's stated goal had been to create a mythology for England. As he wrote to Milton Waldeman years later: *'I had a mind to make a body of more or less connected legend...which I could dedicate simply to: to England; to my country'* [49]. And, following a meeting in 1914 with three of his friends at Christopher Wiseman's family home, the so called Council of London, Tolkien made his first steps in this great undertaking with the poem, *The Last Voyage of Eärendel.*

Tolkien had been greatly influenced by the Finnish mythology, *The Kalevala*, and, as he explained to W.H. Auden in 1955, his own legendarium was an attempt to reshape some of that work. But, whereas the author of *The Kalevala*, Elias Lönnrot, primarily gathered his stories from existing folktales, Tolkien proposed to write his own legends and link them to actual history. As Christopher Tolkien states at the beginning of *The Silmarillion*: *'my father came to conceive The Silmarillion as a compilation, a compendious narrative, made long afterwards from sources of great diversity (poems, and annals, and oral tales) that had survived in agelong tradition'* [50].

However, even in the very early stages of constructing his mythology, Tolkien recognized the importance of devising a plausible method by which his legends might be recorded so that they could legitimately be considered to have passed through long periods of time to the present day. As Tolkien would have been well aware, many ancient tales initially passed from generation to generation orally, a practice that is much in evidence in *The Lord of the Rings* where numerous stories are either retold or created as the tale unfolds. Aragorn himself perpetuates this tradition when he recites the tale of Beren and Lúthien on Weathertop and this tale is still being retold millennia later by the elf maid Vëannë in *The Cottage of Lost Play*. It is the very inclusion of stories such as these which enhance the impression, so pervasive throughout *The Lord of the Rings*, of it being a tale that is at the culmination of a very long history, one still remembered in half forgotten tales from an ancient past. Indeed, one fortunate consequence of the inclusion of Númenor within the mythology was the resultant evolution of the Second Age which considerably elongated the time period separating the events of the First Age from those at the end of the Third and so enhancing this impression further.

Over time, this repeated retelling would inevitably result in inconsistencies and distortions of the stories themselves and any created mythology would need to reflect the changes and erosions that would occur as the stories were passed from generation to generation. Also, at some point, these stories would inevitably be written down in books and this would then become the principle means by which the tales would survive far into the future. *The Red Book of Westmarch* and its surviving copies immediately bring to mind ancient extant tomes of stories such as *The White Book of Rhydderch, The Red Book of Hergest* and *The Black Book of Carmarthen*, while much of our history has been gleaned from ancient compilations like *The Annals of Cambriae* and *The Anglo-Saxon Chronicle*. Works of this type inspired Tolkien to invent similar books of his own such as *The Annals of the Kings, The Annals of Valinor, The*

Grey Annals and many more. With the damaged and so incomplete *Book of Mazarbul,* he even went so far as to actually create the burnt pages himself.

If the ancient stories were to be written down, this would also necessitate the presence of writers whose involvement would require some degree of explanation if the mythology was to command the desired level of credibility. Often the people who recorded history were not those who actually lived through the historical events themselves. As Aragorn explains to Éothain in *The Two Towers*: *'For not we but those who come after will make the legends of our time'* [51]. Rather, many books were the works of monks, often painstakingly compiling their own historical accounts many years later and from whatever records were available to them. Verlyn Flieger describes perfectly the position Tolkien was in: *'An entire primary mythology cannot be written, it can only be written* down *or written* about *'* [52]. Rather, she states, Tolkien needed *'a credible, non scholarly observer who could be inside the story but not of it, and who could both experience and explain it'* [53].

For over three decades, it was the intrepid traveller, Eriol, and his later counterpart, Ælfwine, who provided Tolkien with the means to achieve this. The initial premise by which the ancient stories of *The Silmarillion* were to find their way to the present time was via one of these men sailing to Tol Eressëa and discovering first hand the lost tales of the Valar and the Elves. Then, through his later association with the lands which became England, the stories would become a part of the English tradition. This vehicle of utilising a travelling writer to record ancient stories was not new. Snorri Sturluson deployed a similar method in *The Prose Edda* where Gylfi, a king in the guise of a wandering storyteller called Gangleri, acquired first hand information about the creation of the world directly from the gods. And yet, the names of Tolkien's counterparts, Ælfwine and Eriol, in spite of their prolonged and intimate association with the legendarium, may well be unfamiliar to many readers of Tolkien's most popular works.

The character of Eriol was created in the winter of 1916, while Ælfwine first appeared in the unfinished piece, *Ælfwine of England*, written circa 1920, although the two characters subsequently existed in parallel for some time. Eriol was a man of the period before the Saxon invasion, while Ælfwine was a Saxon of the tenth century. The essential difference between their roles was the manner by which the old tales came to be a part of the English tradition and the roles these two men would play in those stories. While Ælfwine was merely a chronicler of events rather than a participant, Eriol, at least in one draft, had a crucial role to play in shaping the events themselves.

Eriol came originally from the land known as Angel, the ancient homeland of the English before they migrated across the North Sea. Coming from a coastal people, he inherited a love of the sea from his father and his wanderlust is explained as a consequence of his being a son of Eärendel, a description given in this context to those restless sea-farers born under the mariner's beam. His parents died in the wars with men from the East, and Eriol became a thrall. Eventually, he escaped and took to the seas, coming to an island in the North Sea called Heligoland where he married Cwen, by whom, according to Tolkien, he fathered the Anglo-Saxon brothers, Hengest and Horsa, semi-legendary characters who were said to be the first Saxons to arrive in England. On his wife's death, Eriol returned to the seas where he met Ulmo in the guise of an ancient mariner who told him of the Isles beyond the Western Sea. In this way, Eriol came to Tol Eressëa where he learnt of the ancient tales of the Elves and the Valar.

Whilst on Tol Eressëa, he married again and fathered another son, Heorrenda. The accounts vary, but in one version only existing in note form, Eriol, driven by home-longing, was to sail with Heorrenda from Tol-Eressëa back to the 'Great Lands', as Middle-earth was known at this stage. His motives for doing this were tangled with his desire to muster Men to the aid of the Elves and so hasten the prophesised 'Faring Forth', an event which, in this instance, refers to the long hoped for uprising of the Elves on Tol-Eressëa against Melkor. As a result, the island of Tol-Eressëa was literally towed to the present geographical location of England, so that, in this particular version, Tol-Eressëa actually became England. But Eriol unwittingly bought about the downfall of the Elves he wished to aid and, by jumping the gun before all was ready, the Faring Forth proved a disaster. The Elves were defeated and eventually went into hiding on Tol Eressëa, or England as it had become, where they faded and became invisible to the eyes of most men. Later, Eriol's sons, Hengest, Horsa and Heorrenda invaded the island in the fifth century and, being descendants of Eriol, they were not hostile to the fairies. They also brought with them the tradition of Elvish lore, thus providing a link between the legends and the land itself, and so creating the desired mythology for England. The fact that, rather like King Arthur, Hengest and Horsa are not fully substantiated historical figures was undoubtedly convenient for Tolkien's purpose.

Eriol witnessed these events from were he dwelt in the village of Tavrobel, the name Tolkien gave to the village that in the present day is Great Hayward in Oxfordshire. Most importantly, here Eriol wrote down everything he had learned and seen in *The Golden Book* although, according to one draft, it was Heorrenda, not his father, who did this. Tolkien was stationed at Great Hayward in the winter of 1916-1917 after his return from France and it is possibly where he wrote *The Cottage of Lost Play* and so 'discovered' the legends for himself.

With Eriol replaced by Ælfwine, the conception of Tol Eressëa was also changed so that the island no longer became England but remained quite separate. Instead, in the period before the beginning of Ælfwine's story, England, or Luthany as Tolkien named it, was still attached to the mainland of Europe, just as in actual prehistory. In this conception, when the Elves were defeated, they retreated to Luthany which, at that time, was ruled by Ing, an ancestor of Ælfwine. Ing was friendly towards the Elves so, although some eventually returned to Tol Eressëa, many remained. Later, Ing attempted to come to Tol Eressëa himself, but he was shipwrecked when he incurred the wrath of Ossë and instead came far to the East, where he became the leader of the Ingwaiwai. Christopher Tolkien confirms that the name 'Ingwaiwai' compares with 'Inguaeones', a Roman term for the Germanic tribe of people who lived along the coast of the North Sea and from whom the Anglo-Saxons were descended.The Inguaeones were one of three tribes, and it is surely no coincidence that the name 'Ing' was at first used in place of 'Ingwë' for one of Tolkien's original three Elf lords. Tolkien associated the 'Ing' element with the West and 'Ingold' was chosen as a name for Aragorn for this very reason.

Meanwhile, the Elves of Luthany, being fearful of the evil Men in the East, separated their land from the mainland by digging a deep channel, the landmark white cliffs of Kent being carved by the silver spades of the Teleri. However, successive invaders still reached the island in boats and, with each invader being less friendly to the Elves, more fled back to Tol Eressëa. The seventh of these invaders, however, were the people of Ing, the Ingwaiwai. As an elf-friend, Ing taught his people to be of similar persuasion, 'Luthany', in fact, means friendship, and it was in those times of harmonious coexistence between Elves and Men that Ælfwine was born.

Ælfwine story is primarily told in some detail in the unfinished, *Ælfwine of England* but it is basically similar to that of Eriol. His people were at war with the Forodwaith, Tolkien's name for the Vikings, and both Ælfwine's parents died in the raids. He, too, became a thrall and consequently endured a life of hard labour. But he inherited his longing for the sea from his mother and, when he escaped thralldom, he travelled far, learning of ships and becoming a great mariner. Like Eriol, he encountered Ulmo, here named the Man of the Sea, who took him to the land of the Ythlings from where he finally reached Tol Eressëa. In this particular version, Ælfwine saw a vision of the island but, when it was lost from sight, he jumped overboard and his companions believed him drowned. Ælfwine's function, though, was to come to Tol Eressëa where, like Eriol, he too heard all the old tales of the Gods and the Elves and recorded everything he learnt in *The Golden Book*.

The mariners, Ælfwine and Eriol, are characters in the mould of renowned sea-farers such asthe eighth-century Maelduin and the sixth century monk, Saint Brendan, both great Irish mariners who sailed the seas off the west coast of Ireland seeking, in Maelduin's case, the killers of his father, and in Brendan's, the Isle of the Blessed. Brendan undertook several voyages into the Atlantic where he is said to have seen paradise and these voyages are commemorated by Tolkien in his poem, *Imran*. Tolkien also mentions him in *The Nameless Land*, a poem published in 1927 which celebrates the unattainable beauty of the lands beyond the Shadowy Seas and which Tolkien later renamed, *The Song of Ælfwine.*Brendan's story, the *Navigatio Sanct Brendani*, is a possible source of the White Tree, such a potent symbol of Tol Eressëa, Númenor and Gondor. Among the many islands and strange things that Brendan encountered, he came across an island where there was a tree apparently covered with white leaves although the leaves were in fact white birds. Notably, in both the later versions of *Imram* and *The Song of Ælfwine,* which were written after *The Lord of the Rings*, this connection is explicit; *'The white birds wheel; there flowers the tree!'* [54]

This, then, was the means by which Tolkien envisaged his legends reaching the present day prior to the writing of *The Lord of the Rings* and before the inclusion of Númenor in the mythology. The importance of Eriol/Ælfwine is made quite clear in the introduction to the *Quenta Silmarillion*. In a note attributed to Ælfwine, the histories were said to have been written by Pengolod the Wise of Gondolin who in turn made use of the writings of Rumil of Valinor, yet it was Ælfwine who wrote down the tales on his return to Britain and who translated them into his own language. Ælfwine was also to feature in *The Lost Road* and, although his role was only sketched briefly, he was to find his way to Tol Eressëa by coming upon the Straight Road, a concept which inevitably only arose in conjunction with the development of the Númenor legend. It is possible that Tolkien even intended Ælfwine to introduce the tales that collectively make up *The Silmarillion* through this completely different conception.

Yet, although Ælfwine and Eriol were of great importance to the mythology, both were eventually omitted from all the major publications. With Númenor now providing a tangible link between the earlier elvish legends and those of the later ages, a different route for recording these legends had emerged which potentially made these characters redundant.

As Tolkien wrote in 1958, *'It is now clear to me that in any case the Mythology must actually be a 'Mannish' affair. (Men are really only interested in Men and in Men's ideas and visions.)... What we have in the Silmarillion etc. are traditions... handed on by Men in Númenor and later in Middle-earth (Arnor and Gondor); but already far back – from the first association of the Dúnedain and Elf-friends with the Eldar in Beleriand – blended and confused with their own Mannish myths and cosmic ideas'* [55].

A further note, possibly written earlier, affirms this shift towards Númenor as the source of the old tales: *'The three Great Tales must be Númenórean, and derived from matter preserved in Gondor. They were part of the Atanatárion (or Legendarium of the Fathers of Men)'* [56]. And repeatedly, the increasing importance of the role of Númenor was evident in Tolkien's writing. *The Annals of Aman*, for instance, written after the completion of *The Lord of the Rings*, was said to have been conceived as a work made in Númenor, the records stated as being drawn from the memories of the Exiled Eldar. In the *Quenta Silmarillion*, *The Lay of Leithian* was said to be, *'the longest save one of the songs of the Noldor concerning the world of old,'* [57] but, in *The Later Quenta Silmarillion* written after *The Lord of the Rings*, 'of the Noldor' has been replaced by, 'of Númenor' [58]. Even the preface to *The Adventures of Tom Bombadil* refers to the High Elvish and Númenorean legends of Eärendil.

However, this change of direction was not without its problems. With the legends of long ago events now being derived from those accounts made by Men from the earlier ages, Tolkien realized there would be implications for how those events would come to be viewed far in the future. Reconciling stories about a flat earth and the making of the sun and the moon from the Two Trees with how those stories would have changed over time as knowledge and understanding increased was problematical.

Tolkien himself explained the situation; *'the 'mythology' is represented as being two stages removed from a true record: it is based first upon Elvish lore and records about the Valar and their own dealings with them; and these have reached us (fragmentarily) only through relics of Númenórean (human) traditions, derived from the Eldar, in the earlier parts, though for later times supplemented by anthropocentric histories and tales'* [59].

In other words, while the inclusion of Númenor was, on the one hand, advantageous in allowing for a realistic dilution and distortion of the ancient legends over a longer period of years, the recorded legends themselves would now have to reflect these distortions. Consequently the next version of the Númenor legend, *The Drowning of Andúnë,* which was written in the mid forties when Tolkien was struggling with these very problems, illustrates the dilemma Tolkien was facing and demonstrates how significantly he was prepared to amend even his most fundamental ideas in an attempt to find solutions. While *The Fall of Númenor* represents the Elvish account of the tale, the *Drowning of Andúnë* tells the story from the Númenórean point of view. Here, much appears which was retained in *The Akallabêth*; for instance, Amandil is now present, as is the suggestion that Elendil and his household were saved as a result of his errantry, but there are also some substantial differences, principally as a result of the story being told from this mannish perspective. So as to emphasise this distinction, the names of places and characters are all given in Adûnaic, a language only devised at that time. The most prominent difference between the tales is that here Númenor is said to exist at the time of a round world rather than the flat earth of the familiar legend. Increasingly, Tolkien was finding he could not ignore the fact the Elves would undoubtedly have known the true cosmology because they would have learnt it from the Valar, and the Elves, in turn, would have instructed the Númenóreans. As a result, the story now reads that the Númenóreans were aware that the world was round because the Eldar had told them this was so, and, if only in a passing idea, that it was Sauron who had taught them that the world was flat. In this conception, Valinor had, therefore, already been removed from the world before Númenor was gifted to the Edain. Consequently, Eärendil came instead to Tol Eressëa to make his plea and it was to Tol Eressëa that the last king, Tar-Calion, set sail. Tol Eressëa was then drowned, along with Númenor.

Christopher Tolkien confirms that these discrepancies between *The Drowning of Andúnë* and *The Fall of Númenor* were no accident. Rather they represented a conscious effort on his father's part to express the vagueness exhibited by Men over the nature and history of the Elves and the Valar in much the same way that would be reflected in accounts of real history, the sort of inevitable confusion that would occur with the passage of time and the handing down of these stories from generation to generation. At this time, Tolkien even went so far as to write a revision of the *Ainulindalë* based on a round earth legend. In this account, and departing even further from that already established, the Sun was said to have been present right from the very beginning of creation. In 1948, Tolkien sent both the 'flat world' and 'round world' versions to Mrs Katherine Farrar who had expressed an interest in reading *The Silmarillion*. Mrs Farrar evidently preferred the earlier version and her preference may well have influenced Tolkien in retaining the original work, but the difficulties continued to trouble him.

Ten years later he wrote: *'I was inclined to adhere to the Flat Earth and the astronomically absurd business of the making of the Sun and the Moon. But you can make up stories of that kind when you live among people who have the same general background of imagination, when the Sun 'really' rises in the East and goes down in the West, etc. When however (no matter how little most people know or think about astronomy) it is the general belief that we live upon a 'spherical' island in 'Space' you cannot do this any more'.*[60]

Noticeably there is little mention of the *Ainulindalë* or the legends of the creation of the Sun and the Moon in *The Lord of the Rings* even though there were still characters in Middle-earth at the end of the Third Age who would have firsthand knowledge of these events. Furthermore, a draft passage where Tom Bombadil mentions that he saw the sun first rise in the West, as it does in the published *Silmarillion*, was dropped from *The Fellowship of the Ring*. Yet, with Númenor becoming an indivisible part of the story, the flat earth legend was inevitably incorporated into the narrative - Bombadil says he was there before the seas were bent, Galadriel laments the width of the Sundering Sea and that Valimar is lost to her, while Treebeard sings of a road that leads into the West.

Certainly, Bilbo never mentions finding any discrepancies between the mannish records at his disposal in Rivendell and the verbal accounts he must have heard from those with long memories who dwelt there still. Bilbo, of course, became the most important writer in all Tolkien's mythology and firmly proclaiming its importance, his and Frodo's work, *The Red Book of Westmarch*, is mentioned in the very opening line of the original *Foreword* of the first edition of *The Lord of the Rings*. Eventually, the task of compiling all the stories of the Eldar Days, passed from Ælfwine to Bilbo, but, whereas Ælfwine learnt the stories firsthand from those on Tol Eressëa, Bilbo used the already ancient records of the Dúnedain kept at Rivendell. These, in turn, had been compiled by the Númenóreans in the days of their close association with the Eldar on Tol Eressëa, and there are clues as to who the compilers of these records might have been. Tar Elendil, the fourth king, was said to have been a great scholar and loremaster who wrote books on the legends gathered by his grandfather, Vardamir Nólimon, the eldest son of Elros, while it was Elendil himself who gave us both the *Akallabêth* and the story of *Aldarion and Erendis.*

However, Tolkien still appeared undecided about entrusting Bilbo with this role completely. In the *Foreword* of the first edition of *The Lord of the Rings*, Bilbo's account is described as 'confused' and yet, by the second edition, Bilbo's work is said to be one of *'great skill and learning'* [61]. By then Tolkien had evidently given the question of records much further consideration since the second edition *Prologue* contains the additional passage, *Note on Shire Records*. This passage introduces considerably more detail about the Red Book and, consequently, Bilbo's importance as the prime compiler of the mythology was confirmed. In keeping with the fate of such tomes as *The Anglo-Saxon Chronicle*, the original Red Book has not survived, but, we are told several copies did, all made by different hands.

Although Ælfwine's role as the principle story gatherer was superseded by Bilbo, Tolkien still seemed very reluctant to let him go, and it is possible that he still intended to find a use for him. Ælfwine reappears after the completion of *The Lord of the Rings* in such works as the *Laws and Customs of the Eldar*, and, although he has all but disappeared as a commentator in the *Annals of Aman* and the *Later Quenta Silmarillion,* he is nonetheless mentioned as the author of footnotes. After completion of *The Lord of the Rings*, he was said to be the author of Túrin's story after having read a manuscript based on the eye witness accounts of a survivor from Túrin's outlaw band which was written by Dirhaval, a man of the House of Hador who perished at the Havens of Sirion. Also, Ælfwine was to have a role in compiling the Númenor legend. The later account, *The Akallabêth*, is said to have been *'conceived as a tale told by Pengolod the Wise (as it must be supposed, though he is not named) in Tol Eressëa to Ælfwine of England'* [62]. This apparently was not changed in any of the drafts and yet in *Unfinished Tales* it is clearly stated that it was Elendil who wrote the tale and that *'it was preserved in Gondor'* [63].

However, Ælfwine's fate was sealed by two statements published in the second edition of *The Lord of the Rings*. First, Findegil's copy of *The Red Book* is said to 'alone' contain the whole of Bilbo's translations, and, secondly, the efforts of Pippin and his successors collecting material relating to Elendil meant that: *'Only here in the Shire were to be found extensive materials for the history of Númenor and the arising of Sauron'* [64]. Inevitably, any future attempts at incorporating Ælfwine's compilations into the structure of the mythology were quite futile.

In the event, therefore, Númenor became both a solution and a problem. Tolkien never did resolve the matter to his satisfaction and Christopher Tolkien removed all mention of Ælfwine when editing the final version of *The Silmarillion*. Faced with the mammoth task of drawing so much material into one coherent narrative, Ælfwine's inclusion may well have proved one layer too many to incorporate in an already convoluted work, although arguably the lack of a framework is to its detriment. The usurpation of Ælfwine was probably quite unintentional on Tolkien's part and it must surely have been a matter of regret that, with the loss of Ælfwine so, too, was lost the original desired link between the mythology and England. However, Tolkien had already devised another, less tangible, but actually more enduring, means by which his mythology would come to be associated with his homeland and in this both Ælfwine and Aragorn had parts to play. It was not only the legends that were to pass to future generations, the descendents of Tolkien's Men were also to survive far into the future and, as we shall see, were even to be found alive today.

Chapter 4: The Divine Plan

In a letter written to Peter Hastings in 1954, Tolkien stated, *'The entering into Men of the Elven-strain is indeed represented as part of a Divine Plan for the ennoblement of the Human Race, from the beginning destined to replace the Elves'* [1]. There can, therefore, be no doubt that inheriting a strand of divinity as a consequence of long ago unions between our distant forefathers and incarnate immortals became a vital tenet of the mythology, and in the fulfilment of this ambitious undertaking, Aragorn and his descendants would come to perform a key role.

The concept was not in itself original and is a recurring theme common to many of the great mythologies of the world. Greek mythology abounds with the offspring of gods and men, while in the Norse myths the god Odin was particularly prolific. Associations with fairy immortals are even more common place, Morgan Le Fey of Arthurian legend being one of the most notorious. John D. Rateliffe notes that Tolkien first encountered the winning of a fairy bride by a worthy mortal in the children's story, *Puss-Cat Mew*, a tale Tolkien remembers as being one of which he was particularly fond [2]. Yet Tolkien's unions between mortal Men and otherworldly immortals reflected a more profound and wholly benign intent from that often found elsewhere. The progeny of his unions were to provide an explanation for mankind possessing a trace of the more ethereal qualities that he otherwise attributed to his Elves. With their innate capabilities enhanced in this way, Men could then aspire to something approaching the level of grace that Tolkien accorded to the Firstborn, whom he described as *'the lesser folk of the divine race'* [3]. That credibility might be stretched if the science behind the biological implications for such pairings was examined too closely was clearly not a consideration and Tolkien was completely dismissive of such modern day concerns; *'I do not care. This is a biological dictum in my imaginary world'* [4].

History, however, is more sympathetic than science, and, historically, it was monarchs who were considered to have the closest relationship to the divine. Tolkien's concept would prove no exception. In fact, Tolkien wrote about kings a great deal; there are several in *The Hobbit* and *The Lord of the Rings*, while *The Silmarillion* is populated with them. Even in those stories set outside of Middle-earth, there is usually a king to be found somewhere and, from the regard in which his kings are generally held by their subjects, even allowing for the occasional exception such as Augustus Bonifacius, it is clear that Tolkien was comfortable with the hereditary and autocratic nature of monarchies. At the time Tolkien began writing *The Lord of the Rings*, his view was typical of that found among the British people despite the recent scandal of Edward VIII's abdication which rocked the British monarchy in 1936. Even today, respect for the institution of monarchy is still widespread in the UK.

However, the perception of the relationship between the monarch and the divine has inevitably changed over time. In the past, kings were largely believed to be descended from gods, the notion of the sacral king being an ancient one found in many societies throughout the world. Even as recently as the seventeenth century, James I held that he was an actual god and he reared his sons to hold the same belief. Such kings were naturally keen to demonstrate their exceptional line of descent to stabilize their positions and so a super-natural ancestor was desirable. The Pharaohs were considered descended from a plethora of gods, and even became gods themselves at their deaths, while the Anglo-Saxons claimed descent from Odin, or Woden as they named him.

The divine ancestry of kings was not, however, universally acknowledged even in the ancient world. The Greek philosopher, Euhemerus, claimed that the gods were no more than exceptionally capable mortals, and Snorri Sturluson adopted a similar explanation in *The Prose Edda* where he claimed that Odin was just an ordinary man who had performed extraordinary deeds. But Snorri took this stance, not to discredit the present kings, but to legitimize them by making them more acceptable to the prevailing Christian Church which threatened to obliterate the Norse myths entirely. With the rejection of the pagan gods, a Christian king was instead believed to have been chosen by God and he only became sacred at his coronation where he was anointed with holy oil by the highest ecclesiastical authority available. He was then considered to be an actual representative of God on earth. The Church of England today still performs this anointing at the crowning of a monarch, a coronation being primarily a ceremony of a religious nature and one which demonstrates the surviving link between the head of state and the head of the church. When Elizabeth II succeeded her father in 1952, one third of her subjects believed that she acceded to the throne by divine right, although the modern monarch serves rather than rules and their position is tenable only with the consent of the people.

In the application of consent, Aragorn was way ahead of his time. When Faramir asked the people of Gondor whether Aragorn should be king and they replied with a unanimous 'yea', this principle was applied to his reign from the first. Yet Aragorn was also simultaneously very much a sacral king. Considered wiser than their subjects, such kings were often comparable with high priests and judges. Solomon was typical, and Tolkien gave similar powers to his Númenórean kings. Consequently, a sacral king was no figure head, and his importance to his subjects was huge. In particular, the life and well-being of the king was directly associated with the fertility and productivity of the land. A common belief dating back to Celtic times was that the presence of a rightful king would ensure a good yield, but if the king was ill or absent, the harvest would suffer accordingly.

For a Númenórean king, this royal link to fertility manifests itself in the well-being and survival of the White Tree, itself a descendant of a divine being and upon whose continued existence the reign of the king depended. Legend had it that if the tree died, so too would the line of kings, a prophecy which in fact did come true, both in Númenor and in Gondor. It was, therefore, a most conspicuous symbol of legitimate kingship and an indicator of the healthy state of the monarchy. Aragorn would, of course, have been acutely aware of its importance and his anxiety over the future of his realm that he confided to Gandalf as they stood at the neglected hallow on Mindolluin, was perfectly understandable. Appropriately, in this holy place where the former kings had given thanks, Aragorn found a young sapling, a descendant of the last White Tree, which he restored to its rightful place in the Citadel where it replaced its long dead predecessor. That the new tree thrives and blossoms so swiftly is further confirmation that the rightful king is now in residence.Not surprisingly, given its legendary significance, Aragorn took this as a sign that Arwen was on her way to him and his fears that his fledging realm might fail to flourish would prove groundless.

Most importantly for establishing Aragorn's right to the throne, Tolkien went to great lengths to create a divine ancestry for him which would legitimize his claim to the kingship in the manner of the sacral kings of the past. In fact, much of the creation of the Second Age revolved around extending his pedigree so that he could clearly trace his line of descent back to Melian, the highest source of the divine in Men in Tolkien's mythology. Such a comprehensive genealogy would not be provided for any other mortal character. Denethor is arguably Aragorn's nearest counterpart at the time of the War of the Ring, but even though he is the hereditary Ruling Steward of Gondor, he is not granted an ancestry prior to the time when his line acceded to that position in the middle of the Third Age. Similarly, although the kings of Rohan were descended from the same stock as the forefathers of the House of Hador who crossed into Beleriand in the First Age, Tolkien never found it necessary to extend their blood line sufficiently so that they were demonstrably descended from Marach, the original leader of that house. Aragorn's ancestry, as the heir of the Kings of Men, was clearly another matter.

Tolkien was not, of course, immediately aware of Aragorn's potential in this regard. As already noted, at one stage he was destined to wed Éowyn and then not to wed at all. However, when Tolkien returned to his time travel theme during the last long hiatus in the writing of *The Lord of the Rings*, the concept became fully realized and the extent of the role Aragorn's heirs might play became apparent. Most of the ingredients necessary for the 'divine plan' to come to fruition were already present in the mythology, but they just lacked the vital lynchpin to hold them all together. Aragorn proved to be that lynchpin.

Descendants of immortals had been in evidence in Tolkien's work even from his earliest writings. Heorrenda, the son of Eriol by his second wife, Naimi, was half-elven, while Ælfwine was the son of Eadgifu, a lady from the West, and was said to possess the gift of 'elfin-sight'.Tamar, the early conception of Brandir, the lame-footed lord of Brethil, was half-elven, being the son of the chieftain and a lady of the Noldor, while even one of the Tooks was believed to have had a fairy wife. Tolkien's desire to include these characters was quite evident, but, at this stage, there was no coherent explanation behind their introduction beyond a general wish to do so, in spite of an early suggestion, never returned to, that the creation of the half-elven was part of a plan devised by the Valar.

This lack of coherency was also found in the original three tales of Men, all of which were in existence by 1920, and which would eventually form a substantial part of *The Silmarillion*. All three stories, *The Fall of Gondolin*, *The Tale of Tinúviel* and *Túrin and the Foalókë*, featured romances between Elves and Men, and, even in the absence of a discernable plan, these relationships were far from incidental to the fabric of those tales. Rather, they were essential elements fueling the stories themselves with even Finduilas' unrequited love for Túrin a factor in his final despair. However, for the fulfilment of Tolkien's stated aim, the most important elements of these stories were the actual marriages themselves and the progeny that arose from them. Through the marriage of Beren and Lúthien, the daughter of Melian and the Sindar king, Thingol, and that of Tuor and Idril, the daughter of the Noldor king, Turgon, the very first steps enabling the divine to enter into mankind became possible.

The love story of Beren and Lúthien was particularly close to Tolkien's heart and was based on his own romance with Edith, his wife. So strongly did Tolkien identify with his characters that after Edith's death he had the name 'Lúthien' inscribed upon her tombstone and, at his own death, his family added the name 'Beren' to their shared grave. Famously, Edith had enchanted the young Tolkien with her dancing among the hemlocks at Roos and these personal memories became the inspiration for Beren's first sight of Tinúviel as she dances at evening time among those same flowers. Although the hemlocks would be replaced by silver birches, there can be no doubt that Aragorn's first meeting with Arwen as she walks at sunset among the woods of Rivendell is a direct descendant of this scene. Aragorn, still giddy from Elrond's revelation about his ancestry, is absently singing *The Lay of Lúthien* to himself when he espies Arwen through the trees. Crying out the name 'Tinúviel', he is as enchanted as his distant ancestor Beren had been millennia before, and his subsequent quest to fulfil his prospective father-in-law's condition upon the hand of his daughter makes Aragorn's own love story readily identifiable with that of Beren.

Beren and Lúthien's tale was extensively reworked from its original conception, *The Tale of Tinúviel*, yet much of its final form was achieved by the end of 1937 when Tolkien began work on *The Lord of the Rings*. Although, at one point, the original Beren found himself slaving in the kitchens of Sauron's precursor, the evil cat, Tevildo, many of the basic essentials remained unchanged. However, in his earliest conception, Beren was an Elf, not a Man, and so the story completely failed to fulfil its eventual function within the mythology. Even so, Elven brides were not won lightly and Beren must still acquire a Silmaril from Morgoth's crown if he is to win Lúthien's hand. At this stage, Beren is considered an unsuitable suitor because he was a gnome from the Bitter Hills who were thought *'treacherous creatures, cruel and faithless'* [5] following the slaying at the Haven of the Swans. When Beren transforms into a man, he becomes even less desirable as a son-in-law to Thingol, who has so little regard for the race of Men that he will not have them in his household. Yet even Aragorn, beloved of Elrond though he was, must nonetheless fulfil his prospective father-in-law's daunting request if he is to claim Arwen as his wife. Beren's encounter with Thingol, however, bears only superficial comparison to Aragorn's audience with Elrond on his return from Lothlórien. While neither father will part with his daughter until stringent demands are met, Aragorn does not have to endure the scorn and derision of Elrond who, as his loving foster father, treats him with a respect not shown to Beren by Thingol. Elrond, being partly of the race of Men himself, has none of Thingol's prejudice, nor is his demand one devised to bring about Aragorn's certain death. But even so, Elrond still sets Aragorn an apparently impossible task to reclaim the dual crowns of his ancestors and death may well have been his fate throughout the many years that he strove to fulfil this condition.

The reluctance of these Elvish lords to allow their immortal daughters to marry mortal Men is understandable, although notably Tuor has no such difficulty. Tuor quickly earned the regard of his prospective father-in-law, so when he came to seek the hand of Idril, Turgon had no objections, seeing Tuor as *'a kinsman of comfort and great hope'* [6]. But in those early days of the mythology, Tolkien had yet to identify the importance of such unions so, although Tuor and Idril were the very first of elves and men to wed, they were to be the first of *many*. Even the distinction between the races was blurred on occasion, and, notably, in *The Fall of Gondolin* where Tuor was, as later, the only actual Man present in the battle to defend the king, Tolkien nonetheless refers to 'men' [7].

Tuor, of course, had the distinct advantage over both Beren and Aragorn of having been chosen by the Valar, Ulmo, although Huor's prophetical words to Turgon that hope will come from their union did not appear until after *The Lord of the Rings*. Yet, originally, Ulmo selected Tuor for no higher purpose than that, as a Man, he was of no interest to Melkor and so more likely to reach Gondolin unhindered. Only later, when the full role of his son, Eärendil, was conceived, did Tuor's coming to the city take on its greater significance. Even so, from the first, Ulmo still aids Tuor on numerous occasions enabling him to succeed where he would otherwise have failed. From providing Voronwë as a guide to putting appropriate words in Tuor's mouth as he speaks to the king, and aiding Tuor's escape from Gondolin by creating mists and fogs, Ulmo's intervention sets in chain a series of events which not only ultimately bring about the defeat of Morgoth, but also ensures Eärendil can fulfil his part in the perpetuation of the half-elven.

Ulmo's involvement highlights a recurring theme whereby these unions between Men and Elves only became possible because of intervention by higher beings. Just as Ulmo puts words in Tuor's mouth, Melian similarly aids Beren when he comes before Thingol. In the *Quenta Simarillion*, Melian is also credited with taking a hand in enabling Beren to gain admission to Doriath, his passing through her Girdle only being possible because she is aware of his great doom. In the published *Silmarillion*, the suggestion is instead that the 'doom' of Beren was greater than Melian's restraining power, but, irrespective of Tolkien's final word on this, at the time Aragorn's tale was devised, Melian's role in bringing together Beren and Lúthien was comparable with Galadriel admitting Aragorn to Lothlórien. Galadriel went out of her way to increase Aragorn's prospects of successfully wooing Arwen even though she would have been aware of the dilemma this would present for Elrond, just as Melian would have been sure of Thingol's reaction.

Tolkien, however, gave Elrond greater insight than Thingol. Elrond was not as confident of Aragorn's failure as Thingol was of Beren's, but neither were his terms set arbitrarily for his own vanity or out of malicious intent. Instead, Elrond was mindful of the larger implications of a union between Aragorn and Arwen for the coming Dominion of Men. Indeed, in *The Silmarillion*, Tolkien retrospectively credits Elrond with wisely knowing that one from the line of his brother's heirs could come *'to whom a great part was appointed in the last deeds of that Age'* [8]. By making his demand of Aragorn, Elrond ensured that, if he must lose his daughter, it was for greater cause than to merely satisfy the lust of his foster son. Furthermore, rather than being a means of deflecting an unsuitable admirer from a beloved daughter, his condition can even be interpreted as a lure to hold Aragorn to his purpose throughout those long years when failure would seem far more likely than success.

The prospective brides also have roles to play in shaping the fortunes of their beloved. Lúthien, in particular, is a great help to Beren. Not only does she twice heal Beren of wounds which could have proved fatal, but her many supernatural abilities prove vital for the success of the quest. Without her skills, Beren would never have gained entrance to Angband or removed a Silmaril from Morgoth's crown. Idril's assistance is more mundane compared with Lúthien's overtly magical talents, but nonetheless essential. None would have survived the assault on Gondolin without her foresight in planning an escape and during the battle itself she was prepared to fight, being attired in mail and carrying a sword. Both Idril and Lúthien are considerably more proactive than Arwen. As the daughter of Elrond, Arwen may well have possessed similar skills to his, especially the power to heal, but the narrative never called for her to use them, and any talents she has are very much toned down. We are told that Arwen watched over Aragorn *'in thought'* [9] when he was abroad, but how much of an aid this might have been is never explained. The use of Ósanwe-kenta, the means by which thoughts can be passed over long distances between individuals, was a convenient plot mechanism in a pre-technological age, but to what extent the Dúnedain possessed this skill is unclear. Denethor, certainly, was credited with being able to read men's minds although whether this referred to merely the perception of the intuitive rather than the utilization of this specific skill is unclear. Aragorn is never shown communicating in this way, although Tolkien did credit the Númenóreans with the ability to communicate with their horses by this method. The rough appearance of the beasts ridden to Aragorn's aid belied their extraordinary ability to empathise with their riders which proved such a boon when persuading them to brave the Paths of the Dead. It would be strange if this handy technique only worked on horses. There are no specific incidents of Arwen utilizing this skill either, and, once war was underway, she employed Halbarad as her messenger. Her most conspicuous contribution to Aragorn's cause appears to have been the creation of the great standard which so fabulously advertised the return of the king as Aragorn rode into battle on the Pelennor.

However, Aragorn did benefit from supernatural aid, if not quite of the same magnitude as that granted to Tuor and Beren. Galadriel was believed by Legolas and Gimli to have been responsible for the summoning of the Grey Company. The rangers may have been few in number, but they were a great assistance and comfort to Aragorn in his greatest trials, as well as being the means by which Arwen's banner came to hand. What other supernatural aid either Galadriel or perhaps Elrond may have rendered in the past can only be guessed at. Both provided considerable practical support and Galadriel, of course, had a crucial role as matchmaker. We witness something of Elrond's power with the flooding of the Bruinen, an act not instigated to directly aid Aragorn alone, but one which undoubtedly did. And of course, Aragorn benefited from the friendship of Gandalf, a divine being himself, for over sixty years.

Collectively, this body of supernatural assistance rendered to the prospective bridegrooms suggests that Tolkien wanted to underline that his three chosen Men - Tuor, Beren and Aragorn - were not just random suitors who had the good fortune to bag themselves an elvish beauty, but were individuals of sufficient worth and stature that the higher beings would demonstrably acknowledge their suitability to participate in the greater scheme by aiding them in their various trials to claim their lofty prizes.

By the time Tolkien completed the earliest version of *The Silmarillion*, sometime between 1926 and 1930, there was no doubt as to the roles the marriages between Elves and Men would play. Not only had Beren and Tuor now become the *only* men to take elven brides, this is where Elrond makes his first appearance in the legendarium. The son of Eärendil and the great-great-grandson of Lúthien, Elrond is descended from all the great Houses of both the Eldar and the Edain and was consequently the ideal character to perpetuate Lúthien's line. At this stage in his development, it was said of his descendants: *'Through him the blood of Húrin (his great uncle) and of the Elves is yet among Men, and is seen yet in valour and in beauty and in poetry'* [10]. 'Húrin' was later replaced by 'Huor and Beren', and although this statement fails to identify which of Elrond's ancestors was responsible for the enhancement within mankind of these laudable attributes, the implication that his elvish blood was a factor is unmistakable. In another amendment, Tolkien again emphasized Elrond's divine ancestry by adding, *'and part of the race of the Valar'* to his earlier description of, *'half-mortal and half-elfin'* [11].

In *The Quenta*, the next version of *The Silmarillion* written not long after, it is reiterated that this link with the divine had become specific to certain individuals.Of Elrond, it is here said that, *'from whom alone the blood of the eldar race and the divine seed of Valinor have come among Mankind'* [12]. Originally, therefore, the next stage of passing the divine seed to Men was to be exclusively Elrond's role, since Elros, as we have seen earlier, only emerged to share this task later. Quite how Elrond would achieve this is unclear since, at this time, he is without a demonstrable line of descent. In spite of this absence of any named descendants, in the early drafts of *The Lord of the Rings*, there were nonetheless a number of half-elven characters in existence. Originally, there were said to be two half-elvish folk of the children of Lúthien among those present at the Council of Elrond, one of which was Erestor who is named as a kinsman of Elrond. At one stage, Erestor was even destined to become a member of the Fellowship where he would represent the half-elven of whom there were presumably a number. By the same token, when Trotter first told the *Tale of Tinúviel* at Weathertop, he said initially of Lúthien, *'she is the fore-mother of many in whom the Elves see yet... the likeness of Lúthien'* [13], further suggesting that the descendants of Lúthien were not uncommon. As Elros' line developed and Aragorn's role became clear, this situation was amended and, not surprisingly, Strider became more circumspect and instead says of Lúthien, *'from her the lineage of the Elf-lords of old descended among Men. There live still those of whom Lúthien was the foremother, and it is said that her line shall never fail. Elrond of Rivendell is of that kin'* [14].

With Elros entering the equation, Tolkien suddenly had greater scope to develop other lines of descent, and, in particular, Elendil's line could now be effectively divorced from that of Ar-Pharazôn and his evil deeds. While Ar-Pharazôn could also count the likes of Tuor and Beren among his ancestry, by establishing a line of descent through Silmariën and creating a separate line through the lords of Andúnë for those who remained true to the teachings of the Elves and the Valar, Tolkien conveniently sidestepped all those of Elros' descendants tarnished by their involvement in the Downfall. It is also interesting to note that although Silmariën was denied the throne because of her sex, she would in fact have acceded when the constitution was later changed by Aldarion, so her not having acceded to the throne herself in no way diminished the royalty of her descendants.

This strategy of sidestepping the undesirable elements was to continue into the Third Age with the descendants of Elendil.Aragorn not only has the best pedigree of any man living at the end of the Third Age, it is also one noticeably lacking any less than stellar characters. It can surely be no accident that Aragorn is descended from all the good guys! His line remained untainted by any of Gondor's troubles and, even when Arnor disintegrated into three feuding realms, Aragorn's ancestors in Arthedain distinguished themselves in the interminable war against the Witch-king and, unlike in Cardolan and Rhudaur, successfully preserved Elendil's line even though nothing remained of his kingdom but ruins.

In fact, the only one of Aragorn's forefathers with any sort of question mark over his character is Isildur, who infamously failed to destroy the Ring of Power when he had the opportunity to do so. But did Tolkien intend this error, catastrophic as it was, to be such a stain on Isildur's character. Certainly, at the Council of Elrond, Aragorn himself refers to *'Isildur's fault'* [15] but Tolkien's later expansions on Isildur suggest we should perhaps view the man in a more forgiving light. The impression of Isildur provided in both *The Akallabêth* and *The Disaster of the Gladden Fields* is one which undoubtedly evokes our sympathy.There can be few more moving pieces anywhere in Tolkien's writings than the moment when, as the Dúnedain face certain annihilation, Elendur urges his father to save himself. Here, Isildur is portrayed as a brave and noble man, acutely aware of his folly and the price that he and all his men, including his three elder sons, must pay for his foolish pride. Similarly, Isildur is seen in heroic mode in *The Akallabêth* when he risks his life to rescue a seed of Nimloth from the court of Armenelos. Admittedly, this is also the same man who condemned the Oathbreakers to three thousand years of torment, but it does seem as if Tolkien attempted to redefine the character post *The Lord of the Rings* rather in the manner in which he did with Galadriel when he belatedly distanced her from the kinslaying at Alqualondë. We are, perhaps, meant to view Isildur as an essentially good man, just one who merely possesses the same human failings as any of us. Certainly, it can appear that Tolkien not only required Aragorn himself to be of exemplary character, but that his entire line of descent should be unblemished also.

The question that then must to be answered is: was Aragorn the sole surviving member of his race descended from Lúthien at the time he acceded to the throne? With Elros electing to become a mortal man, his prospects of propagating the seed of Eärendil obviously became considerably greater than those of his brother. While Elrond's descendants numbered precisely two sons and a daughter at the end of the Third Age, Elros' descendants throughout two long Ages would have been many. But can we say precisely how many were still extant in Aragorn's time? Elros himself had four offspring and, while Tolkien only provided an extended genealogy for his eldest son, the family clearly flourished, and this in a race of people that was known for not being generally prolific. However, the line of the kings was lost with Ar-Pharazôn and, of Elros' other descendants, only Elendil and his two sons were known with certainty to have escaped the drowning of Númenor. In all likelihood there were others of his line among the survivors and it is, of course, theoretically possible that some of Elros' descendants were among those Faithful who had already returned to Middle-earth to escape persecution during the Second Age.

We do know that in Gondor, even a thousand years before the War of the Ring, none of Anárion's line remained with a sufficiently undisputed claim to be able to take the throne. With greater opportunity to intermarry with 'lesser' men than Isildur's people in the North, the Númenorean blood of the Southern Dúnedain soon became unidentifiable. Even the Stewards, who could claim to be as Númenorean in origin as any, were still not of royal descent. As Faramir observes: *'We of my house are not of the line of*

Elendil' [16], an important distinction it seems since even Denethor, as lordly as he was, believed that it would take ten thousand years for a Steward to be accepted as a King. However, this lack of royalty in the Stewards' line was an amended view on Tolkien's part. Originally, while still not of the direct line of descent from Elendil, the Stewards were nonetheless said to be *'ultimately of royal origin, and had in any case kept their blood more pure than other families in the later ages'* [17]. And, in an early account of Faramir's speech to Frodo at Henneth Annûn, Faramir claimed that there were still those in Gondor possessing elvish blood as a result of the kings of old being half-elven. In a rejected scene, Sam is wide eyed at the thought that this captain of Men might be descended from Elves, yet there is no mention of his being similarly impressed by Aragorn! This notion of there being the descendants of Elros still living in Gondor was introduced before Arwen and her unique marriage to Aragorn entered the story and its removal from Faramir's speech must surely signify a playing down of this possibility on Tolkien's part.

The idea that there were Men in Gondor of elvish descent did, however, persist into *The Lord of the Rings*. Imrahil possessed sufficient elvish blood for this to be plainly evident from his physical appearance, although the explanation for his ancestry in the shape of the story of Mithrellas, his elf-maiden foremother, only appeared later. Importantly though, Tolkien made a clear distinction between the elvishness of the lords of Dol Amroth, which derived from the Silvans, and that of his three great pairings between Men and Elves where the Elves were either from the Noldor or the Sindar. As Tolkien confirms at the beginning of *Appendix A*, there were quite definitely only three unions between the Edain and the Eldar: Lúthien and Beren; Idril and Tuor: Aragorn and Arwen. It is, therefore, doubtful that there were any of the line of Elros or of Elendil still living in the South at the time of the Ring War.

In the North, the situation with the descendants of Elros was rather different. The Northern Dúnedain generally remained 'purer' than their Southern kin, but, unlike their more numerous cousins in the South, the Northern Dúnedain were perilously few in number. The heirs of Isildur had long become extinct in Cardolan and Rhudaur, but they survived, and in an unbroken line of succession at that, in the old kingdom of Arthedain and were still splendidly represented at the end of the Third Age by Aragorn himself. Moreover, while Aragorn was the last of the direct line, he was not the only Dúnadan descended from Elros extant at that time; Gilraen's father, Dírhael, was also said to be of the blood of Aranarth, the first Chieftain. And if one other branch existed then it is quite probable that there were others, even if only of remote and far distant kinship to Aragorn. Halbarad is one whom Aragorn actually named as a kinsman, although we do not know if this title merely referred to his being of the Dúnedain and so kin in a tribal sense or if he had a closer, more specific blood tie. That all hope for the Dúnedain rested with the progeny of Arathorn and Gilraen, as Ivorwen believed, does, however, suggest that Aragorn was, in effect, the last of his line capable of restoring the kingship, irrespective of the possibility of there being the occasional fourth cousin three times removed still living somewhere in Eriador.

Aragorn himself was still some sixty or more generations distant from Elros. The genes of Lúthien would need to be of a dominant nature if they were to survive undiluted through so many random divisions, assuming, of course, that Aragorn's Númenórean blood had not retained its purity as a result of inbreeding, an unlikely flaw in one so hardy! Aragorn, on his death bed, named himself the last of the Númenóreans and it seems he was right to do so since he was more of a throwback to the kings of old than any of his ancestors from the intervening years. Indeed, the eulogy Tolkien provided for him as he lay in state says as much. It was doubtless no accident that he was said to bear a striking resemblance, in both appearance and temperament, to his esteemed ancestor, Elendil, especially since Tolkien further endowed him with a great likeness to Elendur, Isildur's eldest son, who was described as the fairest of all Elendil's seed. These similarities, coupled with the very fact that Tolkien mentioned them at all, can be taken as a barometer of Aragorn's purity of descent.

At the end of the Third Age, therefore, we can safely say that Aragorn had, effectively, become the sole remaining source in Men of the blood of the divine Melian. But if this line was to continue, Aragorn must marry, and for him to wed his chosen lady, he first had to acquire the kingship of both Gondor and Arnor. As the descendant of Elendil, this should not have been a problem since intrinsic to the nature of kingship is the principle that it should be an inherited position and this is how the succession of all the monarchies in Middle-earth operate. Even the position of Steward in Gondor is not a democratically-elected post. Denethor is a king in all but name, except that he must bow to one should he return. In the Shire, perhaps as a result of typical hobbit good sense, Mayors are elected, although both the Thrain and the Master of Buckland are inherited positions. The inevitable drawback of this method of choosing a ruler is that the heir might prove totally unsuitable. With the modern tradition of kings being little more than figure heads, the suitability of the monarch is almost irrelevant, although in early modern Europe where royal titles were inherited regardless of suitability, an undesirable heir could be potentially disastrous. One solution was that the people could choose their king from the available heirs. Among the Haladin of Brethil, the position of chieftain was hereditary, but the people also had a voice in choosing between which of Haleth's descendants occupied that position. That the sons of Eärendur, the last High King of Arnor until Aragorn, divided the kingdom because of unresolved dissent among the brothers, suggests that the rule of the realm was not always automatically handed to the eldest son. Where a system of choice operated, inevitably those candidates who were victorious in battle or who fulfilled some prophecy or had the ability to heal would be prime candidates. As if to ensure there could be absolutely no doubt about his claim or his suitability, Tolkien endowed Aragorn with all of these desirable characteristics and no siblings!

Aragorn's claim to the throne of Arnor is never in doubt, but the reaction to the naming of him as Isildur's Heir at the Council of Elrond shows that, while he may be eligible to become king through his bloodline, this in itself is not enough. Many of those present were already well aware of Aragorn's background, but of those to whom this came as a surprise, none exactly fell at his feet! But neither does Aragorn expect the crown to be handed to him on a plate. He has, after all, known he is Isildur's heir for nearly seventy years, and has been actively striving to attain the position of king for the last forty, ever since Elrond placed regaining the duel crowns as a condition of his marriage to Arwen. But he is crippled by a lack of manpower to implement his position and repel the inevitable assault from Sauron that would descend upon his race should he openly declare his intent. His people are few and scattered, as demonstrated by only thirty being able to come to his aid. What plans Aragorn might have dreamt up to restore the kingship prior to the Ring entering the equation can only be guessed at, but it will take more than an authoritative introduction on the part of his foster father to land him his inheritance.

Claiming the crown of Gondor will arguably be even more problematical. If all that was required was for Aragorn to introduce himself, he would have done so years before when, in the guise of Thorongil, his popularity with the people of Gondor was riding high and he had succeeded in earning the esteem of his comrades in the armed forces and that of the aging Steward, Ecthelion. As it is, Aragorn is hindered on several fronts. First, he has to prove himself to Boromir, the Steward's heir, who on meeting him doubts his worth as a potential king. The two men continue to differ throughout the quest, but

Boromir's dying request to Aragorn to go to Minas Tirith and to save his people suggests that Aragorn has successful changed Boromir's opinion of him, although there is always the possibility that Boromir's thoughts might have been quite different had he not been in extremis. There is also the question of the validity of Isildur's line to the succession in Gondor. Regardless of whether Isildur ever intended the line of Meneldur to permanently rule the southern kingdom independently of Arnor, Aragorn's claim on that realm is hampered by the legacy of Arvedui whose own pursuit of the crown of Gondor was rejected, in spite of his being Isildur's heir and also married to Anárion's descendent, Fíriel, the daughter of King Ondoher.

Not the least of the hurdles that Aragorn must overcome if he is to win this argument is the matter of the presence of the Ruling Steward. Certainly Denethor has no intention of giving way to Aragorn. Although he implies to Gandalf that he would step down should a king return, he refuses to acknowledge the legitimacy of the line of Isildur: *'I am steward of the House of Anárion. I will not step down to be a dotard chamberlain of an upstart. Even were his claim proved to me, still he comes but of the line of Isildur. I will not bow to such a one, last of a ragged house long bereft of lordship and dignity'* [18].

Here Denethor is taking the same line as his ancestor, Pelendur, who was the prime mover in the rejection of Arvedui's claim for exactly the same reason. Denethor and Aragorn, of course, have a history and Denethor's old jealousy and uncertainty came to the fore again as Aragorn approached the city. In the event, neither Denethor nor Boromir is in a position to block Aragorn's ascendancy to the throne, but Aragorn also more than adequately proves his mettle and his suitability for the role. His claim to be Isildur's heir is irrefutably proven by his use of the Palantír, by his commanding the Army of the Dead and by his ability to heal. And with his glorious arrival at the Pelennor proving the turning point in the fortunes of the battle for the city, it would have taken a very brave incumbent steward to deny him his throne.

Once he is king, Aragorn is able to claim his bride. It is perhaps important to note at this point that all three unions between Men and Elves in Tolkien's mythology were genuine love matches. The fulfilling of his plan was no cold selective breeding programme where the characters are treated as prize cattle. All three men were instantly smitten, and both Lúthien and Idril very rapidly fell for their suitors. In *The Fall of Gondolin*, Idril's fate was said to be bound with Tuor's as she gazed at him from a window above, even though

Tuor, as he stood before the king dressed only in bear skin appeared no more than a *'way-worn suppliant'* [19]. There was clearly no need for Galadriel's fancy garb here! Although in the later, *The Quenta*, Idril's heart was said to have 'turned' to Tuor, she nonetheless gave her heart significantly faster than the more cautious Arwen who took nearly thirty years to commit to Aragorn. Tuor, of course, did not have the longer life of Aragorn in which to await such elvish indecision. Tolkien did boost the chemistry a little by ensuring that all three elven ladies were exceptionally beautiful and all three Men were mighty warriors, physically impressive specimens as well as heroic and tenacious. It was important that they should merit the considerable sacrifices that their elven ladies must make to wed a mortal.However, the Firstborn as a people will ultimately benefit too from these unions. With the Elves departing from Middle-earth, or fading to eventually become the flimsy fairies of fairy-tales, Arwen's descendants would become their predominant means of continuing to influence mankind long after the last ship had sailed. The heirs of Aragorn and Arwen were, therefore, the custodians of both their legacies.

Tolkien's choice of Midsummer's Day for the marriage of Aragorn and Arwen underscores the supernatural implications of their union, and forms part of a natural sequence progressing from their betrothal some thirty nine years earlier on Midsummer's Eve. Midsummer has long been thought a magical time when it is believed that the boundary between this world and the world of faerie becomes thin so that encounters with fairies are more likely, a myth taken up by Shakespeare in his comedy *A Midsummer Night's Dream*. Many ancient stone circles were aligned so that the sun would strike between the stones in a certain way at midsummer, and Stonehenge is still a place of pilgrimage at this time of the year. John the Baptist was born on midsummer's eve, and midsummer is also the Festival of the All-Father, with Father's Day being celebrated in the UK on the Sunday closest to the summer solstice. The date also has its dark side. Balder the Norse god of light was slain by his brother, Hodur, at midsummer, while Túrin, in his original tale, unwittingly married his sister on this day. That Tolkien chose midsummer for the union of Aragorn and Arwen may also have something to do with the date being considered a time of joy, a celebration of courage and manliness and, for older women in particular, a time of increased fertility!

The marriage of Aragorn and Arwen would prove a watershed for the passing of the divine to mankind. As Tolkien himself said of their marriage, *'the long-sundered branches of the Half-elven were reunited and their line was restored'* [20]. But, crucially, the line did not end there. Aragorn was undoubtedly a great and successful king, not least because he fulfilled one of the most important functions of any ruling monarch, that of providing an heir to ensure the succession. We know little of his son, Eldarion, but, in *The Peoples of Middle-earth,* there is an intriguing prophecy concerning his heirs which was originally tagged onto the end of an early draft of the Appendix concerned with the heirs in Gondor.

'Of Eldarion son of Elessar it was foretold that he should rule a great realm, and that it should endure for a hundred generations of Men after him, that is until a new age brought in again new things; and from him should come the kings of many realms in long days after. But if this foretelling spoke truly, none now can say, for Gondor and Arnor are no more; and even the chronicles of the House of Elessar and all their deeds and glory are lost.' [21].

Writing of Lúthien's heirs even before work began on *The lord of the Rings*, Tolkien's intent for her descendants is unequivocal: *'For her line is not yet extinguished, though the world is changed'* [22]. This prediction was reinforced by Aragorn himself at the camp near Weathertop when he told the hobbits that the line of Lúthien would not fail.Legolas, too, said the same thing in the chapter *The Last Debate.*The prophecy of Eldarion was eventually omitted from the Appendices, possibly because Eldarion had yet to be introduced as Aragorn's son in the chronology, but from Aragorn's own prediction alone, we can be sure that his descendents were to endure far into the future.

~oo0oo~

So, what do we know of these 'heirs' who ruled for a further one hundred generations? Tolkien was not very encouraging when he wrote in 1964 that *'the dynasts' descended from Aragorn would become, just kings and governors - like Denethor or worse'* [23]. One suggestion proposed by Stratford Caldecott in his paper, *Tolkien's Project*, was that Tolkien might have intended re-writing the legend of Arthur so as to trace his ancestry back to Aragorn and Lúthien as a means of preventing the *'Norman-Plantagenet 'hijacking'* [24] of the Arthurian legends which so appalled him. There may well be some justification in this suggestion since, as has already been shown, Tolkien was no stranger to experimenting with fusing his mythical heroes with those on the fringes of history as a means of threading his own story into existing legends. Certainly, the Inklings were actively considering possible links between old legend and modern history during World War II and, in 1945, C.S. Lewis published *That Hideous Strength* which features characters said to be descended from King Arthur.

This blending of myth and history was particularly in evidence in *The Lost Road*, which, as mentioned in the earlier chapter would feature a succession of Elf-friends, beginning with characters from the present day and continuing back in time to conclude with Elendil in Númenor. The intermediary chapters were to recall episodes from throughout history, but, in the event, only short pieces materialised, primarily the story of Ælfwine, who was already well established in Tolkien's legendarium. Ælfwine would feature in the Anglo-Saxon episode set in the tenth century and his story would also incorporate the legend of King Sheave, more of which later. Other episodes would follow, each one recalling an earlier period in history before ultimately leading to Middle-earth as we know it. What is interesting about the proposed Elf-friends who were to appear in these various chapters is the implication that they were actually descendants of Elendil. The present day character, Alboin, on seeing a vision of Elendil thought that the face reminded him of his father. Elendil then confirms this connection by saying to him, *'I was of Númenor, the father of many fathers before you. I am Elendil, that is in Eressëan "Elf-friend", and many have been called so since'* [25].

We can but speculate as to the content of the stories and the roles that Elendil's descendants might have played, although we do know something of their broad nature. There would have been a Lombard story featuring the historical king Alboin, who was described in glowing terms in the poem, *Widsith*. A tale based on the Irish legends of the semi-divine Tuatha-de-Danaan would follow, and it is possible their story would be told by Finntan, who was said to be the oldest man in the world and a survivor of the biblical flood of Noah. With his great age of five thousand years, he may well have been destined to fill a role as witness to historical events in a similar manner to that of Ælfwine. Other historical episodes would follow, including a tale from the Ice Age featuring old kings found buried in the ice, before, ultimately, the stories would lead to Middle-earth and to Elendil.

Tolkien returned to this time travel theme in 1945 when he wrote *The Notion Club Papers*. In this work, Ælfwine would again feature prominently, but now the link between the principal characters and Elendil becomes explicit. Set in contempory England, *The Notion Club Papers* features a series of conversations between its members, a group of Oxford academics, the eponymous Notion Club, which has obvious parallels with the Inklings. Two of their number, Alwin 'Arry' Lowdham and Wilfred Trewin Jeremy, are quickly revealed as descendants of those who witnessed the drowning of Númenor. Lowdham is no less than a descendant of Elendil himself, his nickname perhaps being a clue to his royal ancestry, while Jeremy's forefather was Elendil's companion, Voronwë, a name more familiar as that of Tuor's guide. These contempory characters are clearly counterparts of those introduced in *The Lost Road,* and in an earlier draft, Arry Lowdham's father, Edwin, is named 'Oswin Ellendil', while Lowdham himself is 'Alboin Arundel', mirroring the Oswin Errol and his son, Alboin, of *The Lost Road.* Edwin even possessed characteristics typical of the Dúnedain, being described as a large, tall, powerful and dark man. A great sea-farer, he had inherited the sea-longing of his ancestors and eventually sailed west in his ship, *Eärendel,* never to be seen again. These present-day 'Númenóreans' are not reincarnations of their ancestors, but Lowdham and Jeremy discover they have an ability to experience past events as witnessed by their various forefathers. The visions they receive of these earlier historical periods come to them with great clarity, more vivid and real than ordinary dreams, since the images originate in inherited memories. This concept is clearly in the realms of science fiction, but even when written before the unravelling of the genetic code by Crick and Watson in the early 1950's, Tolkien nonetheless still manages to convey the concept with a degree of plausibility.

The Notion Club Papers may well have been little more than a distraction for Tolkien while he was stuck with progress on *The Lord of the Rings,* yet his note of 1945 to *'do the Atlantis story and abandon the Eriol-Saga, with Loudham, Jeremy, Guilford, and Ramer taking part'* [27], suggests he was seriously considering returning to this time travel method of bringing his ancient stories to the present day even whilst in the midst of finalising his ideas on *The Lord of the Rings.* The concept of a travelling Englishman discovering hitherto forgotten legends was hardly new, being the premise upon which the mythology evolved in the first place. This route, with Lowdham and Jeremy witnessing historical events through the eyes of their ancestors, would also once again place the mythology firmly in England as here it is Englishmen who are the descendents of Elendil and his companion. Tolkien even had a legitimate premise by which the adventures of these two characters would eventually become known since the minutes of the Notion Club meetings recording these events were to be discovered in a basement in Oxford in 1989.

Initially, Lowdham and Jeremy visualise images from fragments of a book, written as it turns out by Elendil, the broken sentences coming to them subconsciously and unbidden. At their meetings, the members of the Notion Club attempt to decipher the text of these fragments which tell of the legend of Númenor. One day, these scraps of information suddenly take on an unexpected and dramatic dimension when a severe storm rips through the UK causing great devastation and flooding in its wake. With a remarkable piece of foresight of his own, Tolkien gives the date of this storm as 1987 and, like the hurricane which laid waste southern England in that very year, this storm arrives without prediction by the weather forecasters! Its coming is, instead, heralded by the appearance of huge clouds in the shape of great eagles, a phenomenon which takes up a recurrent theme from *The Lost Road*.

Lowdham and Jeremy subsequently disappear for a while during the Oxford summer recess, but on their return, they have some extraordinary tales to tell. On their travels, they came to Ireland where they caught a glimpse of Tol Eressëa and met a strange man described as wild and ragged, but tall and rather impressive who spoke of ghostly visions of a black ship carrying tall men far inland that had come out of the sea on the crest of a great wave in the *'days before the days'* [28]. The two travellers eventually came to Porlock in Somerset were they beheld events which occurred in that part of the West Country during the reign of Alfred the Great's son, Edward. The scene is set in 918AD and Lowdham's and Jeremy's ancestors are among the Saxons waiting to make war upon the invading Danes. Lowdham's forefather is Ælfwine who, in this later conception, is, therefore, a descendent of Elendil. The sea-longing has grown strong within him and he recalls his past voyages, his journeys to 'Iraland' where he always sought tales of the sea, and, linking up with *The Lost Road*, he tells of mariners like Maelduin and Saint Brendan and others who told of a land of Men which long ago had been 'cast down'. According to the legends, those who survived had come to 'Eriu,' a name for Ireland, and the descendents of these men were said to have lived on in lands on the shores of the ocean. But they were said to have, *'dwindled and forgot, and nought now was left of them but a wild strain in the blood of men of the West'* [29]. All were, according to Ælfwine, still identifiable by their undiminished longing for the sea.

There is something very haunting and moving about these passages and, as the following excerpt from a letter written to W.H. Auden in 1955 suggests, these images resonated with Tolkien on a very personal level: *'a man of the North-west of the Old World will set his heart and the action of his tale in an imaginary world of that air, and that situation: with the Shoreless Sea of his innumerable ancestors to the West, and the endless lands (out of which enemies mostly come) to the East. Though, in addition, his heart may remember, even if he has been cut off from all oral tradition, the rumour all along the coasts of the Men out of the Sea'* [30].

The 'tale' Tolkien is referring to here is, of course, *Lord of the Rings*, but this lure of the sea and of the lands that lie beyond the known lands was a powerful and motivating motif for him. Not surprisingly, it infuses much of his work, from the sad ending of *Ælfwine of England* to the departure of Legolas and Gimi on the death of Elessar. Of particular interest here is the 'rumour' of these men that came out of the sea which must equate with the survivors of Númenor. But Tolkien seems ambivalent about how he came to view the fate of these tall, mysterious men, the descendents of those from a long vanished world. On the one hand, there is the eventual, rather sad, marginalising of these men as described in the passage above, while, on the other, there is the legend of King Sheave.

Sheave is Tolkien's modern name for the legendary Scandinavian king known historically as Sceafa or Scef, which translates as 'sheaf' in Old English. Tolkien first introduced Sheave in *The Lost Road* where his story was to be incorporated into that of Ælfwine, while *The Notion Club Papers* contains a further passage featuring the life of this mythical character. Historical evidence is sparse, although Alexander M. Bruce has compiled every known reference to the name 'Scef and' the closely allied, 'Scyld', from a wide variety of sources. The names and their derivatives appear in a range of legends and are found among a diversity of characters from Snorri Sturluson's grandfather of Frothi to the sons of Odin or Noah. Although the historical authenticity of the character is unproven, a king named 'Sceafa' is mentioned in the Old English poem, *Widsith*, and there is some consensus on the legend among two of the principle sources, namely the *Anglo-Saxon Chronicle* attributed to Æthelweard, and *The History of the Kings of England* by the twelfth century historian, William of Malmesbury. Both tell a similar story of the coming of a mysterious child in a boat. Alone and asleep on a sheaf of corn, he is adopted by the people who rescue him and he eventually grows up to become a great king who is invariably of great benefit to his people.

In *The Lost Road*, Christopher Tolkien gives a translation of Malmesbury's description of how a sleeping child arrived at Scandza, an island of Germany:

'He was regarded as a marvel by the people of that country, and carefully fostered; when he was grown he ruled in the town which was then called Slaswic, but now Haithebi. That region is called Old Anglia, whence the Angli came to Britain.' [31].

Incidentally, Tolkien chose this place, the home of the Anglo-Saxons, as the region from which Eriol's folk originated. Æthelweard, too, records Scef's arrival in a similar manner to Malmesbury: *'This Sceaf came with one ship to an island of the ocean named Scani, sheathed in arms, and he was a young boy, and unknown to the people of that land; but he was received by them, and they guarded him as their own with much care, and afterwards chose him for their king.'* [32].

Most famously, the first fifty-two lines of the eleventh century poem, *Beowulf* are devoted to telling a similar story, although for one Scyld Scefing, a name interpreted as either 'Scyld the son of Scef' or 'Scyld of the Sheaf'. This is possibly the same character or, at least, a character performing a similar function since Scyld was said to have founded the Danish dynasty, the Scyldings. Tolkien's own legend of Sheave has parallels with all three versions. His child-king also arrives by boat asleep on a sheaf of corn, although uniquely, and in keeping with the theme in *The Lost Road* of which the story was originally to be a part, his coming is heralded by clouds shaped like eagles. Sheave was also taken as king by the people who cared for him and he, in turn, brought great prosperity to that people. The tale is echoed in that of the shipwrecked Ing coming to the land of the Ingwaiwai, and also has some parallels with the thirteenth century legend of King Horn, who, as a fatherless lad, was set adrift in a boat before also becoming a king eventually. Like the Sceafa Longbeardum in *Widsith,* Tolkien's Sheave became king of the Lombards, and, also after the manner of *Widsith* where their later king, Albion, is described in glowing terms, Sheave, too, was given an exemplary epitaph by Tolkien.

> *At his throne men found comfort and care's healing,*
> *justice in judgement. Generous handed*
> *his gifts he gave. Glory was uplifted.*
> *Far sprang his fame over fallow water,*
> *through Northern lands the renown echoed*
> *of the shining king, Sheave the Mighty.* [33]

King Sheave taught the people who adopted him many skills and crafts, and it is likely that it was legends in this tradition which were the inspiration behind the coming of the Númenóreans to Middle-earth. In the early years of that island race, before they became the tyrants seen in the later days of Númenor's decline, the Dúnedain came benignly to Middle-earth purely as teachers bearing corn and wine, and were considered gods by the men who welcomed them. As Tolkien noted, the legends of Númenor were based on a *'special personal concern with this tradition of the culture-bearing men of the Sea, which so profoundly affected the imagination of peoples of Europe with westward-shores'* [34].

Sheave's story undoubtedly functions as an echo to recall the legends of the mythical Scef and Scyld, and, in 1944, Tolkien wrote to his son, Christopher, that he had been, *'getting a lot of new ideas about Prehistory lately (via Beowulf and other sources of which I may have written) and want to work them into the long shelved time-travel story I began'* [35]. It may well have been the story of Scyld Scefing that Tolkien was referring to here since both *Beowulf* and *King Sheave* feature the departure of the hero in a funeral boat, a detail lacking in the accounts of both Malmesbury and Æthelweard. Sheave, however, was said to have come from a western land described as, *'beyond the ways of men since the world worsened'* [36] which could equate with the reshaping of the world following the drowning of Númenor. If this is the case, the legend can not be considered purely as a metaphor for the returning Númenóreans and must be presumed to have arisen in a later time frame.

Although Tolkien first wrote of Sheave as part of *The Lost Road*, more can be discerned about the role he envisaged for the character from the later passages included in *The Notion Club Papers*. In this work, Sheave's story is recited, not by Ælfwine, but by his companion, Tréowine, the Anglo-Saxon forefather of Jeremy. Tréowine was said to be the son of one 'Céolwulf' who claimed to *'come of the kin of the kings that sat at Tamworth of old'* [37]. Tamworth was the Saxon capital of Mercia which was sacked by the Danes in 874 and, while Tréowine's father may have been an altogether different character, it is interesting to note that there were two Mercian kings by the name of Céolwulf. The first was the brother of Coenwulf or Kenelph, the king who succeeded Offa's son, Ecgfrith, to the throne in 796. Coenwulf's son, Kenelm, should have followed his father in the year 821, but Kenelm was murdered by his sister, who was herself deposed by her uncle, Céolwulf. The immediate ancestry of the second Céolwulf is unknown although he is believed to have been a descendant of the first. The last of the Mercian kings, little seems to be known about him, although his death, given variously at either 881 or 879, would place him in the correct time scale to be Tréowine's father. Regardless of whether this was Tolkien's intention, ifTréowine's 'Céolwulf' was descended from kings, as claimed here, then he was probably of Offa's line, and Offa, in turn, is known to have been a descendant of the semi-legendary Cerdic, the first Anglo- Saxon king of Wessex and also the ancestor of the English king, Alfred the Great.

The Saxon kings kept detailed records of their genealogies but, at that time, Cerdic's ancestors could only be traced as far back as Woden. However, his genealogy was later extended further, primarily for political reasons to bolster the prestige of the West Saxons over the Scandinavian kings of northern England. Certainly these ancestors of Woden were, according to Tolkien's former tutor, Kenneth Sisam, *'a fanciful development of Christian times'* [38]. However, the extended genealogies of these Saxon kings are found in more than one source and their existence on the fringes of history makes them, if anything, even more compelling. Æthelweard, who was himself a descendant of Alfred's brother, Æthelred, in his Latin version of the *Anglo-Saxon Chronicle* under the entry for 857 AD, extended Woden's ancestry back to one 'Geat' who was said to be the son of Taetwa, son of Beow, son of Sceldi [Scyld], son of Sceaf; these last three characters being very similar to those found in *Beowulf.* Under the same entry, Æthelweard further added: *'It is from him [Sceaf] that king Ethelwulf derives his descent'* [39]. In other versions of the *Anglo-Saxon Chronicle*, the two Abingdon Chronicles, again, probably added later,the entry for 855 AD also has Scef included in the genealogy of the kings, although separated from 'Sceldwa' [Scyld] by five additional generations. Here, he is further named as a son of Noah, making him a direct descendant of Adam. Asser, the biographer of Alfred, also lists 'Scelwea' among Alfred's ancestors, while William of Malmesbury cites Sceldius son of Sceaf, son of Beowius, son of Tetius, son of Getius among the ancestors of the West Saxon kings.

The historical verification for such claims may be debateable and undoubtedly it can not be ruled out that the various sources were compiled without reference to the same works. Æthelweard's records, for instance, are known to have been dependent upon other sources until about 892. What all this does mean is that Scef, or Sheave as Tolkien named him, could, theoretically, through his descendant Alfred the Great, have been an ancestor of the British monarchs. Tolkien was well aware of this connection and he acknowledged Scef's possible role in his 1964 letter to Christopher Bretherton. When writing of the coming of corn and culture heroes of legend, he added:

'One such Sheaf, or Shield Sheafing, can actually be made out as one of the remote ancestors of the present Queen' [40]. It seems inconceivable that Tolkien would not have had this link in mind when he included Sheave in his time travel stories. Tolkien certainly knew all the intricacies of Scyld Scefing's genealogy intimately, as can be seen from his detailed analysis of the ancestry of the ancient Danish king, Heremod, published in *Finn and Hengest* [41].

For our purposes, however, Tréowine's recital of the tale of Sheave suggests that, if deploying the framework adopted by *The Notion Club Papers*, Sheave is intended to be Tréowine's ancestor. In fact, if Sheave equates with the legendary Scef or Scyld, this assumption can also be made merely on the basis of Tréowine being kin of the Tamworth kings. Consequently, Tréowine could further claim to be, if very remotely and at many removes, of the same bloodline from which arose the present Queen of England. While interesting, this in itself does not further our understanding of what became of Elendil's descendants since Tréowine is quite definitely a descendant of Voronwë, Elendil's companion, and not of Elendil himself.

However, and this I feel to be important, Tréowine does not tell Sheave's tale in its entirety and it is left to Ælfwine to complete the story. And Ælfwine, in this conception, *is* Elendil's descendent. Furthermore, the final passage of Sheave's tale which Ælfwine recounts here was only added to Sheave's story in 1945. This passage was published in *The Lost Road*, because, and this is crucial, Christopher Tolkien believed that all the work on Sheave was written at the same time, that is, before work began on *The Lord of the Rings*. In *Sauron Defeated*, however, he concludes that this particular passage, which provides a more positive view of the fate of Sheave's heirs, was, in fact, written in the mid forties, some eight years later.

So, circa 1937, Tolkien originally said of Sheave's descendants that: *'His children were many and fair, and it is sung that of them are come the kings of men of the North Danes and the West Danes, the South Angles and the East Gothfolk'* [42], but he also added, *'many in the beginning lived to a great age, but comingunder the shadow of the East they were laid in great tombs of stone or in mounds like green hills'* [43]. This would seem to be consistent with Sheave being the inspiration for the culture-bearing Númenóreans mentioned above.

In the later passage, however, written circa 1945, Sheave's role as the founding father of all the great dynasties of Europe has been greatly expanded.

Seven sons he begat, sire of princes, men great of mood, mighty-handed and high-hearted. From his house cometh the seed of kings, as the songs tells us, fathers of the fathers, who before the change in the Elder Years the earth governed, Northern kingdoms named and founded, shields of their people: Sheave begat them: Sea-danes and Goths, Swedes and Northmen, Franks and Frisians, folk of the islands, Swordmen and Saxons, Swabians, Angles, and the Longobards, who long ago beyond Mircwudu a mighty realm and wealth won them in the Welsh countries, where Ælfwine, Éadwine's heir in Italy was king. All that has passed! '[44]

That this particular passage, which so gloriously illustrates the extent of Sheave's influence on most of the peoples of Western Europe, is recited by Ælfwine as he finishes Tréowine's tale and not by Tréowine himself is, to me, significant. Ælfwine described Tréowine's verse as being in the old style, *'the work of some old poet, maybe, though I had not heard it before'* [45], the implication being that the story may not even have been Tréowine's after all. And Ælfwine, in spite of his unfamiliarity with the tale, be it the nature of the verse or the content, is nonetheless able to step up to provide the final chapter. It may be impossible to draw definitive conclusions here, but it certainly appears as if the ability of Ælfwine, and that of Lowdham too, to experience the inherited memory of their ancestors was responsible for this sudden piece of insight which provided both characters with this clear vision of the parts played by their many forefathers throughout history. If this is the case, then we can further say that Ælfwine could, in this context, have been a descendant of Sheave and, since Ælfwine here is the ancestor of Lowdham who is himself descended from Elendil, this inevitably begs the question; does this, in turn, also make Sheave a descendant of Elendil, and, therefore, inevitably, of Aragorn as well? The answer to that, unfortunately, can be no more decisive than, 'perhaps' since Tolkien never states as much, and the whole point of Sheave is that he is of unknown parentage.

However, descent from Elendil is the recurring theme of both Tolkien's time travel stories which feature Sheave's tale and it seems too much of a coincidence that Tolkien amended the conclusion to this episode, and in such a manner, at the very time when he was pondering how to proceed with *The Return of the King*. And while it may be futile to search for connections which may never have been intended as more than echoes, Sheave and Elendil must, at the very least, be considered to have fulfilled parallel roles.

The similarity between the legacies of both characters becomes particularly compelling if we compare this later description of Sheave's heirs with that of Eldarion's found in *The Peoples of Middle-earth* where Tolkien said that from Eldarion *'should come the kings of many realms in long days after'* [46]. Kings who spawned dynasties on such a grand scale were rare and it is worth remembering that Aragorn's marriage to Arwen, which finally elevated him to the lofty status he came to enjoy and placed him in a position where he too was able to found a great dynasty, only entered *The Lord of the Rings* at the time Tolkien amended Sheave's story.

What is less clear is what Tolkien meant by the 'Elder Years' in the context of the Sheave legend. If we assume Elder *Years* equates with Elder *Days* then, according to the definition given in *The Tale of Years*, this era ended with the First Age and, even if the later meaning is used which extends that period to the end of the Third, then Sheave would, of necessity, predate both Elendil and Aragorn. I suspect, however, that the term can be applied in a looser sense since Tolkien was writing of actual history. If 'Elder Years' could be considered to extend to more recent times than Tolkien's own mythology and include the mythical eras of heroes like Sigurd and Beowulf and even Arthur when otherworldly beings still dwelt openly upon the earth, then it becomes perfectly plausible, and indeed very fitting, that Sheave should be a descendant of both Elendil and Aragorn. Sheave's tale, being that of another great king of renown, forms the ideal bridge spanning the gap between the end of Tolkien's mythology and the start of history proper. Tolkien himself believed Scef was included within the Beowulf story to provide a suitably heroic background for the legend. He refers again to the influence of such traditions at the beginning of his published lecture on *Sir Gawain and the Green Knight* in *The Monsters and the Critics*, so it is possible that he intended to utilize Scef's tale in a comparable way in his own mythology. Had *The Lost Road* and *The Notion Club Papers* ever been completed, then Sheave's story may well have provided a similar heroic backdrop to Ælfwine's adventures. As it is, the legend of King Sheave provides a glorious postscript for Tolkien's heroes from the Third Age, just as Aragorn's story does to the legend of Elendil from the end of the Second, and Aragorn, in turn, was well placed to fill the role of Scyld Scefing's in Sheave's own story had that role ever emerged.

However, the urge to extrapolate is irresistible and, if Elendil could be considered the forefather of Sheave, then the natural consequence of this is to further conclude that Aragorn could have been the ancestor of all the monarchs of Western Europe! Tolkien does not of course go so far as to suggest that his own fictional king was an ancestor of the present Queen of England; his prophecy concerning the heirs of Elessar is sufficiently vague and non-committal to ensure this could never be a charge, but he is undoubtedly blurring the boundaries between actual myth and his own invented myth in a way that is completely consistent with how he created his entire legendarium. But what we can say is that once Tolkien discovered Trotter's true identity, his ranger-king provided the means for him to achieve an ambition that had long been part of his larger plan but which had previously lacked a mechanism for implementation. By his restoration of the monarchy and by his marriage to Elrond's daughter, Arwen, Aragorn came to be the ideal instrument by which Tolkien could finally achieve his goal of establishing a stable foundation for the blood of the Eldar and of the Divine to perpetuate within mankind. Although in the present day we might be lucky to glimpse little more of the Dúnedain than an occasional sighting of tall and mysterious men wandering the fringes of the Western Sea, Tolkien undoubtedly intended their legacy to be considerably more widespread and influential, and what better way to achieve this than for their descendants to number members of all the royal Houses of Europe. But, irrespective of whether Sheave was an intermediary for the blood of Elendil to infuse the ancestral peoples of the Western world, that an ordinary Oxford man like Arry Lowdham possessed in his genes a strand of the divine, passed to him from his far distant foremother, Lúthien, is surely sufficient evidence in itself of quite how far reaching Tolkien intended this bloodline to become.

Aragorn's story, therefore, far from being the incidental event that its sidling to the Appendices might suggest, was in fact, actually fulfilling a vital function of Tolkien's mythology. This may not have been the role Tolkien originally had in mind for his hobbit-ranger, but, when the pieces to the puzzle of Aragorn's identity finally fell into place, the full extent of his potential, as well as the implications for what could be achieved with that potential, became apparent. As a result, Aragorn acquired a new and completely unexpected role, one which extended far beyond that required of him within the bounds of *The Lord of the Rings* itself. What he ultimately achieved was no mean feat for a man who started life as a hobbit with wooden shoes.

Chapter 5: A Peerless Hero

The question of precisely who is the hero of *The Lord of the Rings* is one which is likely to spark lively debate. Frodo, obviously, many will say; no, it is Sam, will say others, while the names of Gandalf and Aragorn are sure to earn a mention. And each will be correct; *The Lord of the Rings* is, after all, teeming with heroes. Yet the heroism of these characters is as diverse as the characters themselves. Certainly, not all possess the exceptional physical prowess of the traditional hero, and the emergence as heroes of the diminutive hobbits demonstrates that heroism can take many forms. Rather, it is how any talents are utilized that matters than the size of those talents. Neither need a hero be undefeated if he has striven to his utmost in pursuit of his goal. The heroism of the Host of the West as they dared to engage the overwhelming hosts of Sauron at the Black Gate would have been no less had they been utterly destroyed. Their heroism was in the undertaking of the task irrespective of their success or failure in completing it. With heroism being largely a moral concept, all heroes must possess values which they are prepared to defend to their utmost so heroic acts are, by their very nature, rarely easy to achieve, and the individuals who do achieve heroic status inevitably belong to an elite group, distinguished and united by their courage and their forbearance.

W.H. Auden in his defense of Tolkien, *The Quest Hero*, maintains that there are two types of hero. The first is the hero of epic who possesses a superior 'areté'. Originally a Greek expression, areté indicates the attainment of excellence through courage and effectiveness. Characters possessing areté were supremely capable, their talents easily visible for all to see and recognize; Auden cites Jason of Greek myth as an example. The other is the sort of hero whose areté is concealed. This is the more humble, less obvious hero who is actually the more common of the two types, often found in fairy-tales, and of which the hobbits are prime examples. Aragorn, however, is only the latter when he actively strives to conceal his areté. Strider does not make the most auspicious of entrances in his drab ranger disguise, but his arête nonetheless quickly becomes apparent. The people of Bree do not think well of him, but even the most parochial Breelanders afford him a grudging respect. Frodo feels uncomfortable under the gaze of his keen eyes and quickly suspects the stranger is not what he appears. While he may not yet resemble his esteemed ancestors preserved in stone in Minas Tirith,

Aragorn himself swiftly demonstrates that there is more to him than meets the eye. Boromir – who possesses his own very conspicuous arête - may be less than impressed at their first meeting, but the man beneath the travel-stained clothes, his undoubted humility not withstanding, is nonethelessin possession of sufficient self knowledge to be aware of his own capabilities, even if others are not. This is a man who long ago earned the regard of the people of Boromir's home land, and his level handling of Boromir's doubts is a sure indictor that he has no need to boast to prove his worth, not even to his potential rival. And once Andúril is aflame in Aragorn's hand and the Star of Elendil shines upon his brow, we are in no doubt as to who can justifiably claim to be the traditional, epic hero of *The Lord of the Rings*.

Indeed, Verilyn Flieger in her essay, *Frodo and Aragorn: The concept of the hero* provides this wonderful summary of Aragorn's many heroic attributes: *'All the positive, glad-hearted, youthful elements of myth, epic, and romance cluster around the man we meet as Strider, whom we come to know as Aragorn. He is the recognised acclaimed victor in the battle against evil, the king coming into his kingdom. He is the warrior, lover, healer, renewer, a hero worthy of the heroic aspects of The Lord of the Rings, whose presence in the story at once contributes to, and justifies, those aspects.'* [1]

Few would deny that the role of the warrior hero belongs to Aragorn. He possesses all the characteristics of a hero who goes to war for a just cause. He is strong, valiant and capable, and carries the trademark long sword, a vital prerequisite of every medieval hero. His brave deeds throughout the Quest are many, preeminent among them his daring to look in the Palantír, his ride through the Paths of the Dead and his subsequent arrival at the Pelennor which culminates with his leading the host of the West to the Black Gate. On the one hand, therefore, Aragorn is a hero out of the same mould of some of the principal medieval heroes from literature. Yet, as Tolkien reminds us, it is as much by his wisdom as by his valour that Aragorn plays his part in the War of the Ring, and this is most conspicuously demonstrated by his rejection of the Ring as a means of achieving his goal. Aragorn's long years of sacrifice spent preparing for his future role, his ability to heal and the benefits he brings to his people as king, further mark him as an exceptional hero. Ultimately, he is a character whose brand of heroism is unique and sets him apart from his predecessors.

Even so, when Tolkien finally made the decision to transform 'Trotter the Hobbit' into 'Trotter the Man', he undoubtedly tapped into the wealth of role models at his disposal to create a baseline upon which to establish the characteristics of his king. Even within his own mythology, Aragorn inherited certain facets of both his character and his story arc from Tolkien's existing leading men: Beren, Tuor and, to a lesser extent Túrin, all possess features which were later acquired by Aragorn. Looking beyond Middle-earth, history and literature abound with tales of heroes with long swords, and Tolkien was no stranger to any of their great deeds. The extraordinary breadth of his linguistic range allowed him to not only study many ancient sagas and tales in his bread-and-butter languages of Old Norse, Old and Middle English, but also in Gothic, Finnish and Icelandic. Of the Roman and Greek myths, he particularly enjoyed Homer. He loved fairy-tales and, although he claimed to dislike it, he knew Shakespeare well.

However, three principle characters dominate the medieval heroic landscape: Sigurd, Beowulf and Arthur. Each a king of great renown, all three of these heroes came to assert an influence upon the creation of Tolkien's own king. Tolkien himself famously did not approve of the academic search for sources, any more than he did comparisons of skeleton plots. Quoting Dasent in his 1939 lecture, *On Fairy-Stories*, he maintains: *'We must be satisfied with the soup that is set before us, and not desire to see the bones of the ox out of which it has been boiled'* [2]. The influence of these 'bones', however, is undeniable, and when, in the same lecture, Tolkien remarked upon his childhood reading preferences, in particular, he confirmed his liking for the tale of Sigurd.

'I had very little desire to look for buried treasure or fight pirates, and Treasure Island left me cool. Red Indians were better:.. But the land of Merlin and Arthur was better than these, and best of all the nameless North of Sigurd and the Völsungs, and the prince of all dragons. Such lands were pre-eminently desirable...the world that contained even the imagination of Fáfnir was richer and more beautiful, at whatever cost of peril' [3].

Andrew Lang's *The Red Fairy Book* provided Tolkien's first introduction to Sigurd, and his early fascination with this tale continued into his school years. In 1911, he presented a paper on the Norse Sagas to King Edward's Literary Society. Of these, he considered *The Völsunga Saga* to be one of the best, and, although apparently finding it inferior to Homer in many respects, he reported that in some it excels, especially the final tragedy of Sigurd and Brynhild.He continued to study the tale of Sigurd as an undergraduate at Exeter College and, on winning the Skeat Prize for English in 1914, among the books he purchased with the five pound prize money was the William Morris translation of *The Völsunga Saga*, which had itself been the basis for Lang's version. The legend of Sigurd also became a significant part of his professional life, and in 1926 he founded the Kolbitar Club with the specific purpose of translating all the major Norse sagas. At Oxford, he taught Old Norse, the original language in which the material was preserved, from 1926 to 1941, as well as the material itself; his Tuesday morning lecture for the Michaelmas term of 1941 was, for instance, *William Morris: The story of Sigurd and the Fall of the Nibelungs* [4]. According to Christopher Tolkien, his father never wrote a critical account of the Saga, but his own version, *The Legend of Sigurd and Gudrún,* was finally published in 2009. A representation rather than a translation, *The Legend* consists of two lays. The first, *The Lay of the Völsungs*, recounts Sigurd's story, while the second, *The Lay of Gudrún*, describes the ongoing saga of his widow, Gudrún. There can, therefore, be little doubt that this is a story that Tolkien knew intimately.

Sigurd's story was preserved by more than one medieval author and consequently there is no single definitive version. The earliest record of his adventures dates from the eleventh century when a number of scenes from the legends were carved on rune stones in Sweden. However, it was not until the thirteenth century that the various written accounts appeared. The German *Nibelungenlied* was penned circa 1200, slightly earlier than the comparable Scandinavian versions, yet it tells of a similar cycle of stories to those of *The Völsunga Saga,* which is the longest and most complete version of Sigurd's story. Written in Iceland in the latter part of the thirteenth century by an unknown author, *The Völsunga Saga* recounts the events surrounding both Sigurd's family, the Völsungs, and the Nibelungs, the family into which he marries. Much is told that occurs before and after Sigurd's life, but it is his story which sits at the heart of the tale. *The Völsunga Saga* was in itself largely drawn from the collection of Norse verse, the *Poetic* or *Elder Edda*, which, in places, describes the story in greater detail, but, although there is substantial continuity between the versions, there are also irreconcilable differences. The original *Elder Edda* manuscript, the *Codex Regius*, which was written in 1270, is, however, incomplete, eight pages having been lost to fire, so it is *The Völsunga Saga* which preserves the most comprehensive version of Sigurd's tale.

Sigurd was the son of Sigmund, a northern king, who was slain in battle by the god Odin before the birth of his son. Sigmund's widow was taken to live in the household of the King of Denmark where her son, Sigurd, was raised with honour in the king's court. His tutor, Regin taught him the many accomplishments that were fitting for the son of a king in those times, and when Sigurd was nearly full grown, and goaded by Regin, he asked the king for a horse, to which the king agreed. The next day in the forest, Sigurd met an old man with a long beard who helped Sigurd acquire Grani, a grey coated stallion, the fastest and best horse in the world. The old man was Odin from whom Sigurd was descended. Regin then sought Sigurd's help avenging his own father who had been killed by the dragon, Fáfnir. Sigurd agreed to help, and, for this task, Regin set about forging him a sword. Unable to make one to Sigurd's satisfaction, Sigurd finally brought him the broken shards of his father's sword which had long been kept safe by his mother and from which Regin now forged a great sword called Gram. But before aiding Regin, Sigurd desired to avenge his own father. The king of Denmark agreed to furnish him with a large army and, in the subsequent battles, Sigurd acquitted himself well, ruthlessly slaying all his enemies, and so his reputation as a warrior began to grow. *'People fled from him as he advanced, and neither helmet nor mail coat withstood him. No one thought he had ever seen such a man before.'* [5]

When he returned home, Sigurd honoured his pledge to aid Regin and, with some assistance from Odin, he succeeded in killing the dragon by skewering its underside. On Regin's advice, he cut out its heart and, roasting it, he tasted the dragon's blood. In this way Sigurd came to understand the speech of the birds and from them, he discovered that Regin could not be trusted. So he beheaded his former tutor and kept all the treasure for himself, but Sigurd also learned from the birds that he would find wisdom if he rode to Hindarfell where the maiden, Brynhild, slept. Mounting Grani, he rode south with the treasure until he came to a ring of fire and a rampart of shields. Passing through these, he came upon a female warrior in a deep sleep. This was the beautiful valkryie and shieldmaiden, Brynhild, cursed by Odin to remain at rest until a warrior came to marry her. But, with a counter vow, Brynhild had sworn she would only marry a man who showed no fear and, in daring to ride through the flames, Sigurd proved himself to be such a man. From Brynhild, Sigurd learned much wisdom and, before Sigurd rode away, they pledged themselves to each other.

Sigurd eventually came to the estate of Brynhild's brother-in-law and was treated with great honour. Brynhild, too, returned there shortly after and embroidered a magnificent golden tapestry depicting Sigurd's great deeds. On espying her in her tower, Sigurd came to her and they renewed their oaths to one another. Seeking to further his renown, Sigurd eventually came to the realm of the Burgundian king, Gjuki, who was the father of three sons, Gunnar, Högni and Guttrom and of a daughter, Gudrún. Now a mighty warrior and renowned dragon-slayer, Sigurd was made most welcome. The queen, Grimheld, a manipulative woman of supernatural power, was eager to keep such a man in the realm, and so she gave Sigurd a drink of forgetfulness. With the memory of Brynhild wiped from his mind, Sigurd married Gudrún and became as a brother to Gunnar and Högni.

The queen then encouraged Gunnar, her eldest son, to seek Brynhild's hand in marriage. To prove his worth, Gunnar must brave the same ring of fire as Sigurd had once done. This Gunnar failed to do, even when Sigurd lent him Grani.Sigurd and Gunnar then changed shapes, as the queen had taught them, and Sigurd passed through the fire in the guise of Gunnar. Unaware that the man before her was really Sigurd, Brynhild agreed to become Gunnar's wife, but once she had come to his home and they were wed, too late, Sigurd remembered his own love for Brynhild and eventually, in a moment of bitterness, the truth behind the deception was revealed by Gudrún.

Distraught, Brynhild turned against Sigurd for his part in the conspiracy. Sigurd, in spite of his anguish and grief over his own lost love, declared that he would give away all his treasure if Brynhild could but find happiness with Gunnar. In the end, he announced that he would even forsake Gudrún rather than have Brynhild die of despair. But Brynhild would not be placated and demanded that Gunnar kill both Sigurd and his young son for his betrayal and for having dishonoured her prior to her marriage; a claim which was not true. Reluctant to break oaths and do the deed themselves, Gunnar and Högni persuaded their younger brother, Guttorm, to slay Sigurd. And so, while Sigurd lay asleep in Gudrun's arms little suspecting that he had earned the ire of the brothers, Guttorm murdered Sigurd. But before he died, Sigurd managed to reach for his sword and with it, he sliced Guttorm in half. Brynhild then killed herself and was burned with Sigurd upon his funeral pyre.

In many ways Sigurd's tale, with its flawed characters and tragic ending, is more reminiscent of Túrin's story than that of Aragorn. All three characters receive the benefits of an exemplary upbringing at the hands of foster fathers, and yet, like Túrin, Sigurd is a man fated to ultimately fail. Early on, he is told of his fate by the dragon in much the same way as Túrin is taunted by Glaurung in Nargothrund. The method by which Sigurd slays Fáfnir is very similar to how Túrin defeats Glaurung and, in the first version of Turin's tale, Tolkien even included the prophecy of the dragon's heart. Just as with Túrin, it is the complexities of Sigurd's love life which eventually bring about his downfall. Like Túrin, he is a man who tries to do the right thing, but is thwarted by the designs of others. Whereas Túrin endures the malice of Morgoth, Sigurd is used by both the evil Grimhild and the morally ambiguous Odin.

Yet, as a great warrior king, Sigurd inevitably also demands comparison with Aragorn. In their simplest context, the stories of Aragorn's and Sigurd's early years are strikingly similar. Both men are of exceptionally noble birth; both, at many removes, are descended from supernatural beings, Sigurd from the god, Odin, Aragorn from the maia, Melian; both lose their fathers in violent deaths when too young to remember them. Both are taken by their mothers to live in the courts of great lords where they are raised with honour and learn much wisdom and lore. Both, on reaching adulthood, receive broken swords which are heirlooms of their line and which must be re-forged before they go on to perform great deeds with them. Just as Andúril, the Flame of the West, gleamed with white fire in battle at Helm's Deep, Gram also appeared *'as if flames were leaping from its edges'* [6]. And both men subsequently have lots of adventures before becoming great kings themselves. Sigurd is clearly a man with a great destiny as this passage from the William Morris translation recounting Sigmund's dying words to his pregnant wife demonstrates:

'...behold now, thou art great with a man-child; nourish him well and with good heed, and the child shall be the noblest and most famed of all our kin: and keep well withal the shards of the sword: thereof shall a goodly sword be made, and it shall be called Gram, and our son shall bear it, and shall work many a great work therewith, even such as eld shall never minish; for his name shall abide and flourish as long as the world shall endure...' [7]

When Master Elrond speaks to the young Estel, he is more reserved yet still he predicts that his foster son may accomplish great deeds with the shards of Narsil. And Ivorwen, in her foresight, urges Dírhael to permit the marriage of their daughter Gilraen to Arathorn as *'great things are to come. If these two wed now, hope may be born for our people; but if they delay, it will not come while this age lasts'* [8].

Sigmund's widow is saved by the Danish King, Alf son of Hjalprek, much as Elrond protects Gilraen and her son on the death of Arathorn. Just as all at Rivendell came to love the young Estel, Sigurd, too, was held in great esteem, as seen in this passage which is again from the William Morris version read by Tolkien as a young man:

'...then was the king glad thereof, when he saw the keen eyes in the head of him, and he said that few men would be equal to him or like unto him in any wise. So he was sprinkled with water, and had to name Sigurd, of whom all men speak with one speech and say that none was ever his like for growth

and goodliness. He was brought up in the house of King Hjalprek in great love and honour; and so it is, that whenso all the noblest men and greatest kings are named in the olden tales, Sigurd is ever put before them all, for might and prowess, for high mind and stout heart, wherewith he was far more abundantly gifted than any man of the northern parts of the wide world.' [9]

And of the grown up Sigurd, we learn that:

'greater was his strength than his growth: well could he wield sword, and cast forth spear, shoot shaft, and hold shield, bend bow, back horse, and do all the goodly deeds that he learned in his youth's days.

Wise he was to know things yet undone; and the voice of all fowls he knew, wherefore few things fell on him unawares.

...His sport and pleasure it was to give aid to his own folk, and to prove himself in mighty matters, to take wealth from his unfriends, and give the same to his friends.

Never did he lose heart, and of naught was he adrad.' [10]

Sigurd was clearly a great and noble king, the foremost of his line, remembered with great affection by his people. By the same token, Elessar was considered the most like to Elendil of all his kin, a man who reigned with the dignity and majesty of the kings of old, and, according to Legolas, loved by all who came to know him. He was the greatest traveller and huntsman of the age, the hardiest and the most skilled of all Men. Like Sigurd, Aragorn was a mighty warrior and great swordsman. We observe him in action at Helm's Deep and again on the Pelennor where, due to his skill and might of arms, few dared to engage him in battle, and the ruthlessness with which he smote an orc as he raced for the doors in Moria was an act worthy of Sigurd. As Théoden acknowledges when the Grey Company joins forces with the Rohirrim at Dol Baran, *'If these kinsmen be in any way like to yourself, my lord Aragorn, thirty such knights will be a strength that cannot be counted by heads'* [11]. And he has proved his worth in the past. As a renowned captain of men, he earned the regard of the hosts of both Gondor and Rohan and he personally slew the captain of the Corsairs whilst leading a daring, and successful, raid on Umbar.

Both men are charismatic figures. Sigurd is eminently personable and deemed worthy of respect by his fellow warriors and, in a tale full of treachery and betrayal, he stands apart as the best of a rather barbarous bunch. Like Aragorn, he is a loyal friend and he comes readily to the aid of others. He is a wise man, learning his wisdom from both Regin and the immortal Brynhild as Aragorn does from the Elves. Both men are supremely capable and possessing indomitable strengths of will; Sigurd daring to ride through the flames of Brynhild's tower as Aragorn dared to ride the Paths of the Dead. Like Sigurd, Aragorn was taller than other men and had the same keen eyes that so disconcerted Frodo in The Prancing Pony. Both men had, in certain measure, the gift of foresight and, if the men of Bree were correct in their assessment of the rangers, both had the ability to understand the speech of birds. Both were aided in their adventures by supernatural advisors; Sigurd by Odin and Aragorn by Gandalf whom Tolkien described as an Odinic wanderer.

Neither man ever succumbed to despair; both maintaining hope in their respective hearts throughout their many adventures. Sigurd's ability to suppress and forego his own desires for the greater good suggests a selflessness that one would associate with Aragorn, and his attempts at finding a diplomatic solution to the impasse in which the characters find themselves demonstrates a greater wisdom and willingness to forgive than any other in the story. Sigurd often appears more an unfortunate victim of circumstance than a perpetrator of the many crimes committed around him. He does not despoil Brynhild when in the guise of Gunnar yet is nonetheless accused of doing so. Aragorn, on the other hand, is perhaps fortunate that Éomer is considerably more sympathetic to the predicament in which he finds himself with Éowyn than Sigurd found Gunnar.

However, Sigurd operates under a vastly different moral code from that which would have been acceptable to Aragorn, and the story of the Völsungs is one conspicuously littered with corpses. For instance, with his blood-brothers, Sigurd was said to have travelled far, *'performing many splendid deeds and killing many kings' sons'* [12]. Such behaviour would be completely unthinkable in Aragorn whose own journey to greatness follows a very different path. For Sigurd, battle is something to actively seek out as a means of proving his might and advertising his great strength; for Aragorn, it is an unwelcome necessity, a means to an end for a man who, had fate dealt him a different hand, would have dwelt peacefully in Rivendell. While certainly ambitious, Aragorn is also capable of a degree of compassion and mercy that Sigurd would never comprehend. Imagine those whose fear undid them on the way to the Black Gate, or the fate of the vanquished once victory was secure, in the hands of Sigurd. While we see glimpses of the very human side of Aragorn's nature, his worries and his doubts, these are failings that Sigurd, who reputedly never knew fear, would be unlikely to even acknowledge. Nor would Sigurd have endured the scorn of the likes of Butterbur or Bill Ferny, and it is impossible to picture him with all his bright armour and conspicuous motifs astride his great horse as a nondescript ranger, patiently guarding the Shire, an unacknowledged hero, dressed in plain greens and browns, blending unseen and without esteem into the background. Where Sigurd has a dragon emblazoned upon all his weapons and his worth in gold is flaunted conspicuously, Aragorn's 'gold' is concealed beneath his lowly façade and he fights his battles wearing only a plain cloak and borrowed armour.

Ultimately Aragorn earns his kingdom not just through might with arms but because of his ability to heal and his willingness to trust in the worth of others. Surely Sigurd would never have resisted the Ring nor would he have allowed so diminutive a figure as a hobbit to determine the fate of everything that he held dear.Sigurd's values are, of course, firmly rooted in the medieval whereas Aragorn's are more contemporary, and it is through these values that he successfully governs his realm. He accepts his crown with humility and rules by the consent of his people, adhering to principles of justice which we would find perfectly acceptable today. Nor could the deaths of these two characters be more different, Aragorn dying at peace and with the utmost grace at a time of his choosing while Sigurd is brutally murdered. Aragorn, therefore, may outwardly be of the same stock as Sigurd, but, in his heart, he is a very different man.

Sigurd, like Aragorn, is not only a warrior but also a lover, and both men fall in love with extraordinary women. Brynhild, like Arwen, is an immortal, but she is cursed to lead the life of a mortal woman by Odin. Aragorn, in spite of his long delay in claiming his bride, is blessed with far better fortune in the affairs of his heart than Sigurd. While Aragorn's union with Arwen is undoubtedly his greatest reward for his endeavours, and is the key to his subsequently blissful and glorious reign, Sigurd's relationship with Brynhild proves his undoing.Sigurd is also loved by two women, one mortal, one not. The golden-haired shieldmaiden, Brynhild, gird in the mail of a warrior and desiring the adventure of battle, inevitably reminds us of Éowyn. She and Sigurd share cups together, much like Éowyn and Aragorn, and Sigurd's waking her from sleep is reminiscent of Aragorn recalling Éowyn in the Houses of Healing, the waking of a beauty by the prince being a fairy-tale staple. Éowyn's desire to seek death on being spurned, if lacking the seething hatred of Brynhild, is nonetheless driven by the same terrible despair. However, while Éowyn's infatuation was an unwelcome complication for Aragorn, Brynhild was Sigurd's true love, as Arwen was Aragorn's. She makes a tapestry displaying his great deeds as Arwen makes a glittering standard in the hope of the deeds Aragorn will yet perform. Like Arwen, Brynhild ultimately sacrifices her life for the man she loves, although, admittedly, under vastly different circumstances.

Although Arwen was only a later addition to the text, Elrond's condition upon Aragorn receiving her hand in marriage must be considered a great motivational force, inevitably spurred Aragorn onwards and a factor in much that he achieved. Furthermore, with the recent publication of Tolkien's own version of Sigurd's story, we find an unexpected source of this demand which provides a previously unseen codicil to any comparison between these two characters.

Both heroes respond to what Joseph Campbell terms in his famous work of 1949, *The Hero with a Thousand Faces*, 'the call to adventure'. Born in 1904 in the American midwest to a Catholic family, Campbell is almost a contemporary of Tolkien's, and he too was very familiar with a range of myths from around the world. In fact, Campbell believed that all myths shared a common fundamental structure and, in essence, repeatedly retold the same single myth, the one great story of mankind, which he termed the 'monomyth'. While there is no evidence that Tolkien was influenced by Campbell, Tolkien also detected the universal truth underpinning all myths and fairy-stories. Campbell, however, went further and identified the various stages of every hero's journey which he believed were universal. Campbell summarizes this journey thus: *'A hero ventures forth from the world of common day into a region of supernatural wonder: fabulous forces are there encountered and a decisive victory is won: the hero comes back from this mysterious adventure with the power to bestow boons on his fellow man'* [13].

Very few myths contain all of Campbell's stages so the system is open to a wide interpretation. Aragorn's story can be slotted into at least some of the categories, if with a bit of juggling. But it is his 'call to adventure' which is of interest here. This could be interpreted as his leaving home at the age of twenty after learning of his ancestry and receiving the broken sword of his forefathers; or it might be his setting out on the Ring quest with the broken sword now symbolically re-forged. Yet Aragorn's true quest is undoubtedly the hand of Arwen. The quest of the humble suitor who dares to aspire to the hand of a princess is another fairy-tale staple and, in his pursuit of Arwen, Aragorn's tale has echoes in many before and since. Beren's story was obviously a prime influence and this, in turn, was influenced by the Arthurian tale of *Culhwch and Olwen* which has received extensive analyse by Lewis and Currie. Culhwch is a young prince who spends his youth with foster parents. When reunited with his father, he is cursed by his stepmother who, in a complete reversal of Elrond's demand that Aragorn shall marry no woman, let alone his only daughter, tells Culhwch that he shall marry no woman *other* than Olwen, the daughter of the giant Yspaddaden. While Olwen is not human she nonetheless appears as one and Culhwch falls in love with the very idea of her. To win her hand, however, Culhwch must first complete a series of seemingly impossible tasks set by the giant – Culhwch's 'call to adventure'. For this, Culhwch seeks help from his cousin, King Arthur, with whose aid he succeeds and he weds his beloved.

However, the 'call to adventure' in Tolkien's version of Sigurd's story was not based upon the work of any medieval writer, but was introduced by Tolkien himself. One consequence of the diversity of source texts recounting Sigurd's story is that there are discrepancies in the telling of Sigurd's relationship with Brynhild. In the *Poetic* or *Elder Edda*, Sigurd initially meets a valkyrie called 'Sigrdrifa' at Hindarfell, and only encounters Brynhild later, while, in *The Völsunga Saga,* he meets Brynhild on both occasions. Here, the chapter where Sigurd and Brynhild plight their troth ends with the lines:

'Sigurd spake, "None among the sons of men can be found wiser than thou; and thereby swear I, that thee will I have as my own, for near to my heart thou liest."

She answers, "Thee would I fainest choose, though I had all men's sons to choose from."

And thereto they plighted troth both of them'. [14]

If these same passages ever existed in the *Elder Edda*, they were unfortunately on those eight pages of the *Codex* which were lost to fire. We will therefore never know precisely what words passed between Sigurd and his valkyrie lover, be it Brynhild or Sigrdrifa, as he bid her farewell in her tower. The surviving text ends with the recounting of Sigrdrifa's councils to Sigurd, but there is no mention of their declaring their love for each other.

Tolkien himself was unhappy with how the stories of Sigurd and Brynhild were merged in *The Volsunga Saga*, and, citing his father's letter to W.H. Auden as evidence, in the *Foreword* to *The Legend of Sigurd and Gudrún*, Christopher Tolkien states that this work was an attempt by Tolkien to unify the lays of the *Elder Edda*. Tolkien obviously favoured the *Elder Edda* over *The Volsunga Saga*, and, apparently, did not hold the artistic capacity of the author of the latter in particularly high regard, considering the combination of the contradictory stories of Sigurd and Brynhild as unsatisfactory. Indeed, the above passage from *The Volsunga Saga* is followed by a simple, and indeed highly unsatisfactory: *'Now Sigurd rides away'* [15].

However, in his own version, *The Lay of the Völsungs,* Tolkien offers a considerably more satisfying solution to this particular problem. He merges the two meetings between Sigurd and Brynhild into just one, that at Hindarfell, and he chose to provide the following words at their parting:

'Here, Sigmund's son, swift and fearless, is our way's parting, to woe or joy.

Here, lord, I leave thee, to my land turning; hence Grani bears thee glory seeking.'

'Why, Brynhild wise, bride of Völsung, when at one are the riders do our ways sunder?' 'I was queen of yore, and a king shall wed. Lands lie before thee – thy lordship win!' [16]

This statement of Brynhild that she expects to marry a king and her demand that Sigurd must depart to win the lordship of other lands, is clearly echoed in Elrond's words to Aragorn stipulating that his daughter *'shall not be the bride of any Man less than the King of both Gondor and Arnor'* [17]. The similarity between these two demands is even more evident in the prose preamble which precedes the Lay: *'the pride of Brynhild causes her to bid Sigurd depart and come back to her only when he has won all men's honour, and a kingdom'* [18].

These verses were believed to have been written in the early 1930's, long before Aragorn's creation so, inevitably, one has to wonder if Aragorn inherited this demand from Brynhild. Interestingly, Tolkien has the prospective bride herself place this condition upon the marriage and not, as in the case of Aragorn, the bride's father. While the terms that must be fulfilled before these marriages can proceed may be almost identical, it should be noted that the motives behind them are very different. Brynhild possesses a pride that Elrond does not, and her stipulation is clearly one of nothing but vanity. Elrond's demand to Aragorn, however, is as a result of shouldering the burden of considerably more complex considerations, by no means all of which centered on his love and concern for his daughter. Nonetheless, these two demands are strikingly similar and, as Christopher Tolkien remarks in his notes, it is *'a development altogether peculiar to the Lay'* [19].

~oo0oo~

The concept of heroism is unique to every age and none these days is required to slay a dragon to be awarded heroic status. Yet the eagerness with which Sigurd actively pursues his adventures is totally in tune with the culture in which he must live where the swiftness of revenge killings is paramount in determining a man's worth. As Brynhild sneeringly tells Gunnar: *'He [Sigurd] killed the dragon and Regin and five kings – unlike you, Gunnar, who blanched like a corpse'* [20]. The beliefs applicable to Sigurd in his era inevitably shaped his decisions and his attitudes to his fate. He is typical of a man adhering to the Germanic warrior code where strength, courage and loyalty are valued above all else. A glorious death in battle was the ideal, and such a death, preferably with his hand on his sword, was the ultimate goal for those hoping to be admitted to Valhalla by Odin and, eventually, to fight in Ragnarök.

Whether the Anglo-Saxons had a similar belief is unknown, but the Germanic heroic code is very much on display again in the poem *Beowulf*. The unknown author of this long, epic poem, written in England sometime between the ninth and eleventh centuries, is believed to have been a Christian, but his tale, containing a mix of historical fact and elaborate fiction, is set in the pagan culture of late fifth century Scandinavia. So, while the author acknowledges Beowulf's divine protector, warriors still seek to perform great deeds so that they will be remembered favorably after death. It is the sort of renown sought by Éowyn, and of which Aragorn did not wholly approve. With hindsight, Aragorn may have been proved wrong in Éowyn's case, but his view that good deeds are worth doing, regardless of whether any remain to witness them, is more that of the Christian who believes he will find his reward after death than of the Norse hero who wants to be remembered well by those who come after him.

The distinction between these two perceptions is highlighted by Faramir in his conversation with Frodo at Henneth Annûn. Faramir cites changing attitudes to war as the principle reason for the lessening of the difference between, what he terms, the High Men, the Númenóreans, and the Middle Men who include the Rohirrim. According to Faramir, the Gondorians are now more like the men of Rohan because they *'love war and valour as good things in themselves, both a sport and an end; and though we still hold that a warrior should have more skills and knowledge than only the craft of weapons and slaying, we esteem a warrior, nonetheless, above men of other crafts'* [21].

This distinction, which Tolkien describes as the difference between martial glory and true glory, represents a fundamental schism in the motives of warrior characters such as Faramir or Aragorn on the one hand, and Boromir or Sigurd on the other. As Aragorn tells Éowyn at Dunharrow, he only seeks war because he must.

Beowulf is a character very much of the mold of the warrior interested in furthering his renown, yet he is also the embodiment of the traditional, epic hero: brave and fearless, loyal and self sacrificing. The legend of Beowulf was particularly close to Tolkien's heart and formed a significant part of his professional life throughout his career. Tolkien published very little on *Beowulf* during the decades he taught his students, although he was apparently *'very generous with his ideas to those who sat at his feet.'* [22] With only fragments of Tolkien's own translation published in his essay, *On Translating Beowulf*, and the very scholarly *Finn and Hengest* focused on the technical detail, our knowledge of Tolkien's views are largely restricted to those he expounded in his acclaimed 1936 lecture, *The Monsters and the Critics*. Here Tolkien deplored the traditional view of the poem as merely a historical document which contained all the 'unimportant things', such as the story itself, at the centre, and all the 'important things', primarily the history that could be gleaned from the work, at the outer edges. Subsequently, Tolkien's view that the poem was worthy of consideration for its own merit came to be prevalent among Beowulf scholars.

When we first meet Beowulf he is already a warrior of some renown. He is physically as impressive as Sigurd, and we are told, *'There was no one else like him alive. In his day, he was the mightiest man on earth, high born and powerful'* [23]. Like Aragorn, Beowulf was fostered as a child into the home of a great lord; he became a brave and skilled warrior who, as a young man, ventures abroad to aid a foreign king. He travels long distances and fights battles that he seemingly has little chance of winning. He becomes an esteemed and beloved king, and, like all noble warriors, he possesses a great sword. In fact, he has several.

A warrior from modern day Sweden, Beowulf goes to the aid of the Danish king, Hrothgar, whose people are under attack from the marauding monster, Grendel. He travels by boat with a small band of loyal men, and is welcomed warmly since Hrothgar knew his father and has also heard good things of his son. Beowulf's arrival at Heorot undoubtedly provided the inspiration for Aragorn's arrival at Edoras. Both men are challenged twice by guards before gaining an audience with the king, and both are instructed to leave their weapons outside, although, perhaps because he carries no sword comparable to Andúril, Beowulf does not question this command in the way Aragorn does. An old but wise king, Hrothgar reminds us of Théoden, while his noxious servant, Unferth, who sits at the king's feet, is immediately reminiscent of Wormtongue. Once introductions are over, Beowulf and his men are offered mead to drink which is brought to them by Hrothgar's queen. As she hands Beowulf the cup, there is more than a little of Éowyn's joy at the arrival of these strangers in her speech as she *'thanked God for granting her wish that a deliverer she could believe in would arrive to ease their afflictions'* [24]. Éowyn, being an unwed maiden, has an additional interest in the newcomer: *'And she now was suddenly aware of him: tall heir of kings, wise with many winters, grey-cloaked, hiding a power that yet she felt'* [25].

Beowulf has no illusions about the scale of the task before him, and is quite prepared to die in the defense of others: *'I mean to perform to the uttermost what your people wanted or perish in the attempt, in the fiend's clutches. And I shall fulfill that purpose, prove myself with a proud deed or meet my death here in the mead-hall'* [26].

His vow is reminiscent of Aragorn's pledge to the hobbits in the Prancing Pony: *'if by life or death I can save you, I will'* [27]. Yet Beowulf is considerably more boastful than Aragorn, and he regales all assembled with tales of his previous exploits. His claim that he, *'battled and bound five beasts, raided a troll-nest and in the night-sea slaughtered sea-brutes'* [28] does, it has to be said, make guarding the Shire look like a stroll in the park for our ranger, although Aragorn chooses never to elaborate upon what manner of dark things which *'come from the houseless hills, or creep from sunless woods'* [29] he has slain in the past. Beowulf's tales are challenged by the scornful Unferth, and the ensuing sparring match over his boasts calls to mind the battle of words between Boromir and Aragorn at the Council of Elrond. Beowulf demonstrates restraint comparable to Aragorn's very even deflection of Boromir's thinly veiled insults, and it has been suggested that Unferth was only included in the poem so as to highlight Beowulf's possession of self control, a trait as desirable in his time as in Aragorn's.

Beowulf may not have Aragorn's modesty, but neither does he make idle claims. That night, Beowulf is able to live up to the expectations his boasts engender and he succeeds in pulling out Grendel's arm, and so fatally wounding the monster. Furthermore, on a point of honour, he insists on fighting the unarmed beast in like manner. Yet, for all his proud retelling of his great deeds, Beowulf is honest about his inability to kill Grendel by the method he had originally intended. The following night, Grendel's mother attacks the king's hall in revenge, and Beowulf, his prowess now acknowledged beyond doubt, sets off in pursuit of this new threat. As he prepares to face this second monster in her underwater home, Beowulf is given a sword by Unferth. This renowned sword uncharacteristically fails Beowulf, yet Beowulf reveals some of the same generosity of spirit displayed by Aragorn towards the fallen Boromir by placing no blame on Unferth. Beowulf eventually beheads the creature with a sword from the monster's own armory and, once the monster is dead, the blade melts leaving only the jewel-embossed hilt, exactly as the Nazgûl blade did in Aragorn's hand.

When Beowulf returns to the king's Hall, he is again hailed a hero and is praised by Hrothgar for his skill and his wisdom: *'I have never heard so young a man make truer observations. You are strong in body and mature in mind, impressive in speech'* [30]. So taken is the Danish king by the young warrior that he is moved to tears when the time comes for them to part, and, because of his love for him, Hrothgar declares his intent to strive for greater harmony and peace between their peoples. Beowulf's qualities have served as a unifying force for good, something also amply demonstrated by Aragorn when he becomes king. And, in earning the love of a foreign lord whom he has served well, Beowulf is foreshadowing the respect awarded Aragorn for his service as a young man to both Thengel and Ecthelion.

Beowulf returns home laden with gifts and acclaimed as an even greater hero. However, after the death of his own king, Hygelac, he refuses to further his own ambitions, and declines a request by the king's widow to take the throne at the expense of the rightful heir. Aragorn, in spite of his own long wait for kingship, displays similar prudence and wisdom by not claiming even what is rightly his until Sauron is defeated. Only when the throne falls vacant again does Beowulf assume the role of king, ruling his people wisely for fifty years. A beloved king, Beowulf is morally principled, his values decidedly more Christian than those of Sigurd.

'Thus Beowulf bore himself with valour;
he was formidable in battle yet behaved with honour
and took no advantage; never cut down
a comrade who was drunk, kept his temper
and, warrior that he was, watched and controlled
his God-sent strength and his outstanding natural powers' [31].

Beowulf's sure and stabilizing reign is thrown into uncertainty when a dragon emerges from his lair and goes on the rampage in his realm. Like Aragorn, for all his strength of arms, Beowulf is not immune to doubt, even though he is now above fear. So, *'for the glory of winning'* [32], he goes forth to fight the dragon, but as he does so, he senses his own death. He does not ask any of his comrades to accompany him into the dragon's lair but, unlike the Dúnedain who brave the Paths of the Dead for their love of their lord, only one of his warriors, Wiglaf, driven by pity, goes with him. Beowulf fights bravely, his third sword, Naegling, breaking in two because of the force he applied to it. Even so, he would not have slain the dragon without the aid of his loyal subordinate, just as Aragorn would not have triumphed without the sacrifices of Frodo and Sam. Yet Beowulf is mortally wounded, and although he dies with great dignity and acceptance, his is not the willing relinquishment with hope that Aragorn achieves in his final hour. However, as his death approaches, Beowulf is satisfied that he has adequately fulfilled all of the requirements of his warrior ethic, primarily that he has committed no malicious deeds nor broken any oaths. The poem ends with the lines:

'They said that of all the kings upon the earth
he was the man most gracious and fair-minded,
kindest to his people and keenest to win fame' [33].

Beowulf and Aragorn are undoubtedly valiant warriors and wise kings. Both are fortunate to be awarded a certain degree of Divine Grace, and the manner of their deaths is important to both their stories. But it is in his 'keenness to win fame', that Beowulf most departs from Aragorn. By insisting on fighting the dragon alone, Beowulf failed to appreciate that a leader who is charged with the protection of his people cannot always enjoy the freedom to behave as a foot soldier. Caution is sometimes prudent. Théoden, too, chooses to ignore suggestions that he is too old to lead his people into battle at the Pelennor. His actions,too, result in his death, but they also redeem his legacy from past failings, and his death is not catastrophic for his realm as he has already appointed Éomer as his heir. Beowulf has no heir so he instructs Wiglaf to care for his people, but his death leaves his lands vulnerable to attacks from marauding neighbours, and the continued stability and security of his realm is put at risk. For all his valour, in the end, Beowulf's pride marred his wisdom, ultimately destroying both himself and his legacy.

Aragorn attempted to explain this duty of care of a leader to Éowyn and earned her ire for his efforts. He, too, takes risks, but he weighs the odds and takes those risks only when he has no choice. Without venturing into the Paths of the Dead or riding to the Black Gate, there would have been no victory. Such risks were necessary. Even when fighting in battle, Aragorn is not reckless, but does what he must. This is not to say he spares himself at the expense of others. At Helm's Deep, he stumbles on the steps and is put in danger because he is aiding those trapped below.

Aragorn, nonetheless, surges into battle at the head of his host when alighting from the Black Ships, and with all the apparent abandon to Théoden when he, too, arrives at the Pelennor. But in this instance, Aragorn is making a very different statement. He is advertising his return, and there is no better way for him to do this than to triumphantly, and conspicuously, lead a conquering army. For all his fine ancestry, Aragorn is still the outsider presenting a challenge to the resident Steward. Allowing any other to lead this charge would have weakened his claim to the throne irredeemably. At the Black Gate, however, his acceptance as king is now ensured and here he assumes the role of a more prudent captain.

Beowulf's behaviour, both in fighting the dragon alone and in tackling Grendel without weapons, boarders on that of chivalry, a concept that became prevalent in the later Middle Ages, andone which is more concerned with personal honour than with true heroism. Tolkien talks about the differences between heroism and chivalry in his short essay, *Ofermod*, published at the end of *The Homecoming of Beorhtnoth*, his fictional version of the Anglo-Saxon poem, *The Battle of Maldon*. Tolkien roughly translates the Old English word 'Ofermod' as 'pride' of the sort which manifests as 'overboldness'. It is a word of condemnation and is apparently only used twice in literature, once to describe Beorhtnoth's behaviour and once when applied to Lucifer. Beorhtnoth's defeat by the Vikings in the year 991 demonstrates succinctly how the overboldness that accompanies chivalric behaviour can turn potential victory into resounding defeat. Beorhtnoth made the fatal mistake of permitting his enemy to cross the river before launching his attack, believing, in his pride, that he could be victorious while still giving ground to the invaders. His actions resulted in a terrible defeat and most of his men were slain. Tolkien makes the point that Beorhtnoth was responsible for the lives of all the men in his command and for the defense of the realm, and, while it was heroic to fight on *'to annihilation if necessary...It was wholly unfitting that he should treat a desperate battle with this sole real object as a sporting match, to the ruin of his purpose and duty'* [34].

Tolkien then turns his attention to what he considers Beowulf's 'ofermod'. He is forgiving of Beowulf's sporting decision to fight Grendel without weapons, even though, by doing so, Beowulf places himself in unnecessary danger, and, by increasing his risk of defeat, the chance of the monster surviving to continue running amok among the Danes is also increased. However, as Tolkien observes, Beowulf is under no obligation to defeat this creature and if he does, it is his own lord who will bathe in his reflected glory, not Hrothgar. Rather, Tolkien maintains, the foolishness of Beowulf is most evident in his decision to personally face the dragon in his old age with just a handful of men. Not only does the killing of the dragon place his subordinate's life in needless jeopardy, Beowulf's desire for a glorious death results in disaster for his people who end up losing their king. It is this desire for fame and glory which underpins the concept of chivalry. Chivalric behaviour, therefore, can become a handicap achieving the very opposite result from that for which the hero is striving. It is perhaps also a shortcoming of the Germanic code that its first virtue is bravery, even bravado. As Wiglaf declares: *'A warrior would sooner die than live a life of shame'* [35]. This does not sit well with the prudence that is required of kings and such an attitude obviously contrasts with the more Christian view that a good king should remain modest and humble, possessing all the qualities of a good father or a good shepherd, qualities amply demonstrated by Aragorn.

Tolkien also explains that the implied altruism of heroic acts is not quite as pure as it might seem since altruistic behaviour is, in itself, to be applauded, and so has its own inherent reward in the glory and renown that it brings. It may well be, of course, that the ensuing renown is completely by the by and the dual motives may run parallel quite comfortably making no difference whatsoever to the actions of the hero who performs the same great deeds regardless of any recognition he might hope to receive. Aragorn's dual quest to claim the crowns of Gondor and Arnor whilst also defeating Sauron is a prime example. Where the existence of pride does become significant, however, is when the pursuit and the acquisition of glory overtake the desire to do good as the prime motive, *'driving a man beyond the bleak heroic necessity to excess'* [36] and to the point where the actions of the hero might actually do harm to the good intent. Here, Aragorn's self-effacing modesty and genuine lack of desire to further his own renown, stands him in good stead.

Only once might his actions be considered the folly of pride. Ill-equipped with no food or water, Aragorn's suggestion that he and his friends must lay down their lives searching for Merry and Pippin in Fangorn can appear a matter of stubbornly doing the right thing at any cost, especially if one considers that everything he subsequently achieves would not have come to pass had he continued in his fruitless search to the bitter end. By such an action, he could be charged with being negligent of his potential usefulness to his people. But Aragorn at this point is in dire straights with no seeming way out. In his own words, he has gone on without hope. He does not know that he is about to be reunited with Gandalf or that more fortuitous courses of action will soon present themselves. Against his current predicament, starving to death trying to achieve the one 'good' option available is not an act of pride. Neither is Aragorn seeking to achieve renown since there are none to witness their sacrifice. His comrades are not directly under his command, and are free to follow their own course, although, as leader, Aragorn's decisions will inevitably influence the choices of those who have stated that they will follow his lead. He is not, therefore, entirely free of responsibility.

Inevitably, Tolkien's experiences in the First World War coloured his attitudes to the recklessness of those in command, and strengthened his sympathy for those who have no choice but to endure the consequences of the rash decisions of their commanding officers. Tolkien found the heroism of obedience and love of the kind found in the foot soldiers to be particularly moving. Indeed, inspiring loyalty of this kind was part of Tolkien's brief as a junior officer in the Lancashire Fusiliers, although he was required to achieve this without the familiarity and friendship of those that he leads that we witness between members of the Fellowship in *The Lord of the Rings*. For Tolkien, such loyalty is summed up by the words of Beorhtwold, an old retainer of Beorhtnoth, spoken as he was about to die and which Tolkien adapted thus:

'Heart shall be bolder, harder be purpose,
more proud the spirit as our power lessens!
Mind shall not falter nor mood waver,
though doom shall come and dark conquer'. [37]

Tolkien considered this form of unflinching loyalty to be *'the finest expression of the northern heroic spirit, Norse or English; the clearest statement of the doctrine of uttermost endurance in the service of indomitable will'* [38], and an echo of these words is found in Tolkien's description of Aragorn as he stands beneath his banner at the Black Gate: *'silent and stern, as one lost in thought of things long past or far away; but his eyes gleamed like stars that shine the brighter as the night deepens'* [39]. However, Tolkien maintains that Beorhtwold's words only hold the power they do because Beorhtwold was a lowly servant. He therefore had none of the pride of his superiors, and this lack of pride heightened his love and his loyalty, qualities which would drive a man to die for his comrades and for what he believes in. It was precisely this sort of love that drove Aragorn's comrades to follow him, no matter the risks to their own lives.

Aragorn, however, is in the strange position of being a leader who has no one under his command, and, as if to ensure that Aragorn never faced any charges like those he places upon Beowulf or Beorhtnoth, Tolkien was always at pains throughout *The Lord of the Rings* to emphasize that Aragorn never commanded any to go with him on his increasingly dangerous missions. Although he assumed the role of leader of the Fellowship on Gandalf's death, all members of the company were free to leave at any time. He reiterates this point as he prepares to venture to the Paths of the Dead, an important reminder given the Rohirrim's perceived recklessness of that mission. It was not even he who summoned his men to his aid in Rohan, and when debating their final campaign, Aragorn once more asserts that he asks none to follow him. He did release those too fearful to continue to the Black Gate, but, in truth, he had no jurisdiction over these men. It was the deference shown by their lords towards Aragorn which allowed his mercy to hold sway. And yet his men do follow him, for, as Éowyn says, they love him. But Aragorn also has his own stated allegiance to fulfil. As he stands beneath his banner at the Black Gate, he is still committed to the oath he made to the hobbits to protect them with his life. Here, he is helping Frodo the only way he can, and so, in one sense, Aragorn's heroism at this point is exactly like that of Beorhtwold. Furthermore, his adherence to his stated oath also explains his determination to find Merry and Pippin.

Undoubtedly, lack of pride is a fundamental characteristic of Aragorn's persona, and the omission of this potentially injurious feature from Aragorn's make-up is quite deliberate on Tolkien's part whose dislike of chivalric behaviour is quite evident. Aragorn's natural, inborn, humility has been further shaped by his upbringing in Rivendell and by spending most of his adult life performing heroic deeds which have routinely gone unrewarded and unrecalled, and often when donning unflattering guises that only earned him the derision of those he aided. If ever an apprenticeship for kingship could mould a character to humility, it would be the long and thankless years in waiting that Aragorn endured working undercover, often alone and in great danger. Is it any wonder that he chastised Éowyn for desiring to abandon her post for the pursuit of glory? Only in his youth when serving both Thengel in Rohan and Ecthelion in Gondor did Aragorn openly earn renown. Yet even here, the renown was awarded to an assumed personality. It was 'Thorongil', the mysterious soldier from the North who became the beloved captain of Gondor, not Aragorn son of Arathorn, the heir of Elendil. It is true that Aragorn stands to benefit more than any other individual if the West is victorious over Sauron. That he is nonetheless prepared to forfeit his last chance to win what might be regarded as the biggest rollover lottery prize in Middle-earth demonstrates that Aragorn's humility is genuine.

Aragorn's lack of pride is all the more noticeable when contrasted with the very conspicuous pride exhibited by some of Tolkien's other 'Men' heroes. Denethor's intransigence and stubborn dependence upon his own wisdom is at the root of his downfall, while Boromir's pride convinces him that he could master the power of the Ring. Beren is arguably Aragorn's closest counterpart in the mythology, yet even he has more pride than Aragorn. Beren's years of fighting in Dorthonion and his retrieving of the ring of Barahir means he is already a hero when he stumbles into Doriath. His quest for the Silmaril, however, is entirely motivated by personal gain since he had no knowledge of the jewel's future role in the defeat of Morgoth. To achieve his ambition, he capitalizes upon the oath of Finrod to gain his aid, a debt which costs Finrod his life while his unnecessary attempt to go beyond Thingol's demand and remove a second Silmaril almost brings ruin to his quest. Notably, in the original tale, the blade of the knife broke as Beren removed the first Silmaril. That this was amended so that it snaps as he tries to remove a second suggests Tolkien is reprimanding him for his presumption.

Only Tuor appears completely untainted in the possession of pride. Tuor is a supreme warrior who slays balrogs by the handful, but when defeat becomes inescapable, Tuor sensibly places the lives of Idril and Eärendil above pointlessly sacrificing his own life in the futile defense of Turgon, who remains determined to fall with his city. By doing so, he not only leads his own family to safety, but a great many of his adoptive people as well. Tuor, however, acknowledges that his wife and child are more to him than all the people of Gondolin, so he is fortunate that the achievement of his own desires runs parallel to his heroic efforts saving others.

The dangers of pride and lack of prudence in a leader are most strikingly illustrated by Tolkien in the tragic tale of his own dragon-slayer, Túrin Turambar. Here, Tolkien vividly demonstrates some of the pitfalls that could have befallen Aragorn had his pride been more and his wisdom less. Although consistently heroic in his efforts against Morgoth, Túrin is flawed in ways that Aragorn is not. In particular, he is arrogant, reckless and thoughtless of how his actions impinge upon others. As we read his story, we oscillate between feeling sympathy for his plight, and irritation at his impetuous and destructive behaviour. On the one hand, his rashness and arrogance directly contributes to the demise of Nargothrond, yet, by his courage and heroism, he saves Brethil from a similar fate. Túrin, of course, had the misfortune to be a direct recipient of Morgoth's malice, and, as Christopher Tolkien points out in the introduction to *The Children of Hurin*, Morgoth's power was such that he could not only distort the truth, he could even design the future. Even so, Túrin's forceful personality also exerts a powerful influence upon the people he encounters, and this, in turn, has a major impact upon shaping the events that came to pass.

Most of the main elements of Túrin's story were in place prior to *The Lord of the Rings*, yet the dichotomy between Túrin's pride and valour becomes progressively more polarised as the story develops, with the original hapless victim evolving into a character whose headstrong self destruction becomes an even greater factor in his downfall. Túrin, like Aragorn, is fostered by the elves, but Túrin never accepts his home in Doriath; his early memories of his mother and his homeland prevent him from forming the degree of attachment to his foster home that Aragorn demonstrates, even before the arrival of Arwen. Feeling the bitterness of exile, he experiences none of Aragorn's joy at receiving an ancestral heirloom, and, while Aragorn is universally loved in Rivendell, Túrin fails to win over Saeros. His dramatic departure from his foster home, fleeing as an outlaw, is very different from Aragorn's loving parting from Elrond. Although Aragorn leaves home abruptly once Elrond has crushed any hope of his taking Arwen's hand, he is always welcome to return, and Rivendell remained a place of refuge and succour for him until his final departure on 25th December 3018.

Túrin is partially shielded from Morgoth's curse while he dwells within the protection of Melian's Girdle, but even in the original tale, its influence upon the events that transpire is clear. Túrin, as he flees his home, bursts into tears and cries *'is there a curse upon me, for all I do is ill'* [40], while the effect is more explicit in the later versions where Mablung remarks of the exchange between Saeros and Turin, *'I feel that some shadow of the North has reached out to touch us tonight'* [41]. He warns Saeros against unwittingly doing the will of Morgoth, but in his refusal to face the consequences of his actions, we see the first of Túrin's many prideful deeds, and once Túrin has left Doriath, his pride continues to directly affect his choices. Now fully exposed to Morgoth's curse, his skill at arms quickly brings him to Morgoth's attention. However, Tolkien repeatedly maintains that by his valour Túrin has the potential to evade the curse, again demonstrating the power of Túrin's own choices even when enduring an unprecedented degree of malice. On coming to Nargothrond, Túrin's over-confidence and impatience again come to the fore. The elves policy of maintaining secrecy by avoiding conflict with the orcs is not to Túrin's liking, and he continually advocates direct combat. Here he lacks the prudence and even the skill of Aragorn and his rangers whose war of stealth in Eriador succeeds in keeping the Shire and the North safe for many years without drawing unnecessary attention to their activities.

Túrin's wilful and arrogant actions are responsible for the fall of Nargothrond, and this is particularly evident in the later versions where he not only totally disregards advice, he does so with extraordinary lack of courtesy to those whose council differs from his. His haughty, even insolent, speech to Gelmir and Arminas makes Aragorn's 'rascal of a dwarf' comment seem mild in comparison. Túrin's reckless behaviour further sets him on the path to ruin when he returns to his former home and finds his mother and sister gone. As a returning lord of his people, Túrin's homecoming could not be more different from Aragorn's triumphant return to the South. Brodda, who is not originally an Easterling, has failed to care for Túrin's mother's house and has stolen her animals, yet Túrin's slaying of him is quite unlawful. In the later versions, Túrin's rage is even more intense, and, as he storms into Brodda's hall, he creates utter mayhem. The resulting slaughter and carnage spells the death of his kinswoman and is disastrous for his people who must endure the retribution of the Easterlings. Such wanton disregard for the well-being of his people would be totally alien to Aragorn.

Túrin's pride reaches its climax as he prepares to face the dragon. He replicates Beowulf's decision to only take a few companions to aid him which, again, contrasts sharply with Aragorn's repeated insistence that he asks none to accompany him. Originally, Túrin seeks a larger company, but when attempts at rousing his men result in only six coming forward, Turin is contemptuous of those too fearful to proceed and *'would have turned his sword against them'* [42]. Túrin's wrath is reminiscent of Wiglaf's scornful dismissal of his companions who failed to aid Beowulf's assault on the dragon, while Aragorn's example towards those too fearful to venture to the Black Gate mirrors the compassion shown by Shakespeare's Henry V. However,

Túrin is only providing the leadership his people believe they require, and among the men of Brethil, *'strength was safety and valour the greatest pride of men'* [43]. Túrin's own regard for such valour, along with his contempt for those not similarly endowed, makes him a very different hero from Aragorn.

Christopher Tolkien described Túrin as possessing severity, a lack of gaiety yet a sense of justice and compassion. It is probably these latter two qualities, together with his boundless courage, which inspire sympathy for the character that might otherwise be lacking. Túrin certainly has the bad luck to be under the eye of Morgoth, whereas Aragorn successfully remains hidden from Sauron until the moment he chooses to reveal himself. But his inherent rashness is undoubtedly in stark contrast to Aragorn's considerable patience. As Aragorn remarks to Gandalf when he cautions him in the use of the Palantír, he has never displayed haste in all his long years of waiting. Túrin's impetuosity, his 'overboldness', invariably overrides any wisdom he acquired from his elvish upbringing. His tale is one of good intentions that produce evil results, whereas Aragorn's story is one of good intentions that convert to good deeds and a successful outcome. Aragorn could be considered fortunate that the crucial events underpinning his story turned out as they did, but he made a major contribution to ensuring that fortune favoured him. As far as he was able, he made his own luck.

~o00o~

Turin's heroism, in effect, occupies a halfway position between embracing the ruthlessness of a Germanic hero like Sigurd, and exhibiting the mercy of a more Christian hero like Aragorn. Yet, for all his pride in his own ability, Túrin is never guilty of the pursuit of personal honour. His renown is a consequence of his actions, not a motivation for them. The acquisition of personal honour is, however, the main tenet of chivalry, a concept which reached its zenith in the Middle Ages and is a feature of many of the Arthurian legends. Here, heroic behaviour becomes formalized by a complex set of codes, all of which must be adhered to by the loyal knight. The courtly world of Arthur is decidedly Christian and very different from that of Beowulf and Sigurd, yet the motivations of the characters are just as much at the mercy of the dictates of their times. Personal honour and a reputation for integrity are paramount.

The complexities of adhering to these, at times conflicting, requirements is vividly illustrated in the fourteenth century poem *Sir Gawain and the Green Knight* which Tolkien knew intimately. Gawain is a supremely virtuous character, and one very concerned with his own honour, who, like Beowulf, ventures into danger out of loyalty to his lord. When a mysterious knight dressed all in green disturbs Arthur's Christmas celebrations, Gawain gallantly steps up to strike a blow in Arthur's defense and beheads the stranger, who then shocks the company by being none the worse for what should have been a mortal blow. But, unlike Hygelac who tried to restrain Beowulf, Arthur permits Gawain to accept the Green Knight's reciprocal challenge to return a similar blow in a year's time and he earns the criticism of his men for placing this popular knight in unnecessary danger. Although a modest man of exemplary character, in his eventual encounter with the seductive wife of his host, Bertilak, Gawain must juggle a league table of knightly virtues as he struggles to maintain his honour in the face of mounting temptations. When he fails, his shame is, characteristically, out of all proportion to his 'crime'. Gawain withholds from his host the magic girdle given to him by Bertilak's wife in the hope that it will protect him from the blow of the Green Knight. Gawain duly turns up at the appointed hour to face his foe who turns out to be none other than Bertilak transformed. Gawain survives the encounter with his honour restored, and it then transpires that the whole challenge had been a set up by Morgan Le Fey to embarrass Arthur and upset Guinevere.

Fortunately such nuances of chivalrous conduct play no part in our understanding of Aragorn's motives. As Tolkien remarked, *'This tale does not deal with a period of 'Courtly Love' and its pretences; but with a culture more primitive (sc. less corrupt) and nobler'* [44]. However, a discussion of Aragorn's heroic literary ancestors would be incomplete without mention of Arthur, who, more than any other character from either history or legend, is the epitome of the heroic king who wields a famous sword. Even so, in his 1951 letter to Milton Waldeman, Tolkien appears to quite emphatically suggest that he was not particularly influenced by the Arthurian legends when creating his own mythology.

'Of course there was and is all the Arthurian world, but powerful as it is, it is imperfectly naturalised, associated with the soil of Britain but not with English; and does not replace what I felt was missing. For one thing its 'faerie' is too lavish, and fantastical, incoherent and repetitive. For another and more important thing: it is involved in and explicitly contains the Christian religion. For reasons which I will not elaborate, that seems to me fatal' [45].

Tolkien's dislike of the pursuit of personal honour and his desire to avoid charges of Christian allegory in his writing were undoubtedly factors behind this denial. It might, therefore, seem futile to search for similarities were it not for the body of evidence which appears to refute this statement. We do know that Tolkien was 'excited' by the legends as a child, although not to the same extent as he was by the tale of Sigurd. Certainly, Tolkien had substantial academic involvement with the Arthurian world. Early in his career, he co-edited the story of *Sir Gawain and the Green Knight* with E.V. Gordon, and wrote his own translation in the early 1950's. He even remarks upon his particular interest in the sources utilised by the unknown author in his introduction. Significant also is the question of the unpublished and unfinished poem, *The Fall of Arthur*. This poem is reputedly nine thousand words long, which, as Lewis and Currie point out, is twice the length of *The Lay of Leithian* and representing a considerable effort for one supposedly disinterested in this material. Lewis and Curry further make the point that Tolkien's comment to Waldeman was, in effect, part of a selling job which he was undertaking at the time in his attempts to have both *The Lord of the Rings* and *The Silmarillion* accepted for publication. Verlyn Flieger, too, makes a strong case for Tolkien being influenced by Arthur, and notes that Tolkien began writing *The Fall of Arthur* some ten years before he wrote that letter to Milton Waldeman and that four years afterwards he still hoped to complete it. She maintains that the strength of his dismissal and denial of Arthurian association is in itself an indication of the influence it was exerting on him.

As to the character of Arthur himself, the debate about whether there ever was a leader of the Britons called Arthur is one that may never be settled. There is no hard evidence to confirm his existence, but whatever the reality, there is no doubting the legacy of literature which has been written about him or the enduring influence of the legend. The character has evolved considerably since his first mention nearly fifteen hundred years ago. Even from the first, the legend was impressive, but if Arthur ever lived, he would have been more a military leader than a king, a sixth century warrior remembered for galvanising the English in their battles against the invading Saxons. While the courtly figure of Camelot with its embellishments the Round Table and the Quest for the Holy Grail is indelibly associated with England, Arthur's roots are Welsh and there are two significant mentions of him in the *Annales Cambriae*. Here, Arthur's famous battle at Mount Badon against the Saxons is dated 516 and the victory is specifically ascribed to Arthur, while the date of the battle at Camlan, where Arthur was fatally wounded fighting Mordred, is given as 537. The timing of the insertion of these entries remains uncertain and the evidence is by no means consistent, with the sixth century cleric,

Gildas maintaining that the victory at Badon instead belonged to Ambrosius Aurelianus, a Roman-British nobleman. In fact, neither Gildas nor Bede, who admittedly was influenced by Gildas, mentions Arthur, omissions that have resulted in speculation that Ambrosius might himself have been the inspiration for Arthur.

The earliest source which identifies Arthur as an actual historical figure is found in the ninth century *Historia Brittonum* which is controversially attributed to the Welsh cleric, Nennius. He cites Arthur as a leader who defeated the Saxons on no less than twelve occasions, and at the ninth of these battles, the battle of Badon, Arthur reputedly killed 960 men single-handedly. Slightly later, in the twelve century, William of Malmesbury in his *History of the Kings of England* mentions Arthur's role in the wars against the Saxons, and states that he *'long upheld the sinking state, and roused the broken spirit of his countrymen to war'* [46].

Fortunately the Arthur of literature is preserved rather better than the historical one. Whereas Beowulf is known to us from just a single source, Arthur features widely in various medieval Welsh poems and prose stories such as those found in the sixth century, *The Book of Taliesin*, and the modern, *Mabinogion*, which includes that of *Culhwch and Olwen* mentioned earlier. Diverse in their nature, collectively these create an image of a supreme and noble warrior who slays all manner of foes and monsters. The very earliest known reference to Arthur is a single mention in the Welsh poem, *Y Gododdin,* which was probably written in the late sixth century, a date which places Arthur in the correct time span for the historical character. The poem tells of a battle at Catraeth in the North of England to which went three hundred warriors, but only one, Gwawrddur, survived. He was said to be among the powerful in battle, *'though he was no Arthur'* [47], and no wonder if Arthur's exploits at the battle of Badon are to be believed.

In most of these early tales, Arthur has only a supporting role, and the legend was only finally fleshed out and formalised by Geoffrey of Monmouth in his twelfth century, part historical, part fantastical work *Historia Regum Britanniae*. Geoffrey expanded greatly upon Nennius's account, and such was the influence and popularity of this version that contemporary studies of the various source texts on Arthur are still divided between those written before and after. According to Geoffrey, when Arthur was fifteen, he succeeded his father, Uther Pendragon, to become king, and with his sword, Caliburn, which was forged on the Isle of Avalon, he successfully defeated the Saxons in a succession of battles before marrying Guinevere, who is described as the most beautiful woman in the entire island. He continued to forge his empire until it covered much of northern Europe, although his motivation for the inevitable killing that this offensive entails appears to be for no higher motive than that all of Europe is now in fear of him. Once he had taken Gaul, he established his court at Paris but returned to Wales for a great feast, to which were invited all the kings of the realms under his now vast domain. But when Rome demanded he pay tribute, according to Geoffrey, Arthur returned to Europe and defeated the Romans at Saussy, though his plan to march on Rome itself was thwarted when he learned that his nephew, Mordred, had married Guinevere in his absence and claimed the throne of Britain. Arthur returned to England and defeated Mordred, but was himself mortally wounded and taken to the otherworldly Isle of Avalon to be healed of his wounds.

Following this popular telling of the story, many more versions of the legend appeared, all of which embellished Geoffrey's already historically dubious account. Wade, an Anglo-Norman born in Jersey, wrote a history of Britain called *Roman de Brut,* adding some creations of his own, in particular the Round Table and Excalibur. Wade's work, in turn, became the basis for Layamon's, *Brut,* which in itself influenced the anonymous Middle English poem *Alliterative Morte Arthur.* Notable also at this time were the versions from France, such as the romances of Chrétien de Troyes, which added significantly to Geoffrey's tale Chrétien introduced Lancelot and his affair with Guinevere and with it the concept of a code of chivalry among Arthur's knights. The poems of the late 12th century French writer, Robert de Boron, form part of the French Vulgate Cycle, and it is here that the legend begins to take on its most familiar form, before finally becoming fully developed with the publication of Thomas Malory's *Morte Darthur* in 1495. Malory's epic is a comprehensive work expanding upon all the legends of Arthur's rise and fall and is considered the last of the significant medieval sources. Although still a noble figure, Malory at times portrays Arthur as less than perfect, his morality questionable, certainly in comparison with Geoffrey's supremely heroic warrior. Malory's Arthur even knowingly commits incest by sleeping with his half sister, resulting in the conception of his illegitimate son, Mordred.

Arthur's popularity fell at the end of the Middle Ages, but in the early nineteenth century there was a revival of interest with Alfred, Lord Tennyson's *Idyll's of the King*, becoming one of the most popular works written at that time. Although based partly upon Malory, Tennyson's Arthur is an idealized hero trying to establish the perfect kingdom, although ultimately failing. The reworking of the Arthurian legend continued to a lesser extent into the twentieth century with works such as those of T.H. White, the first of which was published in 1938. Although support for the concept of chivalry declined in the aftermath of the First World War, in the 1930's, the Order of the Fellowship of the Knights of the Round Table was formed in Britain to promote Christian ideals and Arthurian notions of medieval chivalry, while the discovery of the early manuscript of Malory's *Morte Darthur* in 1934 further reawakened public awareness of the character.

The role of Arthur in all his many tales may have changed considerably with the numerous re-workings of the legend which were inevitably adapted to suit the mood of the times, but the romantic notion of a noble figure, brave and dignified, is what has stayed with us throughout the many and varied portrayals. The popular image of Arthur as a great and valiant king who also happens to wield a magic sword has so indelibly entered our subconscious that it is perhaps no wonder that upon encountering Aragorn we are immediately reminded of him. Which of the diversity of tales surrounding Arthur had the greatest influence on Tolkien is a matter of conjecture and one I will leave to better informed minds than mine. According to Carpenter, *The Fall of Arthur* is a reworking of the *Morte Darthur*, which tells of how the king and Gawain go to war in Saxon lands but are summoned home by news of Mordred's treachery. Tolkien's personal preferences, we know, lay with the Medieval and the Welsh, and it is on these accounts that academic studies also tend to concentrate.

With a breadth of tales spanning a millennium, there is no one character to analyse and the early Arthur of history bears little resemblance to the later king of Camelot. As Tolkien suggested himself in his lecture, *On Fairy-Stories*, Arthur's prolonged boiling in the Pot of Tales had long since distanced the fictional Arthur from any historical one. The early Arthur is a supreme warrior protecting Britain from the invading Saxons who hunts all manner of monsters. His role is partially comparable with Aragorn's protecting of the Shire and the slaying of the many things that would freeze the heart of Butterbur if he did but know of them. But this Arthur is a leader of an elite group of warriors who possess supernatural qualities. For instance, Cei can grow to the height of the tallest tree and provide heat for his companions in the cold weather, while Nennius's portrayal of Arthur as a military leader who slew 960 in a single battle suggests the early Arthur was also credited with at least some superhuman talents.

Aragorn, too, has exceptional characteristics, but even a warrior of his capabilities would still struggle to match Arthur's reputed tally in battle. For a man a few days shy of his eighty-eighth birthday, Aragorn demonstrates phenomenal stamina during the pursuit through Rohan, and while his longevity and his other talents such as his healing ability and his foresight, are still fantastical, they remain believable. Tom Shippey cites Aragorn as an example in *The Road to Middle-earth* when he utilises Northrop Frye's five 'modes' of literature to determine how Tolkien's heroes relate to their environments and the rest of humanity. He suggests that *The Lord of the Rings* lies between 'myth' and 'high mimesis' as 'romance' where *'heroes are characteristically 'superior in degree [not kind] to other men and to [their] environments"* [48]. In other words, unlike some of Arthur's companions, Aragorn always remains a recognisable man, if one whose exceptional talents allow him to stretch, but not break, the usual rules that govern the limitations of man's relationship with the natural world.

As Arthur's story evolves, similarities between the characters begin to become apparent. Both Aragorn and Arthur are rightful heirs to fallen fathers, the last of their line, and, in the later versions, bereft of their kingdoms and raised in secret by eminent foster fathers; Arthur by Sir Ector, Aragorn by Master Elrond. Fostering is a common feature of fairy-stories, and Sigurd, Beowulf, Turin and, belatedly, Tuor were also raised in this manner. In fact, many of Tolkien's characters lose one or both of their parents when very young. Frodo's parents were drowned when he was a child; Éowyn and Éomer were orphans, raised by their uncle Théoden; Boromir and Faramir lost their mother, and throughout *The Lost Road*, the various tales were to be of fathers and sons with no mention of any mothers or wives. Given the tumultuous times in which these characters lived, such losses might reasonably be expected. Perhaps the boating accident which resulted in the deaths of Frodo's parents was rather more contrived so as to free Frodo from domestic responsibilities, since parents, spouses and dependents do not encourage adventurers to be adventurous.

There is some historical basis for a culture of routine fostering of children; it was common for children of Celtic families to be raised by an uncle, and Tolkien adopted a similar practice among the families of his First Age Men. The fostering of Húrin and Huor by their uncle Haldir in Brethil was said to be traditional and in the *Quenta Silmarillion* Morwen wished to foster Turin, not, as later, for his protection, but *'after the manner of that time'* [49]. In the Third Age, with the loss of the kingdom of Arthedain, it further became the tradition that the heir of Isildur should be fostered at Rivendell, both as a means of providing an education and to keep the heir safe. Moreover, there is a strong element of the autobiographical in these numerous fosterings. Tolkien's own father died when he was very young and, with his mother's premature death, Tolkien became an orphan at the age of twelve. He and his brother, Hilary, were then raised by the Catholic priest, Father Francis Xavier Morgan, who became as a father to the boys. According to Carpenter, Father Francis was *'a very noisy man, loud and affectionate, embarrassing to small children at first'*. [50] He might not immediately recall an elf-lord, but in his prohibition of the marriage of Ronald and Edith, we undoubtedly see the roots of a similar ban set by Elrond on his own foster son.

Like Aragorn, Arthur only learns of his inheritance upon reaching manhood. Both become brave warriors, winning many battles to create vast empires. Both become noble kings, beloved by their subjects. According to Geoffrey's description, even as a lad of fifteen, Arthur *'was of outstanding courage and generosity, and his inborn goodness gave him such grace that he was loved by almost all the people'* [51], a description that could equally apply to Aragorn. Both Geoffrey's Arthur and Tolkien's Aragorn strived long and hard against overwhelming odds before they succeeded in bringing peace and prosperity to their respective kingdoms. Geoffrey claims that Arthur *'restored the whole country to its earlier dignity'* [52] while Aragorn renewed his ancestral realms and restored the dignity of the Dúnedain.Both completed their long struggles before they both married beautiful women. Probably though, the two factors which most contribute to draw Aragorn and Arthur together in our minds are their possession of famous swords and their having mighty wizards as counselors.

Aragorn's broken sword had been an heirloom of his line since the Second Age when it came into the possession of the lords of Andúnië. Forged by the dwarf, Telchar, in the First Age, it had remained broken for over three thousand years until its re-forging fulfilled the prophecy that this would occur when the Enemy's Ring was found. Arthur's sword is also an heirloom, and, according to Geoffrey, it was peerless, having been forged on the Isle of Avalon. Although Andúril is not called upon to deliver a final heroic blow in the way its predecessors were, a common theme of the swords of Arthur, Sigurd and Aragorn is possession of their own inherent light, one which Tolkien also attributes to other notable weapons in Middle-earth such as Gurthang and Sting. However the most notable similarity between Excalibur

177

and Andúril is not the sword itself, but its sheath. In Malory, the sheath of the sword gifted by the Lady of the Lake conferred invincibility upon its wearer by ensuring his injuries from blood loss in battle would not kill him. Galadriel's gift to Aragorn may not be as powerful, but Andúril's new sheath will prevent the blade drawn from it being *'stained or broken even in defeat'* [53]. The legend of Arthur's royalty being revealed by his pulling the sword from a stone is similar to the legend of Sigurd's father drawing his sword from a tree, and this use of the inanimate as proof of kingship is replicated in Aragorn's success with athelas on first coming to Minas Tirith. It is a motif found elsewhere, most noticeably in the late thirteenth century story of Havelok the Dane. The handsome and humble lad is unaware that he is the son of king Gunther of Denmark, but it is known that the rightful king produces a flame from his mouth in sleep and so Havelock's destiny is revealed.

Both the later Arthur and Aragorn were befriended by powerful otherworldly advisors who act as counsellors to the kings in waiting. The differing accounts of Merlin's involvement with Arthur are as varied as Arthur's own story and there are many inconsistencies. Merlin has, at times, been human, at others, unworldly; he has variously been a poet, a prophet, a lover, a wizard and a magician. In Geoffrey's *Historia* he is even credited with the building of Stonehenge.Nor has he always been a benevolent force, and the assistance he renders to Arthur is highly variable. The actual character of Merlin is an invention of Geoffrey who appears in both his *Historia* and his later work, *Vita Merlini.* But Merlin's roots go as far back as the late sixth century and he is based on a historical figure who was reputed to have gone mad after witnessing the horrors of war. Consequently he lived a solitary existence in the wilds with only animals for company. The character is called 'Myrddin' in the *Black Book of Carmarthen*, and the name is included in one of Tolkien's purchases with his Skeat prize money; John Morris-Jones' *Welsh Grammar, Historical and Comparative* where there is a discussion on its philology. According to Tolkien's notes in *Sir Gawain and the Green Knight*, Myrddin existed at a later date than Arthur, but, due to Geoffrey's invention, the two became forever associated with one another.

Geoffrey took the figure of Myrddin and attributed to him aspects of the story previously ascribed to Ambrosius by Nennius, effectively amalgamating the two characters. According to Geoffrey, Merlin was the son of a noble woman and a demon. As a boy, he was destined to be sacrificed by the Celtic king, Vortigen, who needed his blood to stop his castle from crumbling, a role

Nennius gave to Ambrosius. Merlin, however, was spared when he persuaded Vortigen that his castle only kept falling down because of the two warring dragons that dwelt beneath it. The precedent of kingly advisor arose when Merlin used his prophetic powers to not only assist Arthur, but also his father, Uther, and his brother who is named by Geoffrey as Aurelius Ambrosius. Incidentally, the character of Aurelius Ambrosius, who has far greater historical credentials than Arthur, is treated so sympathetically by Geoffrey he could also be a role model for Aragorn. A son of Constantine II, Aurelius was considered too young to accede the throne when his father was assassinated so both he and Uther were taken to Brittany for their safe-keeping, and were reared by King Budicius. When Aurelius eventually returned to Britain, he defeated Vortigen and became king, an event prophesied by Merlin. The courage of Aurelius was dreaded by Hengest and the Saxons, and the man was so brave and hardy that none would challenge him to single combat. *'What is more, he was liberal in his gifts, regular in his attendance at divine services, modest in all his behaviour and unwilling to ever tell a lie. He fought well on foot and even better when mounted; and he was most skilled in commanding an army'* [54]. He also demonstrated compassion towards the defeated Saxons before devoting his energies to rebuilding his realm and renewing the peace.

The later Merlin of Robert de Boron was, like Geoffrey's, also a son of a devil. He was freed from this satanic influence by baptism, but because of his unusual parentage, he retained the power of prophesy. Boron also makes Merlin a shapeshifter who is transformed into many guises before finally appearing as an old man with a long beard. His version includes Merlin's role in the taking of the infant Arthur to be raised in secret by Sir Anton. Here Merlin is also responsible for the setting in stone of the magical sword of Arthur's true father. Malory further enlarged the role of kingmaker with his Merlin being at the forefront of most of Arthur's deeds.

As noted earlier, the divine persona of Gandalf probably has more in common with Odin than with the sometimes far more dubious character of Merlin, and it has to be said there are far fewer similarities between Merlin and Gandalf than there are differences. Furthermore, Scull and Hammond suggest Gandalf and Aragorn should be viewed more as colleagues than as tutor and pupil [55]. Yet Aragorn defers to Gandalf in all matters expect in his decision to look in the Palantír, and, when Gandalf speculates to Pippin that Aragorn may have done just that, he credits him with possessing the wisdom to make his own decisions. Certainly, the young man of twenty-five who first made the friendship of the wizard might have needed considerably more guidance than the hardened ranger we meet at the time of the War of the Ring. Indeed, Gandalf's role as counselor is acknowledged by Aragorn himself on Mindolluin where he expresses his desire to still have the counsel of his dear friend. Yet, Gandalf, as far as we know, never actively canvasses on Aragorn's part as Merlin does for Arthur. Such overt interference was not part of his remit which was directed more towards providing guidance and encouragement, although Aragorn readily proclaims the victory of the West as his, and Gandalf shares the honour of placing the crown upon his head. And, if the first version of the provenance of the Elessar is favoured, then Gandalf did indeed play a small, if vital, role as Aragorn's kingmaker. Before he departed from Valinor, Gandalf was given the green stone of Eärendil by none other than Yavanna. This he passed to Galadriel when he came to Middle-earth, but he predicted that it was *'not for you to possess. You shall hand it on when the time comes....one shall come who is to receive it, and his name shall be that of the stone: Elessar he shall be called'* [56]. When Galadriel does, finally, give the stone to Aragorn, she tells him to take the name foretold for him.

Despite their similarities, the stories of Aragorn and Arthur diverge drastically when it comes to their deaths. Being a just and beloved king and a great hero to boot was not sufficient to ensure the longevity of Arthur's kingdom. It was in the defense of his own personal honour, that most dangerous of chivalric necessities, which wrought Arthur's downfall. Arthur was a devout Christian who, according to both Nennius and Geoffrey, even bore an image of the Virgin with him into battle. Aragorn would have lived five millennia before the coming of Christ and yet, with his supremely virtuous humanity, Tolkien ensures he adheres closely to Christian ideals of behaviour, and he enjoys a long reign and a successful marriage as a result. By contrast, in spite of following a conspicuous code of chivalry and religious teachings, problems with fidelity are at the root of many an Arthurian tale and Arthur's marriage is no exception. Arthur does not share Aragorn's good fortune in his choice of wife, and Guinevere's adultery, at first with Mordred and later with Lancelot when Mordred shifts roles and he become Arthur's illegitimate son, proves the catalyst which precipitates Arthur's downfall.

Evolved from the Welsh, Gwenhwyfar, Guinevere has been associated with Arthur since her first appearance in the Welsh Triads where she was the daughter of Gogfan the Giant. There is a suggestion of otherworldliness about her and her name has been interpreted as meaning 'white fay'. Like

Arwen, she was very dear to her father, later named, Leodogrance, and was considered the most beautiful of all women, but, while Arwen was prepared to sacrifice her immortality to marry Aragorn, Guinevere would not forgo the charms of her suitors for the sake of Arthur. That her infidelity invariably occurs with one of Arthur's knights only compounds the betrayal. The details of her adultery are inconsistent and in some versions, Guinevere is even portrayed as a tragic heroine. However, according to Carpenter, this was not how Tolkien chose to describe her in *The Fall of Arthur.*

> *'lady ruthless,*
> *fair as fay-woman and fell minded,*
> *in the world walking for the woe of men.'* [57]

It is unthinkable that Halbarad, dutifully carrying Arwen's standard to his chieftain, would ever do as Lancelot and embark upon an affair with his lord's betrothed, after all, the temptations in *The Lord of the Rings* are not for those of the flesh. Even so, the possessiveness and desire elicited by contact with the Ring might still have proved as disastrous for Aragorn as Guinevere's adultery did for Arthur. It was possessiveness, if of a different magnitude, which wrought the demise of Tolkien's other returning king, Thorin Oakenshield, whose stubborn refusal to part with his family heirloom, the Arkenstone, had disastrous results. Of Aragorn's 'knights' two of his company fall prey to this particular 'sin'. First, Boromir's attempt to seize the Ring from Frodo could have proved disastrous for the Quest, but he repents of his folly, is forgiven by Aragorn and, far from derailing the Quest, his actions help galvanize Aragorn to subsequently make the right decisions which ultimately prove crucial for his success. Potentially far more disastrous for Aragorn and his pretensions of kingship is the claiming of the Ring by Frodo at the Sammath Naur. Again, Aragorn is fortunate; disaster is nonetheless averted by the pity shown previously to Gollum by both Frodo and Bilbo and Aragorn survives the war to establish his kingdom.

Furthermore, while Arthur's kingdom failed, Aragorn's was held to have endured long into the future. In many versions of Arthur's story, he did not produce an heir, and although several sons are mentioned throughout the diverse breadth of the legend, only Mordred appears to have been of any consequence, although any issue of his, if mentioned at all, are consistently said to have been slain. Recent attempts have been made to demonstrate that Arthur's heirs survived, but none have proved conclusive. By contrast, as we have seen, Tolkien ensured that Aragorn's son, Eldarion, was a worthy successor to his father whose heirs would fulfil the prophecy in the Appendices of *The Lord of the Rings* that Aragorn's line would never be extinguished.

Aragorn, for all his superficial similarities with Arthur, in the end, has a very different fate. He does not fall in battle, but is rewarded for his selfless endeavors by being granted a long lifespan in which to rule his kingdom in great bliss and glory. His is the fairy-tale ending in which he earns the right to his bride, and his lady love remains true and faithful to the end of his days. Arthur's fate is more that of Frodo's. The victor in battle, but severely wounded, he goes across the sea to be healed of his injuries on the otherworldly Avalon, 'the lonely isle' of which Avallónë and Tol Eressëa are direct descendants.

In Arthur's story, there is a suggestion of his return and the belief that Arthur will one day drive the English and Normans from their lands is known in Wales as the 'Breton Hope'. The belief became so popular in the Middle Ages that Henry II made strenuous efforts to find Arthur's grave so that the myth could be disproved. The bones of Arthur and Guinevere were supposedly discovered at Glastonbury a year after Henry II's death in 1191, but this inconclusive find did nothing to squash belief in the 'Hope'. Reputedly, even the Spanish king Phillip II on his marriage to Mary Tudor declared that he would resign his kingdom should Arthur return.

The returning king is a common theme of folktales; the Danish king, Ogier, for instance, is said to be asleep, maybe even in Avalon, waiting to return to Denmark, while the Irish legend of Fionn mac Cumhaill tells of a wise warrior with healing powers sleeping in a cave under Ireland who will return when his country's need is greatest. In the fourteenth century poem *A Dispute between a Christian and a Jew*, Arthur and his knights are apparently also residing underground but in a manor house beneath a hill, and in the thirteenth century, Gervase of Tilbury told how the Bishop of Cantania's groom came across Arthur lying on a couch in a plain which was reached via a narrow path on the side of Mount Etna. The subterranean also features in the Arthurian poem, *The Spoils of Annwn*, where Arthur sails to an underworld kingdom to retrieve a magic cauldron. Verlyn Flieger notes the word 'annun' was of particular interest to Tolkien [58] and these subterranean otherworlds inevitably bring to mind Aragorn's ride through the Paths of the Dead. Aragorn may not be the exact same king returning from the past but his return brings the same benefits for his people as those anticipated in these other legends.

Furthermore, his subsequent ride from the Stone of Erech to Pelargir has its roots in the widespread folk-lore belief in the 'Wild Hunt' which features a phantom chase occurring at night, often accompanied by the sounds of horses' hooves and the blowing of horns. One such hunt is said to occur near Cadbury Castle in Somerset, a possible site of Camelot, where there is a track known as Arthur's Hunting Causeway and where Arthur is supposedly heard on occasion leading a midnight chase. Although not associated with Arthur, but well known to Tolkien, another of these hunts is described in the medieval tale of *Sir Orfeo* which also features a king venturing into a subterranean, otherworldly kingdom.

~oo0oo~

While we meet Aragorn primarily as a ranger in his days of battle and strife before he comes into his inheritance, his heroism is not only to be found in his skill with a sword and it is, perhaps, in his later role as king that we should properly judge his purpose within the context of the story. Aragorn may play a crucial part in the War of the Ring, but once the battle against Sauron is over, his true work of preparation for the Dominion of Men is just beginning. It is only as monarch that he can fulfil his role as Envinyatar, the renewer of his People, and after he became king, his wisdom and diplomacy brought huge benefits to all the people of Middle-earth. With Gondor in decay and the former kingdom of Arnor effectively nonexistent, to him fell the task of rebuilding his ancestral kingdoms and healing the hurts dividing the war torn lands. He not only restores peace and prosperity, he also restores the line of kings, the veneration of his people and also their spiritual affiliation with God. With the Dark Lord defeated, the implementation of his rule, which extends over a domain covering much of Middle-earth, is of paramount importance in defining the character of the new age.

His heroic achievements as peacemaker are particularly reminiscent of those of Charlemagne, a Catholic king and a renowned empire builder. Tolkien himself remarked that while most readers noticed the similarities between Aragorn and Arthur, few spotted the connection to Charlemagne. Nothing is known of Charlemagne's early life, but he is as much a legendary king in Europe as Arthur is in Britain, although Charlemagne's deeds, unlike Arthur's, are largely based on historical record. The eldest son of Pippin III, he embarked on a military campaign in the late eighth century which saw him established as a mighty emperor of most of Western Europe, ruling a domain easily comparable to that presided over by the King of the West. Like

Aragorn, Charlemagne came to power at a time of turmoil. The Franks of Charlemagne's homelands were returning to barbarism, the pagan Saxons in the north were still troublesome while the Roman Catholic church was slowly recovering from the defeat by the Lombards in the south. However, after a thirty year campaign, Charlemagne became the ruler of most of Western Europe, his realm forged from the ruins of the former Roman Empire, and, like Aragorn, he had the task of rebuilding a land ravaged by war and unrest. Tolkien notes that the scale of Aragorn's kingdom was comparable with that of Charlemagne's and he maintained that, if the Shire and Rivendell were at the latitude of Oxford, then Minas Tirith was at about the latitude of Florence. Tolkien underlines the comparison by remarking of *The Lord of the Rings* that *'the tale ends in what is far more like the re-establishment of an effective Holy Roman Empire'* [59].

Charlemagne was a more successful king that Arthur, and in this he is more like Aragorn. He was a most efficient organizer who succeeded in bringing order and stability to his realm, and was arguably an even more competent administrator than he was a military leader. His emissaries kept him well informed of everything that took place in his lands, and he genuinely believed that those who governed did so for the benefit of the people. His reforms were aimed at improving the lot of his subjects, and he succeeded in improving agricultural methods as well as promoting commerce. He laid the foundations for modern Europe and was canonized in Rome by the Pope for his efforts. His descendants endured long and could be found among the French and German monarchies. Charlemagne, in his old age, crowned his own son before taking to his bed and dying seven days later. Like Aragorn, he had a peaceful passing at the end of a long life, and his death was widely lamented by his people.

Yet Charlemagne was not averse to killing those that opposed him, and his successes came at a heavy price. He was ruthless in his determination that all should convert to Christianity and during his long campaigns, those who resisted were slaughtered in their masses. At Verden in 782, he beheaded four thousand five hundred Saxons in a single day because they refused to be baptized. The worlds in which these early heroes lived were undeniably brutal with suffering and cruelty meted out on a scale difficult to reconcile today. Edward I, the very tall medieval king of England, is another competent administrator and military tactician who has earned modern criticism for his actions suppressing his enemies, here the Welsh and the Scots. He was far less successful in his foreign campaigns than Charlemagne, and his nickname of 'Longshanks' is probably all that Aragorn inherited from him.

Tom Shippey claims that the heathen element of these heroes, particularly those of Sigurd and Beowulf, would have been no less repulsive to Tolkien who would have regarded the heroic literature of the pre-Christian past with, on the one hand, *'great professional liking, and on the other extreme ideological aversion'* [60]. Shippey further suggests that, being aware of these difficulties, Tolkien created his twentieth century myth as a means of reconciling these two irreconcilables. The challenge Tolkien, therefore, set himself was to create noble pagans in a post-Christian age who possessed a sense of ethics comparable to ours, but without the moral support provided by formal religion.

Aragorn's personal qualities, in particular his compassion, certainly appear to mark him as a Christian hero, although it is too simplistic to label Aragorn as a Christian king. Not only has many a Christian committed atrocities in the name of his God, the roots of modern humanitarianism found in the ethics and philosophies of the ancient Greeks predate the coming of Christ by several centuries. Tolkien's determination to avoid bringing the religion of the primary world into Middle-earth proves a bonus for Aragorn whose sense of natural ethics remains untarnished by formalized religious doctrine. Instead, his morality has been refined and honed by his education among the Elves whose own values, in turn, were directly influenced by the Valar themselves. Perhaps Tolkien's ideal is better described as Northern heroism and courage coloured by Christian values since Aragorn undoubtedly possesses a rather more contempory heart that his medieval counterparts. This modernisation was essential as a hero who is merely good at killing would not satisfy the modern reader. He must also possess characteristics with which the reader can readily identify. So, while Aragorn has the physical prowess of the traditional hero and performs similar spectacular great deeds, he also provides us with ample opportunity to appreciate his humanity and his humility. On claiming his crown, Aragorn demonstrated a very modern form of statesmanship by pardoning his former enemies and by awarding autonomy to the realms under his dominion. Here, Aragorn shows his worth as a leader and also his own freedom from the further dogma of political idealism. Tolkien suggests that the 'taint' of politics was a factor in Denethor's downfall, since his prime motive was less the defeat of an evil tyrant than the preservation of Gondor's power. Had he proved the victor over Sauron, Denethor, who despised 'lesser' men, would have treated the vanquished allies of Mordor very differently.

Aragorn's mercy, however, did not extend towards the orcs which he was prepared to annihilate. It must be remembered that the orcs represented an unprecedented threat to all mankind, and this threat was of an altogether different magnitude from the usual political battles of Men. Of the defeat of Grendel, Tolkien remarks that all men could unite in rejoicing at his death because he was a monster. The same could be said of the orcs which were a threat comparable with, say, an aggressive alien invasion such as we might find in science fiction, except, that the orcs were not alien. Their existence stemmed from the same Music that created all of Eä. In *The Silmarillion*, the origin of orcs is given as corrupted elves, but Tolkien was not entirely happy with this. In a 1954 letter to Peter Hastings, he states that the orcs were *'fundamentally a race of 'rational incarnate' creatures, though horribly corrupted'* [61]. Later, in the same letter, he describes the orcs as *'Morgoth's greatest Sins....creatures begotten of Sin, and naturally bad'*. He does, however, stop short of describing them as 'irredeemably bad' since even orcs were a part of our world, which, Tolkien maintains, *'is God's and ultimately good'* [62]. Whatever redemption Tolkien may have thought possible, he does not say, but, with their wills so driven by the evil spirit of their master, earthly redemption was probably an impossibility, and Aragorn would have been negligent in his duty of care to his people had he attempted any form of modern-day rehabilitation, a step too far, even for one as fair minded as Aragorn.

Where we most strikingly recognize Aragorn's modernization is in his ability to heal. This feature of Aragorn's heroism may be less dramatically heroic than his feats as a warrior or even as an empire builder but, at its most demanding, implementing this skill required courage and sacrifice on his part, since his efforts saving the lives of others placed him in actual physical danger. Aragorn's technique of using herbs as an aid to healing is not in itself uncommon; Gawain was portrayed by Chrétien as a healer with an unsurpassed knowledge of these plants. Aragorn, too, is at times seen using the sort of first aid skills and herbal lore that would be expected of the competent traveller, skills he would have gained through his years as a ranger or even at the hand of his foster father. Initially, his use of athelas appears to be healing of this sort, and we see glimpses of Aragorn's talents as he treats his injured companions throughout the Quest. While there is no suggestion that Gawain's skill was anything more that the result of learned techniques, the healing skills of another Arthurian healer bear some comparison with those of Aragorn. Credited by Malory with healing the seven wounds of Sir Urre whose injuries have been cursed never to heal by the mother of his slain opponent, 'Launcelot' succeeds where the skills of a hundred other knights failed because he was *'the best knight of the world'* [63].

Were it not for his adultery with Guinevere, there would be a case to make comparison between Lancelot and Aragorn. Even from his first introduction, Lancelot is endowed with unique talents. Just as only Aragorn can hope to pass through the Paths of the Dead, Lancelot alone can raise the lid of a tomb said to need the strength of seven to do so.Lancelot was reared away from his kin by the otherworldly Lady of the Lake and becomes the bravest of all Arthur's knights. Lancelot, too, receives the unrequited love of a lady, although Elaine dies of despair at his rejection. However, regardless of his courage and heroism, Lancelot's betrayal of trust inevitably undermines his better qualities and any inspiration that came from this paradox of virtue of French origin likely only spurred the creation of his antithesis.

Furthermore, unlike Lancelot's healing of Urre which came about solely through the power of prayer, Aragorn's healing skill is multifaceted. His strange chant over the Morgul blade on Weathertop, an incantation that remains unexplained, appears to evoke the supernatural, but it is in his healing of Faramir, Éowyn and Merry following the battle of the Pelennor Fields that the full extent of his abilities is finally revealed. Athelas forms the tangible part of his armory and the herb has a long association with the Dúnedain, having returned to Middle-earth from Númenor. It was also the herb used by Lúthien in *The Lay of Leithian* to heal Beren although, as already noted, when this detail was introduced is unclear. Originally, Beren is healed of his maimed arm by nothing more than Tinúviel's love and the tears she wept over him which appear to be part of the healing process. In the *Lay of Leithian*, however, Lúthien's healing of Beren is enhanced by the use of this herb which is fetched for her by Huan, so that now Beren is healed, not only by her love, but by a combination of her skills and her love. Aragorn's possession of healing skills therefore owes as much to his being a descendant of Lúthien as to the use of the herb itself and is a direct consequence of his being, as Tolkien put it, *'not a pure 'Man''* [64]. Lúthien herself no doubt acquired her skills from her mother, Melian, who served the Valar, Estë, the healer of hurts, in Valinor. To some degree, this skill was passed to her descendants, so Aragorn's skill, while innate, was not unique. Elrond possessed skills greater than his, and we know his sons were similarly gifted. Those of Anárion's line also inherited the gift of healing. Ioreth, for one, had not forgotten that the hands of the king were the hands of a healer. Aragorn's healing skills were, therefore, an intrinsic part of him, acquired because of his inherited divine characteristics, his ability to heal inexorably linked to his kingship.

This ability of kings to heal is well established in history. It was one of the talents of the sacral king and a consequence of their divine descent. Alternatively, the gift of healing was believed to have being conferred on the king at his coronation when he was consecrated with Holy Oil. Medieval English kings were thought to possess the 'Royal Touch' and were able to cure certain diseases. Edward the Confessor, the last Saxon king, famously had the gift of healing and the tradition survived in England well into the seventeenth century with Charles II and James II still laying hands on those suffering from scrofula, a skin disease also known as 'King's Evil' because of the supposed ability of the monarch to cure it. The tradition finally ended with William III.

The precise details of how Aragorn performs his healing are unclear. To the leaves of athelas, Aragorn adds his own breath, and this is sufficient for him to counter the malign affects of the Black Breath in Éowyn and Merry. But Aragorn is required to give more of himself to save Faramir who is the closest to death. It is as if Aragorn must venture into some otherworld to retrieve him from that fate. To those standing beside him, observing, he appears to walk *in some dark vale, calling for one that was lost* and to take part in *some great struggle* [65]. His experience might be similar to the spirit journey experienced by shamen, healers who, by connecting with a spirit world, manage to restore the life balance within their patients. To do this, the shaman's own spirit leaves his body to engage in a dangerous battle with evil forces, one which potentially also places the healer at risk. That Aragorn emerges *grey with weariness* [66] would suggest that something of this nature occurred during his efforts to save Faramir.

Aragorn attends Éowyn next, but while he has the power to heal her body, he admits that some other healing must come for her injured spirit; his healing skills only extend as far as curing the physical needs of his patients. Merry is the least in danger of the three and appears to recover remarkably unscathed, his first concern being food! We do not actually witness Aragorn recalling Frodo and Sam after their rescue from Mount Doom, but we can assume that this task proved his greatest challenge of the Quest since Gandalf later tells the hobbits that Aragorn put forth *all his power, and sent you into the sweet forgetfulness of sleep* [67]. Tolkien himself explained Aragorn's healing skills as being *a blend of magic with pharmacy and "hypnotic' processes*

[68], the latter presumably being responsible for the hobbits prolonged rest.

After his strenuous efforts in the Houses of Healing, Aragorn could be forgiven for finding some hard-earned rest, but instead, Aragorn worked long into the night performing similar miracles for any who needed them. He did all this at the end of a long battle fighting hand-to-hand combat which, in turn, followed days of riding hard with very little sleep. He must have been near collapse when he finally sought his bed, but his willingness to unstintingly give of himself is a perennial feature of his heroism. And following Aragorn's feats in the Houses of Healing, word quickly spreads throughout the city that the king has returned and the prophecy that by the healing hands of the king shall the true king be known is proven to be true. In effect, any problems Aragorn might have anticipated over his claim to the throne are finally dispensed with once knowledge of his ability to heal becomes well known. The pertinent point, of course, is that athelas was not generally considered to be of any worth and so Aragorn's skill with it was revealed as exceptional. This ability of a king to elicit the healing power of a herb otherwise considered of no value echoes the skill possessed by Charlemagne who used sow thistle to cure those suffering from the Black Death.

~oo0oo~

Aragorn's heroism is consequently far broader than his military success. As he rides into battle at the head of a great army on the Pelennor fields, we witness a supremely heroic moment which marks Aragorn as great warrior, a suitable heir to the likes of Sigurd, Beowulf, Arthur and Charlemagne. His achievements are of such worth that songs were sung in Gondor and Arnor long after his death. But he is not only a hero because he is lethal with a sword in his hand, an orc could be credited as such. Instead, his valour in battle is amply counter balanced by his life-enhancing ability to save lives, and by the healing that he brings to all the peoples of Middle-earth.

Furthermore, Aragorn's lack of pursuit of personal honour reflects his adhering to a very different code from the warrior ethic of his medieval counterparts. Rather, it is what he seeks to achieve and the manner in which he achieves it that makes him heroic. Unlike some of his literary predecessors, Aragorn does not go to war in search of personal renown and the accomplishment of great deeds. Instead, he fights to protect his people and defeat an evil enemy. That he will simultaneously earn great rewards if he achieves this does not diminish his heroism because he is patently prepared to forgo his personal desires for the greater good. As Arthur Ashe is reputed to have once remarked; *'true heroism is remarkably sober, very undramatic. It is not the urge to surpass all others at whatever cost, but the urge to serve others at whatever cost'* [69]. We only have to recall Aragorn's humility and his voluntarily enduring years of thankless labour, performing countless, untold, but worthy, tasks, and sacrificing the years of his youth to do so to see that he fulfils this criterion. Aragorn's long years learning the ropes as he waits for his throne and for his princess, provide ample justification for the great rewards he eventually receives. Tolkien clearly valued this form of heroism as he considered his mother to be heroic for the hardships she endured as a result of her decision to raise her sons in the Catholic faith.

Tolkien famously commented that his story is about the ennoblement of the humble. He was referring, of course, to Frodo and Sam, yet, with his long journey from despised vagabond to the ruler of most of Middle-earth, Aragorn could also qualify to be included in such company. Although it was his destiny to be king, he nonetheless humbly placed himself as subordinate to Elrond and to Gandalf, acknowledging their greater wisdom. Also, his humility was blatantly genuine. When Frodo and Sam awoke in Cormallen, Sam could not guess the identity of their new king and, when Gandalf warned Pippin against speaking of Aragorn to Denethor, the hobbit failed to appreciate the implications. Aragorn's areté did not come between him and his friends.

However, Aragorn's personal qualities are still recognised by those around him and he is loved for them. As Michael J. Colvin notes, those who chose to follow Aragorn to the Black Gate did so because he has bent their hearts and not their wills. What is more, this loyalty he inspires proves no small factor in his success. His repeated protestations that he asks no one to go with him, not only free him of any charge of recklessness towards those for whom he is responsible, but also allows us to appreciate the extent that those who know him are prepared to jeopardise their own safety in support of him. Even the freed slaves manning the Dromonds worked tirelessly for him and their aid proved to be crucial. Aragorn's form of heroism, therefore, actually succeeds where that of so many of his predecessors ultimately failed.

Within the mythology, Aragorn's heroism is most comparable with that of Elendil, one of the greatest heroes from any of Tolkien's Ages. Aragorn may never be required to fight hand to hand with either a monster or a demon, but, like Elendil, he showed his heroism by resisting the teachings of Sauron, by being victorious in battle against an evil tyrant, by caring for his people and, if not by creating new realms, by peacefully rebuilding and restoring his ancestral ones. Like Elendil, Aragorn was superbly equipped to rise to the challenges that life threw at him because Tolkien gifted him with the best credentials possible to enable him to succeed. Túrin, even without the curse of Morgoth, could never achieve the heroic status of Aragorn; nor even could Beren or Tuor, both great heroes and exemplary characters though they are. Arguably, none of the heroes discussed here could be for the simple reason that, as noted earlier, Aragorn is not quite a pure Man. While Aragorn, like Elendil, undoubtedly has the outward appearance of a Man, concealed behind his travel-stained clothes is not just a returning king, but a Man who possesses a greater part of the Divine than any other Man alive in his time. Because of this albeit very small strand of his being which sets him apart, within Aragorn there consequently lay the potential to be the very 'best' Man of his time, a potential not available to anyone else. He has the capacity to become the wisest of kings, the best of healers, the most heroic of heroes as well as the most humble, the most self sacrificing and the most generous of Men.

Yet possession of this extraordinary ancestry does not undermine or diminish the scale of his achievement; far from it. That he actually achieves these considerable accolades is nonetheless quite remarkable. Tolkien compares the character development of men as like that of a seed which possesses *'innate vitality and heredity'* [70] and which will flourish according to the patterns hidden within it. But he acknowledges that this is too simple an explanation and suggests that man must also be 'gardener'. So, while Aragorn's maximum potential is predetermined by his genes, there is never any guarantee that he will fulfil that potential. Aragorn has the right to exercise his free will as much as anyone else in Middle-earth and, being human, he could so easily have made bad choices and failed. One only has to consider the story of *The Fall of Númenor* to remember just how far from grace those of Aragorn's bloodline were capable of falling. Although created as examples of the very best of men, most of them, as Faramir told Frodo, *'fell into evils and follies'* [71]. For all their enviable gifts, their 'superiority' was not guaranteed. This option to fail must inevitably also have been present within Aragorn himself, because, as noted earlier, Lúthien's bloodline did not confer any immunity against committing evil or willfully ignoring wisdom. Even without the temptations of the Ring, Aragorn might have fallen prey to any normal shortcoming, any baser instinct. That he does not is in itself the greatest measure of his heroism.

The danger for Aragorn is that his 'superiority' could set him apart, not only from his peers, but also from the reader. The lofty heights in which he comes to reside, his 'remoteness', especially when compared with the accessibility of the hobbits, is one of the reasons Aragorn's feats are not always as well regarded as they might be. As Verlyn Flieger reminds us, Tolkien's goal was *'realisation'* by which he means *'making real'* [72], and, to this end, she notes that Tolkien purposefully played down Aragorn's extraordinary characteristics so as not to alienate the reader. It is certainly true that Aragorn's capabilities and background are only gradually revealed to us, and, had we known all we do about him from the outset, he might not have earned our admiration or affection to the degree that he does.

Aragorn, however, balances his 'superior' qualities by being one of the most tolerant characters anywhere in the mythology. He treats the other races with equal courtesy, and the respect he has for all the peoples of Middle-earth is evident in every encounter. Even in death, he chooses to lie between Merry and Pippin rather than among the great kings from the past. And it must be remembered that even Aragorn cannot be entirely without flaws. His is a Man, after all! But even his apparent shortcomings can be interpreted favourably. He is impatient with the long-windedness of Ioreth and the Master of the Houses of Healing, yet, given the need for haste in saving lives, Aragorn is remarkably restrained, and it is left to Gandalf to express the exasperation he must surely feel at their verbosity. Similarly, his impatience with Butterbur, rather than expressing any real contempt for the inn keeper of whom he actually appears quite fond, reflects his being in a tight spot trying to win the confidence of the hobbits. His doubts and his apparent dithering might appear as weakness rather than the prudence of a man determined not to make a disastrous decision, while his haughtiness with Théoden's doorwarden demonstrates the great store he places upon his sword rather than any disrespect for his host.

Aragorn has been criticized as being too good to be true; a curious jibe in a story which features so much that is fantastical! William Ready is one early critic who is very dismissive. Suggesting he has some of the qualities of a noble horse, he rues Aragorn's lack of a dark side. *'Man needs more than a dash of pity to be his exciting self; a sharp taste for sin must be in him too, if he is to be wholly vital'* [73]. Although Aragorn's treatment of Gollum certainly indicates that he is a man quite capable of being brutal when need demands it, his goody goody reputation can still be a turn-off for those who prefer obviously flawed characters like Boromir, or those with less lofty pretensions like Faramir.Such reactions may be understandable, but this is to completely miss what Aragorn is about. The more we consider comparable characters, the more it becomes apparent that Tolkien intended Aragorn to represent near human perfection. His refining of Aragorn's speech, his provision of an elven bride, and the pains he took belatedly developing his back story, all point to the regard in which Tolkien himself came to view his own creation. Aragorn has none of the flaws of other kings-with-swords such as Beowulf, Sigurd or Arthur, and, while much of Tolkien's knowledge of history and literature found a way into his legendarium, some of it consciously and some of it unconsciously as it filtered through his imagination, he nonetheless made his characters very much his own. So, despite his skill in arms recalling other great warriors, and his achievements echoing those of other empire building kings who manage peace time just as effectively as they do their wars, it proves impossible to recall any other mortal hero who possesses all Aragorn's exemplary heroic qualities and his supremely virtuous personality. Aragorn is unique, without peer, and purposefully so, for he still has one final heroic act to perform.

Earlier, I mentioned Joseph Campbell and the stages of the hero's journey which he claims are universal.To discuss fully the remainder of Campbell's theory in relation to Aragorn would require a further chapter and would achieve little. Many of his stages are only tenuously applicable, although the last most definitely is not. According to Campbell, no hero should fear death, and *'reconciliation with the grave'* [74] is Campbell's last prerequisite for hero status. In this heroic requirement, Aragorn excels, and his death is of such importance to our understanding of the character that it is the subject of the final chapter.

Chapter 6: The Importance of Hope

When the infant Aragorn is brought to Rivendell on the slaying of his father, Elrond chooses to name his foster son, 'Estel', a pseudonym which proves particularly apt for the young Dúnadan. The very first of many aliases, it was not only a childhood nickname, but remained the form of address used by Arwen for her husband throughout their married life. Introduced very late in the composition of *The Lord of the Rings*, we only learn of this particular title in the *Appendices* where, being now fully aware of Aragorn's achievements, we are better able to appreciate the appropriateness of Elrond's choice. 'Estel' is defined in *Hiswelókë's Sindarin dictionary* as meaning *'hope, trust, a temper of mind, steady, fixed in purpose and difficult to dissuade and unlikely to fall into despair or abandon its purpose'*. Most of these characteristics are obviously very readily identifiable with Aragorn who, by demonstrating extraordinary steadfastness and strength of will under circumstances when despair would have claimed a lesser man, not only maintained 'hope' for himself throughout his hard and difficult life, but, by achieving his goals and becoming king, he also brought 'hope' to his people.

This was no small matter. In the late Third Age, the Dúnedain were a people teetering on the brink of extinction, all their former power and glory a mere distant memory. Had Sauron not been defeated, there is no doubt they would have been utterly crushed and subject to the most unspeakable retribution from the Dark Lord, who hated these remnants of Númenor with a malice equalled only by that directed at the remaining Elven communities. Gilraen's tragic despair at her last parting from her son before her death, so hauntingly expressed in the linnod, *'I gave Hope to the Dúnedain, I have kept no hope for myself'* [1], must have been shared by many of her people who had seen husbands slain and sons lost during the Dúnedain's long war of attrition they seemed destined to eventually lose. Widowed young and old with worry for both her people and her son, any hope Gilraen possessed at the time Elrond chose 'Estel' as a name for her son had long since been lost during those intervening years.

'Hope', however, had a predetermined affiliation with Aragorn even before his birth. His grandmother, Ivorwen, supported the marriage of Aragorn's parents against the judgement of her husband, Dírhael, because she had foreseen that 'hope' may be born for their people through that union. Elrond, too, recognised Aragorn's potential and knew that he would play a vital role in determining the fate of the Dúnedain. As Elrond told his foster son on the eve of his leaving home, *'A great doom awaits you, either to rise above the height of all of your fathers since the days of Elendil, or to fall into darkness with all that is left of your kin'* [2]. So strong was Elrond's conviction of Aragorn's future role that he forbade him the distractions of marriage, not just to his daughter, but to any woman until he had fulfilled that prediction.

Furthermore, 'hope' and its inevitable counterpart, 'hopelessness', are undoubtedly major themes found throughout Tolkien's mythology. Predominantly introduced to us at times of great strife, the characters we meet generally have their backs to the wall fighting an overbearing enemy against whom they have little chance of success, so much so that hopelessness and despair would seem more the order of the day than hope. As the Noldor depart from Aman in an attempt to reclaim the Silmarils, their task is explicitly pronounced 'hopeless' by Mandos, a weighty proclamation made as it is by no less than one of the Valar. When Men appear on the scene, they are caught up in the same drama, although they have their own dark past from which they are fleeing. Relief, if only temporarily, is found in the help brought by Eärendil, himself a symbol of hope. But after Morgoth is banished at the end of the First Age, Sauron arises to continue his master's work, and his meddling in the affairs of the Númenóreans precipitates the calamity of the re-shaping of the world. Hope returns with the victory of the Last Alliance where Elves and Men unite once more and Sauron is exiled for a time. His Ring of power may be lost, but, as Frodo tells Boromir, there is no hope while the Ring still remains. Nonetheless, the Third Age ends in victory and in hope for the future, although the defeat of Sauron will not bring a lasting end of the troubles facing Men. Gandalf makes it clear to the captains at the Last Debate that Sauron is but one emissary. Other evils will arise even if never again in incarnate form. Hope, for the characters inhabiting Middle-earth, seems always likely to be thwarted.

Hope is nonetheless spoken of frequently throughout *The Lord of the Rings*, though it is immediately apparent that the probability of achieving any expressed hope, be it an expectation or a desire, is widely variable, ranging from the fairly likely to the seemingly impossible. At the Council of Elrond, Aragorn remarks that he 'hopes' never to look upon Gollum again, and this would seem anattainable aspiration given the great difficulty he had finding him, even though, as it turns out, Aragorn does in fact catch glimpses of Gollum later in the Quest. This is clearly colloquial, everyday usage, and when Merry suggests that the worthies of Bree will be discussing Frodo's antics in a hundred years time, they read nothing into Aragorn's apparently throw away reply of, *'I hope so'* [3].

On other occasions, expressions of hope are made when the desired outcome is more immediate. As the companions prepare to spend a potentially perilous night at Weathertop, Strider reassures Frodo by saying: *'There is still hope'* [4]. While undoubtedly in grave danger, they are not yet in the clutches of the Nazgûl, and Aragorn, who has past experience of the Ringwraiths, knows it is possible to escape an encounter and live to tell the tale. Later, at the Mitheithel Bridge, the finding of the Elven jewel *'brings hope'* [5] to him. The jewel is a clear indicator of an Elf having ridden that way, and the placing of such a gem might be a method of signalling utilised by the Rivendell scouts in the past. In such situations Aragorn's expression of hope is based on external evidence which indicates that there is a reasonable chance that the desired outcome or expectation is possible.

Such optimism is clearly compatible with the statement in *The Tale of Aragorn and Arwen* that hope dwelt ever in the depths of Aragorn's heart. But how can we reconcile this perennial possession of hope with his appearing to lose all hope when in more dire circumstances? After Gandalf's fall, he laments: *'What hope have we without you? ...We must do without hope?'* [6] Gandalf was not only the leader of the Quest, but had been Aragorn's mentor and guide for over sixty years. Few would argue that his loss is not potentially calamitous, or that Aragorn's apparent despair is unjustified. And yet Aragorn nonetheless continues to lead the Company forward in spite of this appearance of there being an absence of hope and minimal chance of success. By doing so, he shows a determination not to succumb to despair which has undoubtedly stood him in good stead throughout his adult life. Such resolve is again demonstrated at the breaking of the Fellowship. With the departure of Frodo and the death of Boromir, Aragorn experiences his greatest crisis of confidence throughout the entire Quest. Faced with a choice devoid of any evidence to indicate the likelihood of success on either course, he declares his intention to pursue the orcs, *'With hope or without hope we will follow the trail of our enemies'* [7]. His fortitude in the face of apparent hopelessness is rewarded by Gandalf's return, and he confirms quite how unexpected was this happy turn of events by remarking, *'Beyond all hope you return to us in our need!'* [8]

Furthermore, Aragorn not only reacts in a positive manner when his current situation takes a turn for the worst and appears devoid of all hope, he also embarks on missions fully aware that the probability of success is heavily stacked against him. When he declares his intention to seek out the Paths of the Dead, the Rohirrim, to a man, are aghast at his decision and do their best to dissuade him, convinced that only certain death will await him. Yet he will not be deterred, and again his conviction that this is the right course of action is rewarded for he does not find death but instead succeeds in arriving at Minas Tirith in time to save the day and greatly enhances his own ambitions in the process. His courage and determination in undertaking such a seemingly futile task is in stark contrast to his mother's tragic despair, yet in the absence of any evidence to support the hoped for outcome despair would appear the pragmatic reaction. But it is not one adopted by Aragorn.

While 'hope' is, therefore, often expressed when there is an evident reason to possess it, when this evidence is lacking, an expression of 'hope' hints at a deeper and more profound concept, that of 'trust'. To possess 'trust', 'hope' becomes more than just an emotional response to a set of circumstances where the prospects of successfully fulfilling a particular desire or outcome can be judged by weighing the known facts. Hope is rather a state of mind, and to possess it, one must remain open to the possibility that there are unseen forces or events operating about which nothing is known, forces which are outside the apparent equation being juggled. Those who possess hope must, therefore, be willing to accept that they do not know everything. This requires a certain degree of humility and a belief that others will play their part, and, in particular, that there are larger, unseen, hands at work whose designs march to their own agenda. In this way, 'hope' cannot be completely crushed or defeated by negative experience, and this is how hope can still dwell in the depths of Aragorn's heart even when the means of achieving his desired outcome appears dismayingly absent. This, in part, is the 'trust' element in the definition of 'Estel' given above, and is one demonstrated by Aragorn throughout the Quest. From that first encounter in the inn, he trusted the judgement of Gandalf that Frodo was the right keeper of the Ring, in spite of indicators to the contrary, and, later, he trusted that Frodo would find his way to Mount Doom, and that the Ring would be destroyed when he got there. This trust might have proved vain, but Aragorn could not have known of the role played by Gollum since even the foresight of the powerful proved inadequate in those dark times.

To modern minds, Aragorn can appear quite a superstitious character. He makes strange chants over enemy weapons and interprets findings such as the timber set ready for a fire at Weathertop as a sign that he should stay put. He also believed in pre-ordained destinies, and he willingly paid heed to any lore that would potentially guide his choices. He listened to the words of Malbeth the Seer, believing that they pointed to the Paths of the Dead being the correct course for him to take, and this lore became a major factor in his decision-making. Such convictions are understandable given that he himself possessed the ability of his race to discern, if only to a limited degree, the nature of future events. Also his elvish education would inevitably have touched upon the *Ainulindalë,* and he would have known of the ultimate source of this foresight - the showing of the vision of Arda to the Valar by Ilúvatar before it became substance.

However, Aragorn would also know that this vision was incomplete, and that the freewill of Elves and Men could introduce unpredictability into the designs of Ilúvatar, leaving him with no sureties that any chosen path would prove the right one. Failure was always a possibility. Had he met death on the Paths of the Dead, his decision to take that route would have aided no one, and if riding to the Black Gate had proved futile, there was no plan B. As a result, Aragorn did not slavishly adhere to premonitions and lore. Although he firmly believed that Boromir's dream was a summons for him to come to Minas Tirith, he was prepared to abandon this course in the end, even though his desire to fulfil the summons contributed to his indecision at that time. But Aragorn did trust that if he played his part, both by his own actions and by allowing others to fulfil their own roles, events would conspire to bring about the desired result, even if by unlooked for means. Such choices obviously had cumulative effects, such as the sparing of Gollum in the past by Bilbo had a decisive effect on the choices made by Frodo later.

Trust, therefore, was a key element in the eventual victory, but becoming so weighed with care that this trust is lost is precisely what happened to Gilraen and to Denethor. Gilraen laboured under a weight of mounting despair that must have been shared by every mother of a son with a great destiny, and she felt the same sword piecing her heart that Simeon warned Mary against when he blessed her infant son [9]. Denethor's despair was, instead, confounded by his pride and his belief that only events shaped by his own hand could prove successful. Aragorn never suffered a similar loss of hope, not even at the Black Gate when Frodo's possessions were shown to the captains of the West and their 'last hope died'. Aragorn, as he stood beneath his banner on the slag heap, was resolute in the face of seemingly inescapable death, *'his eyes gleamed like stars that shine the brighter as the night deepens'* [10]. There is defiance in his stance which only increased as the predicament in which he found himself deteriorated further. Even seemingly facing the end of all his hopes, this is not a description of a man in despair. Nor is it resignation or acceptance either. Aragorn must, therefore, still possess hope.

Yet to what hope is Aragorn aspiring; how can hope still be dwelling in his heart at such a juncture when we have been told that all hope has died? In part, even in the face of the apparently overwhelming evidence that defeat is imminently inevitable and that Frodo's mission has failed, Aragorn still trusts that there can still be some other outcome, as indeed there is. And this is not vain wishful thinking either, since Sauron, for all the boasting of his lieutenant, does not appear to have the Ring. A further explanation is found in the *Appendices* when Aragorn does finally die, although a full appreciation only became possible post-*The Lord of the Rings* when Tolkien clarified the precise meaning of 'Estel'. We then discover a deeper interpretation of hope, one which has a special significance applicable to Aragorn, and particularly to the manner of his death. As Aragorn stands beneath his banner at the Black Gate, hope may be dwindling for this life, but not for the next.

~oo0oo~

On first reading, Aragorn's extraordinary and sometimes misunderstood passing can be difficult to understand. That he willingly lies down among the tombs of Rath Dínen and appears to simply lose the will to live may seem an ignoble death for such a great hero. It is as if he simply gives up; commits suicide, even. This is no traditional warrior's death after the fashion of those of Beowulf or Arthur. Nor was it Aragorn's fate to fall gloriously in battle like Théoden, or even in atonement like Boromir. Yet, as noted previously, by dying in the manner he does, Aragorn exhibits one of Joseph Campbell's prerequisites of any mortal hero, that of reconciliation with the grave. For a man about to attempt to die by his own will, Aragorn is remarkably calm, at peace with himself and accepting of his fate. He hands his crown to his son and tries to comfort his wife who clearly shares none of his conviction. No sooner has he said his farewells to his family than he passes in great peace, as if he has but fallen asleep.

Importantly, Aragorn's action is no sudden impulse, but long planned on his part. Even his choice of date, his birthday, must be considered significant since Aragorn is one of the few characters to be given a precise date for his birth and for his death. Not only is the consciousness of his decision emphasised by his electing to die on his birthday, the date of March 1st was probably chosen as it is well known as the date of both the birth and death of Saint David, the patron saint of Wales. David was a gentle and devout man who spent most of his life in his monastery. A bit of a puritan, he worked his monks hard and allowed them nothing to drink but water; no Barliman's brew here! David was, however, descended from kings on both sides of his family, his mother possibly even being a niece of King Arthur. As a child, she took him to live with the monks who taught him much and, when he was older, he travelled far and wide, teaching and preaching about Christ. A renowned healer, he was well loved since he performed many miracles, including restoring the sight to the blind. David was a great age when he died, over one hundred, and was keen to depart this life to dwell at peace in the presence of God. When, therefore, an angel visited him and told him he would die in one week's time, he was glad.

Symmetry in dates did appeal to Tolkien, and it may be worth noting that the date of the conception of Christ, March 25th, was also the date of Christ's Crucifixion. And it probably *is* significant that on that particular birthday, Aragorn was precisely two hundred and ten years old, exactly the three fold span of years Tolkien allotted to the Númenóreans which, in turn, is three times the Biblical span of three score years and ten. It is as if Tolkien was determined to demonstrate that Aragorn was at pains not to exceed his due time on earth by even one day. However, this idea appears to have only occurred belatedly to Tolkien since he originally gave Aragorn's age as one hundred and ninety years in the first edition which was only changed to two hundred and ten in the second.

Still, it is no exaggeration to claim that the entire key to understanding the character of Aragorn lies in the manner of his death. Tolkien always maintained that death was the real theme of his work, and in a draft letter of 1956, he confirms the importance of Aragorn's passing.

'I am only concerned with Death as part of the nature, physical and spiritual, of Man, and with Hope without guarantees. That is why I regard the tale of Arwen and Aragorn as the most important in the Appendices; it is part of the essential story, and it is only placed so, because it could not be worked into the main narrative without destroying its structure.' [11]

Later that same year, he reiterated this point and further explained that Aragorn's story is only placed in an appendix because, *'I have told the whole tale more or less through 'hobbits"* [12]. Tolkien clearly felt it was important to include an idealised, perfect death in his masterpiece, and Aragorn, being a descendant of the Númenóreans whose history was moulded by their attitudes to death, became the prefect candidate for the role. Why he should want to include a death of this nature can partly be explained by his religious beliefs and partly by his personal experiences of one of the worst killing fields in history – the First World War. The losses in that war were on a scale difficult for us to comprehend today, yet, at the time, those losses were felt deeply in every community in the country, and Tolkien's story was typical. Robert Blackman records that 243 former schoolboys from Tolkien's direct peer group at King Edward's School and 141 former students of Exeter College were among those killed, while John Garth notes that junior officers like Tolkien were dying at a rate of one a minute. It is no wonder that Tolkien described his final parting from Edith before he left for war as being like a death. Tolkien himself served in the battle of the Somme and witnessed the unimaginable carnation inflicted upon an entire generation of youth. By the end of the war, all but one of Tolkien's closest friends was dead.

The horror that Tolkien witnessed would have stayed with him to the end of his days and yet, in contrast to the brutal and premature deaths suffered by so many of his friends, Tolkien ensured Aragorn's passing at the end of his long life was one of peace, and, importantly for the reconciliation of the tragedy of war with his religious beliefs, one of hope. In fact, Aragorn's possession of hope is the crucial factor in his death since Tolkien purposefully does not provide his Men with any sureties of what comes after their death. The absence of proof is quite evident in Aragorn's words to his wife as his death approaches: *'I speak no comfort to you, for there is no comfort for such pain within the circles of the world'* [13]. However, Aragorn undoubtedly believes that some sort of existence awaits him beyond the life that he has known, the Circles of the World as he named it, and by dying as he does, he reveals the strength of his hope - his trust - that he is not about to face an absolute end.

As Tolkien stated in an unpublished letter begun in 1963, *'although no one knew the purposes of the One in regard to Men beyond the end of the world, or beyond their death, Aragorn trusted that they were good, and that if he and Arwen bound themselves in obedience to that trust they would be reunited'* [14].

In effect, Tolkien uses Aragorn to set the standard. It is as if he is saying, if you have the Faith, the Trust and the Hope, this is how you do it. This is especially so when we remember that their lack of foreknowledge of their final fate places Tolkien's Men at a disadvantage in comparison with his Elves. For the Eldar, 'heaven', in the shape of Valinor and Tol Eressëa, is well defined, conspicuous and real even to the point where the boundary defining what precisely constitutes life can seem blurred in Tolkien's world. But these habitations are strictly for the Firstborn, mortals only being permitted to come there under rare and exceptional circumstances. There is nowhere comparable described for Men in *The Lord of the Rings*, and few details are given in *The Silmarillion*. In part, this lack of information is a result of the Elvish perspective of *The Silmarillion*, and the Eldar mostly remain aloof to the troubles of Men. In so far as they considered the fate of Men at all, the Elves believed that the spirits of Men would reside for a time in the Halls of Mandos. Indeed, it was to Mandos that Beren was said to have come at death before he departed from the world, but he came to a different part of those halls from where the spirits of the Eldar rested and of their fate afterwards only Ilúvatar and possibly Mandos and Manwë were believed to have any knowledge. Once again, Tolkien's wish to avoid bringing explicit Christian motifs such those found in the Arthurian legends into his created world, resulted in his purposefully not intruding too closely into the territory occupied by genuine religion. He therefore deliberately left his Elves and Men, and, inevitably his readers, largely ignorant of this aspect of his mythology. Aragorn was no exception.

Nonetheless, in spite of the conspicuous absence of overt religious practise in Middle-earth, Tolkien famously described *The Lord of the Rings* as a *'fundamentally religious and Catholic work; unconsciously so at first, but consciously in the revision'* with the religious content instead *'absorbed into the story'* [15]. One such revision was the very late inclusion of the name 'Estel', a replacement of the earlier 'Amin'. Nonetheless, many of Tolkien's races do have some sort of allegiance to higher beings. The Elves predominantly revere the Vala, Varda; the Dwarves esteem their maker, Aulë, while most Men are enslaved to Sauron. Notable exceptions are Hobbits and the Men of Bree who appear to be without any religious affiliations of any kind. Of other Men, the Rohirrim honour Bema, their name for Oromë, but the Dúnedain alone hold faith with Eru, even though at the end of the Third Age the sole expression of this appears to be the Standing Silence.

In this pre-Christian, largely pagan world, Aragorn would undoubtedly have been acutely aware of his Númenórean heritage and familiar with the traditions of that people. The ancestors of the Númenóreans, the Edain, were already spiritually superior clans even before they received instruction from Eonwë at the end of the First Age. They had repented of the sins committed by their kin and, consequently, they had largely escaped the influence of Morgoth, while their Númenóreans descendants would further benefit from their friendship with the Eldar. The Númenóreans were monotheists who believed in the true God and *'held worship of any other person an abomination'* [16]. Although they acknowledged the supreme lordship of Eru, even in the heyday of the Kings of Men religious practise was still limited to the king giving thanks at the summit of the Meneltarma on just a few occasions in the year. However, in keeping with their piety of thought, if not conspicuous culture, for two thousand years the aging Númenórean kings gave up their lives very much as Aragorn did. A Númenórean declined rapidly once old age was upon him, and, according to a note in *Unfinished Tales*, Aragorn would have passed from full vigour to decrepitude in a span of just ten years. When still hale and in full health, the king handed the sceptre to his sons, just as Aragorn handed his crown to Eldarion, before proceeding to die at will and without compulsion. Aragorn's death, while extraordinary in the early years of the Fourth Age, was, therefore, by no means unique.

However, it is important to note that Aragorn's willing departure was a concept which only arose with him. Although within the context of the mythology Aragorn follows in the footsteps of Bëor and the early Númenóreans by giving up his life willingly, prior to *The Lord of the Rings*, this feature of their deaths was entirely absent. Bëor is said to have merely died of old age, and this is consistent throughout all the early texts. Nor is there any mention of the Númenóreans dying in this manner in any of the accounts of either *The Fall of Númenor* or even the later *The Drowning of Andûnë*. Aragorn's death was, therefore, influential in shaping the resultant legend of Númenor. Conversely, the Númenórean belief that their ultimate fate after death lay *'not within the world'* [17] was in existence long before Aragorn spoke of the 'Circles of the World', although the nearest Tolkien came to describing the Númenórean perception of an afterlife is only found in *The Drowning of Andûnë*. In this Mannish perspective of the legend, the Númenóreans were said to believe in a land somewhere in the West, but not the True West, which was inhabited by wraiths. Here, the dead would come, *'bearing with them the shadows of their possessions'* [18].

With the influence of Morgoth never entirely mitigated, this piety could not continue and, in time, most Númenóreans became increasingly fearful of death. As the trust possessed by their forefathers began to waiver, they sought to prolong their existence, even sacrificing the lives of others in the belief that the remaining years of their victims would be transferred to their own spans. And with the loss of trust, so too was lost the ability to die at will. Generally, therefore, the Men in Tolkien's legendarium did not perceive their fate positively, and they faced death with the same fear and with the same reluctance to take that final step into the unknown darkness that has been the fate of Men since Adam first took the bite of the apple. As Tolkien said of Beowulf, *'He is a man, and that for him and for many is sufficient tragedy'* [19].

Presumably Aragorn's ancestors, being from among the Faithful who committed none of the atrocities of the King's Men, fared better in this regard and would have retained the ability to give up their lives for longer. But how many of Aragorn's line died with the same grace as he is unknown. Although nowhere stated, it was probably as a consequence of the breaking of the Ban to sail West, which Tolkien described as Man's second Fall, that dying by freewill ceased to be an option for all the Númenóreans, whether of the Faithful or not. Noticeably, Tolkien subsequently makes no mention of any of Aragorn's line, be they the kings of Arnor, Arthedain, or the Chieftains of the Dúnedain, dying in the manner of the early Númenóreans. Elendil and Isildur both fell in battle, as did Aragorn's immediate ancestors, Arathorn and Arador. Of those who died of old age, we know only that they mostly lived out their lives peacefully in Rivendell, but of their actual deaths, nothing is said. But in Aragorn, who was undoubtedly an exemplary and virtuous character, one in whom *'the dignity of the kings of old was renewed'* [20], the manner of his death was a manifestation of that virtue, and he is consequently permitted to die as his ancestors before him in more enlightened times. As he said himself, to him had been given the grace to go at will. Tolkien confirmed his correlation between virtue and acceptance of death in a draft letter to Rhona Beare where he explained that *'a 'good' Man would or should die voluntarily by surrender with trust before being compelled (as Aragorn did)'* [21].

With his unrivalled education at the hand of Elrond, Aragorn would not only have been familiar with all the Mannish lore relating to death, he would also have known that of the Elves. And the Elvish view of death in Men was very different from how it was generally perceived by Men themselves. The Eldar, in spite of their longevity, did not consider the mandatory, and therefore inevitable, deaths in Men to be something inferior to their immortality, but instead, viewed death as an essential and intrinsic part of Men's nature.

Escape of the Eldar, unlike for Men, was unavailable to them, even if slain, since they could still be 're-housed' in a new body. The Elves, therefore, rather than seeing death as a punishment, regarded it as a 'gift', and, with the endless wearing of time becoming an increasing burden to them, they came to regard this ability of Men to escape from the world with no small degree of envy, a conscious irony given the envy of the Númenóreans for the longevity of the Firstborn. Indeed, by creating two races with such vastly disparate longevities, Tolkien was able to explore how death would be viewed from the perspectives of these two peoples who, although seemingly very different, are both essentially aspects of humankind. Writing in 1956, Tolkien confirms: *'The real theme for me is about something much more permanent and difficult: Death and Immortality: the mystery of the love of the world in the hearts of a race 'doomed' to leave and seemingly to lose it; the anguish in the hearts of a race 'doomed' not to leave it'* [22].

Paradoxically, while Aragorn was able to adhere to this Elvish perception and die with the dignity of his ancient kin, it was the half-elven Arwen who reacted to his death in typical Mannish fashion with grief and despair. Indeed, nowhere are the different fates of Elves and Men brought into focus more acutely than in the few, but crucial, marriages between members of these two kindreds. Elves and Men are sufficiently similar to be able to enjoy a normal marital existence in life, but, with the fate of Men at death unknown, such relationships were never without sacrifice if both partners were to share the same ultimate fate after death and not be permanently sundered in different afterlives. One member must, therefore, abandon the fate into which they were born and adopt that of their chosen partner.

When Arwen accepted Aragorn's proposal of marriage, she was in the fortunate position of being able to exercise the prerogative of the half-elven and voluntarily embraced mortality as the only means by which she could share a life with the man she loved. Romantic love in Tolkien's world is invariably such an all-conquering force that the consequences of such choices are less intolerable than an eternity without the chosen partner. In making her choice, Arwen, as she herself foresaw, was following the example of her foremother, Lúthien. For Lúthien, the pain of separation from Beren at his death was so great she had no hesitation in abandoning her life to be reunited with him in death, and her grief was such that she was able to move even Mandos to pity. Eric Schweicher even goes so far as to suggest that Lúthien may have chosen mortality to experience the wonder of death, so positive was the Elvish view of Men's passing. And it does seem that it is the Elven partner who must relinquish immortality if they desire to remain with their mortal spouse since choosing immortality is never an option for Men. It is only through adopting this course that a Man and an Elf can hope to remain together after the end of the world, and escape from the bonds of time. Implicit within the choices, of course, is the trust that, by becoming mortal, they will still have an existence together after death.

In the case of Lúthien, the matter of the choices available to her and Beren at death underwent several changes before Tolkien settled upon his final option. Originally, in *The Tale of Tinúviel* where both characters are still Elves, neither has a choice in the matter and it is left to Mandos to pronounce their fates. In the *Quenta Silmarillion*, both Beren and Lúthien are given the choice of either dwelling in Valinor for a time or of returning to Middle-earth as mortals, from where they would eventually depart together to an unknown fate. However, dwelling in Valinor would only be a temporary arrangement since Beren, who is now a Man, must still depart from the Circles of the World at death which would mean ultimate separation from Lúthien. In the next draft, written immediately prior to *The Lord of the Rings*, the final text is reached and Beren no longer has the option of going with Lúthien to Valinor.

The exceptional fate of Tuor, who also wed with the Eldar, appears to fly in the face of everything that Tolkien later devised for his eschatology. By stating that Tuor's fate is sundered from other Men and that he joined with the Noldor, Tolkien suggests that Tuor must have remained within the Circles of the World, the only Man ever to do so. Certainly, there never appears to have been any suggestion of Idril abandoning her immortality as Lúthien and Arwen do. Rather Tuor's unique position seem to be a legacy from the early days of the legendarium when Tolkien had yet to firm up his ideas on the fates of those few characters whose marriages presented this unique difficulty. At first, Idril and Tuor were to be parted when the call of the sea drew Tuor so far from land that he disappeared completely, leaving her behind. While from the same period, there is a note suggesting that it is instead Idril's fate that is unknown while Tuor is in Valinor. Elsewhere, Tuor is said to be with Ulmo, and there is even a hint of Eärendil's future role in an alternative scenario where, sailing in Tuor's ship, 'Swanwing', Tuor and Idril *may be seen going swift down the wind at dawn and dusk'* [23]. By *The Quenta*, however, their fate was as it remained with Tuor and Idril sailing West together.

Being half-elven, Arwen did not need any special dispensation to determine her fate and she was able to make her own choice, but having chosen to die as Men, she became truly mortal, just as Lúthien did. However, although Arwen chose to share Lúthien's fate when she married Aragorn, she seemed ill prepared for the grief she found at their parting. Aragorn, for all that he is mortal, does not share the reservations of his wife as his death approaches. Instead, it is Arwen who is distressed and lacking any of the acceptance demonstrated by her husband. During her six score years dwelling among Men, she inevitably lost many mortal friends, such as Faramir and Elanor, and for a millennia she witnessed the Chieftains of the Dúnedain spend their declining years at Rivendell, and yet, Arwen failed to truly appreciate what death meant to Men until faced with losing her own beloved. Like Aragorn, she would have grown up aware of the Elvish traditions of death as being the natural and preordained fate of Men, a stance which no doubt coloured her assessment of the Númenóreans as 'wicked fools' for failing to accept their lot. By her own admission, she had never considered the inescapably stark fact that death means an end to life whether it is considered a gift or not. With no lore available to aid her understanding, she is quite naturally as distraught as any mortal of her time facing the imminent demise of a loved one. And following Aragorn's death, such was her grief and despair, she eventually returned to Lothlórien to die alone upon Cerin Amroth, the very site where she had long before renounced her immortality.

Yet the depth of Arwen's despair serves to underscore the contrasting strength of Aragorn's conviction. Although acknowledging his own uncertainty of what lies before him, Aragorn demonstrates, and in quite remarkable fashion, his unshakable faith in an existence beyond the circles of the world. Consequently, his death became the means by which Tolkien chose to introduce into *The Lord of the Rings* the fundamental religious concept of the supreme Hope of all, that of life after Death.

In Aragorn, therefore, Tolkien created a Man who had the faith and the trust to rise above the doubts and uncertainties of his kin, and instead to treat death according to the beliefs of both the Eldar and the more enlightened of his ancestors. While Aragorn would have been assured of the existence of the Blessed Realm – the first hand accounts of people such as Gandalf, Glorfindel and Galadriel alone would have been sufficient confirmation –his ignorance of the fate of Men was a necessary prerequisite if his faith, trust and hope were to be precisely that. This strength of faith which Tolkien gave to Aragorn represents the sharp focus of what Tolkien meant by hope, and it is only when facing death where there are no sureties of any kind that Aragorn is able to demonstrate his strongest and most potent hope of all, enabling Tolkien to draw together his two greatest themes of hope and death so that the latter becomes the means for the ultimate realisation of the former.

~oo0oo~

However, do we know if Aragorn's 'hope' was justified? What might have become of him on leaving the Circles of the World? With few clues to go upon from within Tolkien's mythology, parallels have to be sought from outside. Tolkien's own views on hope were inevitably shaped by his Catholic upbringing; 'Hope' is, after all, one of the three theological virtues, the other two being 'Faith' and 'Trust'. A particularly important influence was the legacy of Cardinal Newman who was closely associated with both Oxford and Birmingham, two cities where Tolkien also spent much of his life. In particular, the Oratory church in Edgebaston where Tolkien worshiped for seven years was built as a memorial for Newman who had established the Oratory school nearby. Newman regularly preached of hope, which he referred to as the patient, subdued tranquil, cheerful, thoughtful waiting for Christ. He himself has been described as a man of resilient hope, and his teachings and prayers would have featured prominently in the sermons Tolkien listened to in his youth. However, for those raised in the Catholic faith, 'hope' alone is not enough and the observance of the proper rituals of religion is crucial for aspirations in the afterlife. As Tom Shippey notes in *The Road to Middle-earth*, Aragorn's death scene is one *'strikingly devoid of the sacraments, of Extreme Unction, of the 'consolations of religion''* [24]. Most importantly, according to Catholic belief, Aragorn has not fulfilled any of the requirements of religion which would enable him to enter heaven. Yet, as Shippey adds, *'It is impossible to think of Aragorn as irretrievably damned for his ignorance of Christianity'*, and suggests that it was to Limbo that Aragorn's spirit most likely departed to await a time when he could be saved along with his baptised descendants.

The state of Limbo was still part of the official Catholic doctrine in Tolkien's day, and it was widely believed in the Middle Ages that it was here that the souls of the just awaited the coming of Christ. Most souls of the deceased were not considered sufficiently pure to enter Heaven at death, so they first underwent a period of purgatory where the soul was purified and a sinner could repent of his sins and receive forgiveness, which is particularly important if repentance has not occurred in life. The Halls of Mandos are Tolkien's equivalent of both Limbo and Purgatory, and there is one rather chilling description in the original *Music of the Ainur* of the halls that men come to at death to await judgement. Vast and empty with just one burning brazier before a black chair, they had dark pillars made of basalt and a roof formed of bats' wings. When their fate had been decided, some men remained there, some were banished and seized by Melkor, but the majority took the black ship, Mornië, from which they caught a glimpse of Valinor as they sailed to the twilight land of Arvalin, located between the Great Lands and Valinor. Here, they were to patiently await the Great End, the prophesised ending of the World. A few fortunate ones went in chariots or on horses to dwell with the Gods in Valinor where they enjoyed an existence of feasting in the Halls of Valmar. This conception of an afterlife appears to owe more to Norse mythology than to Catholic teaching; the plains of Arvalin being loosely comparable with Freya's field, and the feasting in Valinor reminiscent of Valhalla. Although this conception was later rejected, from this description it is clear that, in Tolkien's world, the fate of men at death was dependent upon past demeanour, and not all are condemned to purgatory.

If parallels are to be made to Catholic beliefs, Aragorn at his death, no matter how exemplary his life or how strong his hope, must still be considered to be in possession of Original Sin. When Adam ignored God's instruction not to eat the fruit of the Tree of Knowledge, the resultant loss of the holiness and grace of God remained in all the fallen descendants of Adam and Eve, of whom Aragorn must inevitably be one. Arguably, the only character in Middle-earth who could be considered to be without Original Sin would be Tom Bombadil who, unlike Elves and Men, was present before Melkor introduced discords into the Music of the Ainur. While Original Sin is believed to be remitted through baptism, in this pre-Christian age, baptism was obviously not an option for Aragorn. Furthermore, a core Catholic belief is that death in men was introduced by God as a punishment for Original Sin, and Tolkien himself referred to this belief in the draft letter to Rhona Beare mentioned earlier. Here he stated that *'death is not part of human nature, but a punishment for sin (rebellion), a result of the 'Fall''* [25].

This explanation of death remains a core subject of debate for theologians, yet Tolkien chose to explain death quite differently in his legendarium. Rather than being something unnatural and only introduced as a punishment, according to Tolkien's conception, death was instead part of the original design of Men, an indivisible aspect of their nature from their first being. It was, therefore, theoretically possible for a man to die and still be described as unfallen, an important distinction if Tolkien's statements concerning 'fallen' man are not to appear contradictory. The following passage, written after completion of *The Lord of the Rings* and describing the beneficial effects of passing 'oversea' for the healing of the few mortals permitted to go to Aman, is, therefore, particularly revealing.

'It was in any case a special grace. An opportunity for dying according to the original plan for the unfallen: they went to a state in which they could acquire greater knowledge and peace of mind, and being healed of all hurts both in mind and body, could at last surrender themselves: die of free will, and even of desire, in estel. A thing which Aragorn achieved without any such aid' [26]

From this passage it is apparent that Aragorn's willingness to die, and the very fact that he was able to achieve death as he did, is confirmation that, at the time of his death, Aragorn had, in life, succeeded in attaining a state of grace where the slate had effectively been wiped clean. Consequently, he was able to die according to how Tolkien envisaged unfallen Man doing so. Tolkien did believe in the sanctification of the pagan, and as Aragorn's death approaches, he cries 'Behold!' and one has to wonder what it is he has beheld! Even without having received any sacraments, the beauty and majesty in which Aragorn lies in death, reflecting the finer qualities he possessed in life, suggests that his trust and his hope were justified and that he has in fact beheld the Beatific vision of God. St Thomas Aquinas, who speculated upon the nature of the Beatific vision, also claimed that beauty is the outward expression of the harmony and the splendour caused by God, and that: *'All things are made, so that they in some way imitate the divine beauty'* [27]. Aragorn's beauty in death could, therefore, be a reflection of how Tolkien perceived God's Grace as it manifests itself at the time of his passing.

Furthermore, there is Biblical support for the idea that it is possible to be saved by one's own conscience even when not in possession of any formal religious doctrine or having received any sacraments. Take Romans 2:14-16, for instance, which states:

'For it is not by hearing the Law that people are put right with God, but by doing what the Law commands. The Gentiles do not have the Law; but whenever they do by instinct what the Law commands, they are their own Law even though they do not have the Law. Their conduct shows that what the Law commands is written in their hearts' [28].

Beliefs such as this provided Tolkien with a plausible means by which his characters can behave in a Christian manner in a pre-Christian age. Newman also distinguished between what he called 'revealed religion' and 'natural religion'; revealed religion being the Judeo-Christian tradition which acknowledges Jesus Christ, while natural religion is that acquired outside of this tradition, yet is still aided by Grace. Tolkien's bestowal of this Grace upon Aragorn was implemented to good effect, and permitted him to enter whatever kingdom of God Tolkien envisaged awaited him beyond the Circles of the World. And there lies the real distinction between Aragorn's death and that of other men of his era. Aragorn is essentially a man ahead of his time, one prematurely granted the salvation which will only come for the rest of mankind with the coming of Christ.

Aragorn does, however, appear to have taken a detour on his way to his final home. When Aragorn took Frodo's hand and left Cerin Amroth, Tolkien mysteriously wrote that he *'came there never again as living man'* [29], the implication, of course, being that he came there after he was dead. This is the very spot were Arwen died the year after Aragorn's death, and it would be wholly in keeping with the nature of the character for Aragorn to search for her spirit. Furthermore, there is a clue to this riddle which lends substance to the view that Aragorn's own spirit returned there before he departed from the Circles of the World. In Túrin's original tale, *Túrin and the Foalókë,* when Húrin, or Urin as he was then named, is released by Melkor, he did not meet Morwen again, nor did he cast himself into the sea. Instead, he returned to his homelands where he died, but after his death, his 'shade' sought her and they long haunted the woods where their children died.

~oo0oo~

The extraordinary manner of Aragorn's death has led to some suggestion that it might be taken as a symbolic reflection of the death of the Virgin Mary. Mary, like Aragorn, relinquished her life by apparently falling asleep, but, while Mary's body was assumed into Heaven, Aragorn's remained solidly earth-bound and subject to the decay of all mortals. Mary is believed by Catholics to be the only real person conceived without Original Sin, a view shared by Tolkien who, in the same letter to Rhona Beare mentioned earlier, describes Mary as the only 'unfallen' person in history. For all the possible symbolism, Tolkien never claims that Aragorn is unfallen, even though he does state that he dies in the manner of 'unfallen' man. In fact, Tolkien states unequivocally that all Men have fallen. Yet, for a concept as fundamental to any mythology as the Fall of Man, no mention is made of this in *The Lord of the Rings.* Even in *The Silmarillion*, it is deliberately something which is *'in the past and off stage'* [30] since Tolkien again wished to avoid any explicitly Christian inferences. Consequently, the fall occurred somewhere in the distant past of those of the Edain who came to Beleriand in the First Age. They had not escaped the fall, but they had repented, and, unlike the men who remained in the East, were not enslaved to Morgoth, their ability to die of their own freewill, just as Aragorn did, being evidence of this.

However, Tolkien maintained that *'all stories are ultimately about the fall'* [31]. This in itself is a revealing comment and is an indicator both of Tolkien's perception of Man's place in the world and of his own desire to explore this perception within his own work. And after completion of *The Lord of the Rings*, he elaborated upon the fall as an aspect of his legendarium in the *Athrabeth Finrod eh Andreth.* Written in 1958 and published in *Morgoth's Ring*, the *Athrabeth* is a revealing and insightful work. Here, Tolkien explored the relationship between the two themes, death and hope within the parameters he had set himself, in what Christopher Tolkien described as a prolonged interior debate. According to Christopher Tolkien, the *Athrabeth* might even have been intended as the final item in an appendix to *The Silmarillion.* In spite of there being contradictions with Tolkien's thoughts related elsewhere, the work is clearly an attempt to define the eschatology of the legendarium and, in particular, it provides us with a further understanding of the significance and aptness of the name 'Estel' for Aragorn. In fact, the earliest drafts of the *Athrabeth* are believed to have been written not long after the introduction of the name into *The Tale of Aragorn and Arwen.*

The *Athrabeth* is set in the year 409 of the First Age, and features a discussion between Finrod, the Elven king, and Andreth, a mortal woman of the House of Bëor. Boron, her lord, has recently died, and Finrod is a visitor at the home of Boron's kinsman, Belemir, where Andreth also dwells. The aunt of Barahir, she is an unwed woman of 48 years considered wise in the lore of the House of Bëor. From Belemir's wife, Adanel, the sister of Hador, she had also learned much lore of the Second House of the Edain. Her views could, therefore, be considered to be representative of those prevalent among the majority of the Edain at that time. Finrod, wise in the lore of his own people, and friend of the Edain, proves an excellent foil for her arguments.

Still grieved at the lost of Boron, inevitably Finrod and Andreth's thoughts turn to death. The ensuing conversation provides us with a summary of Tolkien's later views as perceived by his two principal races, Elves and Men, and explains how those beliefs coloured what hope they had for an existence beyond that experienced on earth. This conversation between a mortal and an immortal is particularly pertinent when we recall that it was Finrod's ring that Aragorn gave to Arwen on their engagement.

Originally given to Barahir for saving his life, Finrod's ring became a symbol of lasting friendship between the House of Finarfin and the House of Bëor, yet it took on a new meaning when Barahir's distant descendant gave that same ring to his elven bride. The ring itself had already appeared in the mythology prior to *The Lord of the Rings*, but, significantly, the detail of the two serpents, one upholding and one devouring a crown of flowers, was only added later. From the serpent of Norse legend that surrounds Midgard, to the warring dragons of Vortigen, the serpent is a potent symbol, variously representing both good and evil; life and death. Even Beowulf's slaying of the dragon has been taken as a symbolic, as well as a literal, encounter with death. That Aragorn chose to give his ring to Arwen at their engagement suggests the opposing serpents represent this age old conflict, and in particular, the difficulties faced by those belonging to the two different kindreds.Perhaps it was not the most romantic timing for this reminder, but it is one which perfectly illustrates Arwen's dilemma. Alternatively, if life is embodied in the precarious existence of the golden flower, the serpents are instead balancing these two inescapable aspects of our being in perfect harmony, itself a most appropriate symbol of Aragorn's hope and trust. This, albeit far distant, connection of Finrod to Aragorn makes him a fitting recipient of Andreth's thoughts.

Andreth is typical of her race in not holding with the view that death in Men is a gift and she is bitter that Elves and Men have such differing fates, although it soon becomes clear that a lack of understanding is a major part of her grief. Later it is revealed that much of Andreth's enmity stems from her having fallen in love with Finrod's brother, Aegnor, whom she believes has spurned her for not having the long life of the Eldar, the unique problems posed by inter-racial romances being one of the triggers for the discussion. Departing from Aragorn's view, Andreth describes death for Men as, *'an uttermost end, a loss irremediable'* [32]. She possesses none of Bëor's acceptance of death, and it is impossible to imagine her giving up her life voluntarily, suggesting that the trust demonstrated by Bëor may not have been universal among the Edain. And in a startling assertion, Andreth claims that Men were not originally doomed to die at all, a claim which potentially undermines Aragorn's achievement of dying as 'unfallen' man. According to the lore of her people, principally *The Tale of Adanel*, Andreth believes Men to have been made immortal, and, echoing the Catholic view, she claims that death is unnatural, only becoming a part of their being after their creation. Furthermore, she asserts that this immortality of Men, unlike that of the Elves, was genuinely unending and that in their true state, Men were *'born to life everlasting, without any shadow of any end'* [33].The loss of their immortality was a consequence of their fall, which she blames on Melkor, who, Andreth claims, 'imposed' death upon Men in his desire to despoil and control them. The shortening of Men's lives, however, was the result of an ensuing punishment by Eru for having listened to Melkor.

Finrod is understandably shocked by this revelation. He had never considered that the power of Melkor was such that it could actually change the nature of one of Eru's Children so significantly. He says: *'if this can be believed, then mighty indeed under Eru were Men made in their beginning; and dreadful beyond all other calamities was the change in their state'* [34]. Finrod, however, remains unconvinced, and believes that this tradition has arisen among Men, partly out of envy of the longevity of Elves, and partly from a fear of death which he sees as another manifestation of Melkor's influence.

By introducing this alternative explanation of death as not being the original fate of Men, Tolkien appears to be questioning the long established view within his legendarium. From the very earliest *Ainulindalë*, death has consistently been the fate of Men. It is said to be a direct consequence of the granting of another gift from Ilúvatar - the power of Men to shape their own lives beyond the designs of the Music of the Ainur, this greater freewill of Men, of necessity, being curtailed by a shorter lifespan. Death was definitely not intended as a punishment, yet, even if this were the case, in the same draft letter to Rhona Beare, Tolkien maintains that, if divine in nature, a punishment and a gift are comparable since the intention is *'ultimate blessing'* even if the means of attaining this is not immediately apparent. In an earlier letter to Father Robert Murray, Tolkien confirms that death *'is not a punishment for the Fall, but a biologically [...] inherent part of Man's nature'* [35] and in that same letter Tolkien makes it quite clear that mortality could not be altered by anyone, not even the One unless *'by one of those strange exceptions to all rules'*. Those 'strange exceptions', would seem to be more applicable to, say, the situation with Tuor who was uniquely allowed to dwell with the Eldar rather than to the whole of mankind.

Moreover, the danger of Men attempting to tinker with their own mortality is in evidence from the earliest stories. Eriol is warned about over-stepping the bounds set by Ilúvatar when he decides to drink limpé, which he hopes will give him the immortality of the Elves. Furthermore, the bedrock of the Númenórean legend from its first conception was that mortality is the natural and unalterable state of Men. Indeed, in *Myths Transformed*, Tolkien elaborated upon what would have become of Men had they ventured to the Blessed Realm. With their mortal spirits trapped within bodies now enhanced and long enduring in the health of Aman, Men would suffer an even greater dread of dying and a more terrible, but still inevitable, death. Even so, while the faithful Númenóreans accepted this belief, those who dissented evidently believed death was the result of Eru punishing them for the rebellion of Men and that everlasting life was theirs for the taking if they were just permitted to come to Aman.

According to these differing traditions, the imposition of death upon Men is evidently believed to have been variously attributed to both Morgoth and Eru. This inconsistency can be taken as a further incidence of Tolkien attempting to introduce the sort of misunderstanding and distortion that would be reflected in our own myths and legends. Both the *Athrabeth*, of which there are said to be a number of versions, and the *Tale of Adanel* are explained as being Númenórean in origin, but there is apparently no definitive version. Discrepancies would be inevitable, although the taking of Melkor as king is consistently cited as the cause of Men's undoing. One has to wonder how much Tolkien's loss of confidence in his own mythology and his invented eschatology was coming to bear here. Certainly, avoiding committing himself on this particular aspect enabled him to reconcile the beliefs of his Men with that held by the Catholic Church that death was imposed on Men by God as a result of the Fall of Adam and Eve. If, however, death became anything other than part of Eru's original design and intent for the second of His Children, the manner of Aragorn's death would completely lose all its significance.

This does not remotely seem to have been Tolkien's intention. Death as the natural fate of Men is consistent with the later view that persisted into *The Silmarilion* that the 'Doom' of Men was at first the Gift of Ilúvatar, but that the fear of death arose from the negative influence of Melkor who had *'cast his shadow upon it [death], and confounded it with darkness and brought forth evil out of good, and fear out of hope'* [36]. Melkor's power was, after all, immense, and great enough to affect the whole of Arda at its marring. Furthermore, Tolkien was at pains to point out that the etiolated existences of mortals whose lives were artificially extended by Rings of Power were entirely unnatural, an existence summed up by Bilbo as being like butter spread too thinly. Writing in 1958, Tolkien warns that we should not confuse serial longevity with true immortality or cling to life unnaturally since, he claims. *'Death is not an Enemy'*, and he cites failure to accept death as *'one of the chief causes of human disaster'* [37]. To illustrate his point, Tolkien suggested comparing the hideous and tortured death of a Ringwraith, an extreme example of a being enduring a serial existence, with that of Aragorn. In Tolkien's mythology, as in life, eternal living could only be achieved for Men through death.

The Athrabeth does, however, provide an insight into the physiology behind how Aragorn was physically able to die of freewill merely by lying down and deciding to do so. The crucial distinction which really defined the biological difference between Elves and Men was the degree of control that their 'fëar', or spirits, could exercise over their 'hröar' or bodies. The spirits of the Elves had far more power in this regard than Men, and it was this power which imbued their bodies with the strength to resist disease, to heal quickly from injury, and ultimately to endure for such a long time on Arda. According to Tolkien, Men had less control over their bodies than Elves, but what control they did have had been greater before their Fall. Finrod guesses that an effect of the Fall upon Men was to reduce this degree of control so that Men could no longer die at will. Elves could, therefore, still choose whether to heed the call summoning their fëar to Mandos at death, while Men, on the other hand, had had that freewill over death taken away. How, precisely, this came about is left uncertain, partly because, once again, Tolkien was aware of the pitfalls of his story becoming too like a parody of Christianity. On the one hand, he suggests that the fëar of Men might have been weakened by their turning to Melkor whose power is wielded through the substance of matter, and so he was able to physically weaken the bodies of Men. Alternatively, Eru, in his wrath at their rebellion, may have changed the nature of Men so that the span of their years was reduced, hence forcing Men to return to him the sooner, that is, to die younger, so that they might more swiftly discover the error of their ways.

Knowing all this makes Aragorn's achievement in giving up his life willingly at a time of his choosing all the more extraordinary. Biologically, Aragorn would have been little different from any of his ancestors, and, yet his ability to relinquish his spirit's hold on his body must have transcended any physical limitations. In part, Aragorn's ability to achieve this was a result of the special grace granted to him which enabled him to not only give up his life, but also restored to him the full Númenórean span of his ancestors. For this to occur, his spirit needed to be enhanced with the necessary strength to maintain his body for a full two hundred and ten years, and then to release it to death at his command. This enhancement was probably achieved by intervention similar to that attributed to Eonwë in *The Silmarillion* or to the Valar in *The Drowning of Andûnë* where the life spans of the early Númenoreans were extended beyond those of other men.

Even so, regardless of being gifted with any special grace, Aragorn still had to possess the trust, the estel, to actually do it, to let go of life and to willingly die. The scale of this achievement is all the more remarkable when we find that even the Valar were not immune to doubt. Included among his notes written at around the same time as the *Athrabeth*, Tolkien states that in summoning the Eldar to Aman, the Valar had 'lacked estel' and should have trusted that Eru would not allow Melkor to damage Arda so badly that it would be uninhabitable for his Children. Aragorn, however, demonstrates no such doubt and appears certain, confident even, both of his fate and of his ability to bring about his own death. Quite how he was aware that this grace had been granted to him is never stated, and his foreknowledge can be taken as another manifestation of the measure of his trust.

In fact, possession of estel in Men was said to be rare; Aragorn's death was, after all, unique in his time, and Andreth is certainly dubious. In reply to Finrod's question of whether she has any hope, Andreth asks: *'What is hope? An expectation of good, which though uncertan, has some foundation in what is known?'* [38] It is at this point that Finrod explains the difference between the two kinds of 'hope' hinted at earlier in this chapter. The hope that Andreth refers to, which is a hope based on reason and experience, the Elves call 'amdir' which means 'looking up'. Amdir is, then, the more prosaic kind of hope, one more easily achieved. If one is hoping for a dry day and the sun is shining in a cloudless sky in the morning, it is reasonable to hope that the afternoon will also be free of rain. 'Estel', however, is a far deeper hope based on trust which, unlike 'amdir', does not come from experience, nor is it undermined by experience.

This distinction can also be found in the theological conception of 'Hope'. Such a hope should not be confused with superficial optimism or 'looking on the bright side'. Rather, theological Hope is seen as a gift from God and is even more important than 'Faith' which is a belief in God and obedience in Him. This is not the same as 'Hope' and 'Trust', although all three are so interrelated it is almost impossible to talk of them separately. Morgoth, for instance, would believe in Eru, but he would find no Hope there. Aragorn may have Faith in the existence of the Blessed Realm and the truth of the *Ainulindalë*, but this would not necessarily instil Hope in his heart. While Faith is the will to continue to believe, Hope is the Trust that having Faith matters. It becomes a surety for those with Faith, and, in this regard, it is very similar to Tolkien's 'Estel'.

Aragorn clearly possessed this trust, this 'estel', and, from the little that we can deduce from both the body of the text of *The Lord of the Rings* and from the *Appendices*, it not only manifested itself at his death, but guided him throughout his life, never deserting him even in his bleakest moments. For it is precisely when 'amdir' is lost that 'estel' kept him from despair. When Gandalf falls in Moria, Aragorn says: *'We must do without hope'* [39], what he actually means is they must do without 'amdir' as their situation now appears to be hopeless, but had Aragorn lacked 'estel', he would never have pressed the Company to continue as he did. Before setting out to the Black Gate, Aragorn remarks that *'hope and despair are akin'* [40], the hope he refers to here is 'amdir' since 'estel' will always triumph over despair. On the ride to the Black Gate, possessing 'amdir' might lack all reason, but Aragorn's greatest courage is that shown in the face of hopelessness when that hopelessness is defined as an absence of 'amdir' but not of 'estel'. In fact, much of Aragorn's life was spent without 'amdir', but his betrothal to Arwen gave his 'estel' a boost as he now had her own 'estel' supporting his - *'with your hope I will hope'* [41]. And in her message brought by Halbarad, Arwen says *'Either our hope cometh, or all hopes end,'* [42], the former being 'estel', the latter, 'amdir'.

Although Finrod attributes a lack of estel in Men to Morgoth's influence, he also maintains that possession of estel is something inherent; an intrinsic aspect of a person's being which explains why it cannot be completely defeated even by adverse experience. If Finrod is right in this belief, then even Aragorn's upbringing at the wise hand of Elrond could not have set estel in his heart had it not been present already. Finrod's claim must also imply that the loss of hope in those like Gilraen and Arwen was another manifestation of Morgoth's evil.Even in Elves, where estel is generally stronger, the strength of their estel was most tested by the uncertainty surrounding their ultimate fate. Although, to all appearances, the fates of Elves and Men are very different, both in fact share the same concern over their final destinies.

Again, this matter is discussed in the *Athrabeth*. Andreth, like most of her race, believes that death for the Eldar has not the same finality it does for Men. Finrod, however, explains that Andreth is mistaken in her belief that only Men fear their ending since the Eldar, for all their apparent immortality, only endure for as long as the world endures. Finrod, like all of his kin, is completely ignorant of their fate beyond this, with many believing they face an absolute and final end at the ending of Arda.

In spite of this alarming prospect, albeit very far distant, many Elves do possess what Finrod terms 'naked estel' which is a trust that their end will not be an absolute end even if it is commensurate with what they believe will eventually be a catastrophic destruction of the world. In effect, this 'naked estel' of Elves equates with the 'estel' demonstrated by Aragorn. Finrod, even though his race has suffered greatly in Middle-earth, justifies his trust because he still believes that all the designs of Eru are ultimately for the joy of His Children. The basis for Finrod's estel is a fundamental belief that Eru will not suffer being deprived of those Children, a faith he describes as the last foundation of estel. In this, Finrod is adhering to an Elvish tradition where Eru demands that all His Children should both believe and trust in him. If Aragorn had been raised acknowledging such beliefs, then his own estel could only have been enhanced and strengthened by such lore.

For the race of Men, however, whose dominion begins with Aragorn on the throne, their 'real world' hope in the shape of the coming of Christ is still far in the future and largely unknown in the world of Middle-earth. In spite of his wish to avoid explicit religion, Tolkien does not completely ignore the beliefs of the primary world and he touches upon this in the *Athrabeth* when Andreth tells Finrod that there are those among her people who believe in the 'Old Hope' that Eru Himself will one day enter into the world and heal Men and all of Arda.

Tolkien also introduced this belief into his reworked Númenórean tale, *The Drowning of Andûnë* where some future redemption for men is predicted: *'we say to you that that trust, if you give it, will not be despised; and though it take many ages of Men...Ilúvatar the Father will not let those perish for ever who love him and who love the world that He has made'* [43].

This view is also alluded to in *The Silmarillion* by the messengers of Manwë: *'The love of Arda was set in your hearts by Ilúvatar, and he does not plant to no purpose. Nonetheless, many ages of Men unborn may pass ere that purpose is made known; and to you it will be revealed and not to the Valar'* [44].

Naturally, this belief in the coming of Eru is another surprise for Finrod as it is not found among the Eldar, but he considers that if any would be capable of thwarting Melkor, then it would only be Eru himself. Tolkien, unsurprisingly, only hints at the coming of Christ; not only is this stance consistent with the 'historical' era in which he is writing, but he once claimed that *'the Incarnation of God is an infinitely greater thing than anything I would dare to write'* [45].

However, this has not prevented there being much debate on which, if any, of the supremely 'good' characters: Gandalf, Frodo, and Aragorn, are Christ-like figures. Each of the three embody in some way one of the qualities of Christ; Frodo his suffering, Gandalf his sacrifice, while Aragorn, as the returning king, might be considered the embodiment of the Risen Christ or Christ Triumphant. He is undeniably the supreme example of his race, not only a great warrior, a king and a healer, but also a priest. He was responsible for the spiritual welfare of his people. Having been raised by Elrond, Aragorn was one of those *'under special Elvish influence'* [46], and consequently more than adequately equipped to restore the worship of God to his people. As priest, his hope and faith should be strongest of any in his realm. But is he a representation of Christ?

Aragorn is without doubt a supremely virtuous character and his story has many parallels with that of Christ. He has endured long years in exile and has suffered in the wilderness. He defeats evil and restores faith in God to his kingdoms. His journey to become the returning king takes him through the Paths of the Dead which is an aspect of his story reminiscent of Christ's Harrowing of Hell. At his death, Christ is believed to have descended into Limbo, where the souls of those who had gone before him were trapped, and released them so that they too might come to heaven. Tolkien gave Aragorn a similar ability to release cursed souls, but, while Christ's descent saved only the just, the cursed saved by Aragorn had to prove themselves and be redeemed from past failings before their release. The arduous and terrifying journey into this otherworld is a crucial part in Aragorn's own transformation from ordinary man to saint-like king and can be seen as representing the symbolic death of the ranger who emerges reborn as the king. The unfurling of the banner at the Stone of Erech is another sign of this transformation which only occurred through the courage Aragorn demonstrated by daring this feared route.

Furthermore, while not the eucatastrophe provided by the destruction of the Ring, the coming of Aragorn as king is a major happy event within the story. The people of Gondor have little hope that their king will ever return, but Aragorn literally carries 'hope' in his hand as he arrives at the Pelennor. Andúril, the Flame of the West, is *like a new fire kindled* [47] and triumphantly heralds the return of the king. A flame brand is traditionally a symbol of hope, and notably the first name for Aragorn's sword was 'Branding'. Aragorn's transformation into king is complete at his coronation. Revealed now as none has seen him before, and with a light about him, it is almost as if a god has descended from another realm to walk among the people.

There are moments when we witness Aragorn behaving in a Christ-like manner. His healing is preeminent among them, and we do see a glimmer of the emerging priest as Aragorn attends to Boromir at his death. Ralph C. Wood, in particular, praises Tolkien's skill in avoiding overtly religious overtones in this scene and explains how Aragorn leads Boromir, who is described by Wood as the Judas of the story, through the stages of the sacrament of penance before he dies. But behaving in a Christ-like manner and being an actual representation of Christ are, of course, entirely different matters. I can express the distinction between the coming of Aragorn as king and the coming of Christ no more succinctly than Deborah C. Rogers does in *The Tolkien Compass*.

'Christ is the true good event. He came, an actual person, in time and space to repair for us ... the relationship between mankind and the extraterrestrial Creator. He does not repair the politics, economics, or ecology of planet Earth. As He plainly said, "My kingdom is not of this world".

But Aragorn's kingdom is of this world. He was born to reign in Middle-earth. Aragorn is parallel to Christ only in that each of them is the man of good events in his story, not in the kind of fortunate conclusion they bring.... Aragorn's good work, then, is that of the restoration of the king on earth. And this is a type, a figure, a symbol, of the happy turnabout of the restoration of man as a race' [48].

In other words, both perform similar roles within their respective stories but that is where the similarity ends. At its simplest level, it could be argued that all the Christ-like characters from *The Lord of the Rings* merely embody the finest characteristics that any good Christian would aspire to, namely: living bravely, doing the right thing even when far from pleasant, putting others first, having faith. Tolkien, being both a Christian and a Catholic, would surely have found the idea of portraying any of his characters as allegories of Christ unpalatable, possibly to the point of blasphemy. And even a mere hundred years after Aragorn's death, we are told a new shadow arises. The message, therefore, is simple. Even a monarch as possessed of grace as Aragorn is no substitute for a true messiah.

Yet one obvious and important symbol of hope in his legendarium which has biblical parallels is the early morning ascent into the sky of Aragorn's ancestor, Eärendil. The light of the Silmaril, named by the Elves, Gil-estel, the Star of Hope, and the only source now of the original hallowed light of the Two Trees, daily heralds the dawn and hints at the coming of Christ, the true light of the future. The name 'Eärendil' was derived from the Anglo-Saxon poem *Crist* which Tolkien first read as a young man. One line in particular had a remarkable impact upon him.

'Eala Earendel engla beorhtast / ofer middangeard monnum sended'
[Hail, Earendel, brightest of angels sent to men throughout Middle-earth].
[49]

Tolkien later wrote that he had *'felt a curious thrill… as if something had stirred in me, half wakened from sleep'* [50] and he subsequently adopted Eärendil as a pivotal figure who came to symbolise hope for both Elves and Men. There are clearly similarities with the morning star referred to in the Bible: *'I, Jesus, have sent my angel to announce these things to you in the churches. I am descended from the family of David, and am the bright morning Star'* [51]. The morning star has variously been interpreted as either the light heralding the coming of Christ, representing John the Baptist, or as Christ himself. The hope encompassed by the star, however, is best expressed by the eighth century scholar and monk, St Bede whose own words telling of this light were inscribed on his tomb in Durham Cathedral.

Christ is the morning star, who when the night,
Of this world is past brings to his saints
The promise of the light of life and opens everlasting day.

Tolkien maintained that Eärendil was specific to his legendarium and not symbolic of the coming of Christ, which he described as *'completely alien to my use'* [52]. However, Aragorn himself refers, if obliquely, to Eärendil during the battle of Helm's Deep when he says to Gamling, *'dawn is ever the hope of men'* [53]. Although Gamling is doubtful, Aragorn is not discouraged and adds, *'Nonetheless day will bring hope to me'*. He is, of course, talking of hope of victory in battle, but his words can be taken to conceal a deeper hope which is symbolically all the more profound spoken as they are in the dark of such a bitter night.

~oo0oo~

There is one final element of 'hope' to consider which is applicable to Aragorn, that of 'desire'. In the earlier quoted passage from *Morgoth's Ring*, Aragorn died, both 'in estel' and 'in desire', suggesting that he not only accepted death, he actively embraced it. Here, Aragorn once again bucks the trend of most mortal men. Rather than desiring death, Tolkien claims in his lecture *On Fairy-Stories* that the desire to escape *from* death is the oldest and the deepest of all desires. In *The Lord of the Rings*, this desire for escape is most apparent among the Elves who wish to leave Middle-earth and to return to their home beyond the Sea. A perpetual yearning in Galadriel, it was the same Sea-longing which afflicted Legolas after hearing the gulls at Pelargir. Although less in evidence, Tolkien also endowed his Men with a similar desire. Tuor and Eärendil were both possessed by it, as were Eriol and Ælfwine, and even Frodo felt this pull when he dreamt of a tall white tower which he suddenly desired to climb so as to see the Sea. Again in *On Fairy-Stories*, when Tolkien uses a metaphor to describe the treatment of *Beowulf* by the critics, it is noticeable that the one possible function he provides for the ignored and vandalized tower built from the stones of the former house was that from it one might see the Sea.

This desire was also apparent when Tolkien wrote of Ælfwine and his companions sailing to Tol Eressëa. As they approached that island, they were overwhelmed with *'unimagined longing'* and they wept for the *'memory of fair things long lost, and each for the thirst that is in every child of Men for the flawless loveliness they seek and do not find'* [54]. In *The Silmarillion* this longing is expressly attributed to Ilúvatar who ordained that Men should *'seek beyond the world and should find no rest therein'* [55]. Naming Men 'the Seekers' in recognition of this trait, it is most vividly evoked in an outline of *The Drowning of Andûnë*. As part of an alternative telling of Eärendil's story, Tolkien wrote of how Men were drawn westward by rumour of a beautiful land beyond the Sea where the Eldar lived.

'*At length Men reached the western shores of the Great Lands, and were halted on the shores of the Sea. The shock and awe and longing of that meeting has remained in their descendants ever since, and the Great Sea and the setting sun has been to them the most moving symbol of Death and of Hope for Escape.*' [56]

Furthermore, when writing to his son, Christopher in 1945, Tolkien articulated his belief that all mankind longs to return to some lost Eden and suffers from a sense of exile at its inevitable lack of attainability.

'*Genesis is separated by we do not know how many sad exiled generations from the Fall, but certainly there was an Eden on this very unhappy earth. We all long for it, and we are constantly glimpsing it: our whole nature at its best and least corrupted, its gentlest and most humane, is still soaked in the sense of 'exile'*' [57].

Tolkien evidently regarded this restlessness within the hearts of Men as an inherent aspect of Man's nature, and Finrod, who is once again Tolkien's instrument to voice his thoughts, picks up on this trait. Being the most intuitive and sympathetic of all the Eldar, Finrod observes that Men do not love the earth in the same way as Elves, for it seems to him that they '*look at no thing for itself...if they love it, it is only (so it seems) because it reminds them of some other dearer thing? Yet with what is this comparison? Where are those other things?*' [58] Answering his own question, Finrod believes this restlessness to be a consequence of Arda being only the temporary home of Men, a summation which not only reaffirms Aragorn's hope at his death, but also the view of the Valar in *The Silmarillion* that the true home of Men is not, '*anywhere within the Circles of the World*'[59]. But as Finrod continues to speculate, he wonders if, in fact, it is to Arda Complete, the prophesised repaired and healed world of the future to which Men unfavourably compare things as they find them in Arda now, marred as it is.

Tolkien wrote several prophecies concerning the healing and re-making of Arda. As with so many of his ideas, the concept has religious roots, and the last two chapters of *Revelations* refer to a vision of a new heaven and a new earth where God will dwell with men in the Holy City in the new earth. In Norse mythology, Odin would gather the slain to Valhalla where they would await the final, terrible battle of Ragnarök where the world would be destroyed by fire, but would rise again from the sea. Evil would be defeated and mankind saved. In Tolkien's mythology the premise has consistently been that out of the catastrophe of the ending of the world would come the eucatastrophe of the re-making of Arda, better than it was before, precisely because of the marring.From the earliest tales, it was prophesised that one day the Elves would march towards Valinorand, with the aid of Men, in particular Túrin, Melkor would be defeated in a great final battle, after which the Trees would be rekindled and their light would '*spread over all the world*' [60]. The healing of the world is also touched on in *The Lord of the Rings* when Tom Bombadil claims that '*gates stand forever shut, till the world is mended*' [61]. Similarly, in *The Hobbit*, Thorin at his death says that he goes to his fathers '*until the world is renewed*' [62] while the Men who alight from the black ship Mornië at Arvalen await the Great End. Aragorn certainly believed in the ending of the world and even chose to utter the words spoken by Elendil when he came to Middle-earth at his coronation: '*Out of the Great Sea to Middle-earth I am come. In this place I will abide, and my heirs, unto the ending of the world*' [63]. Elendil had, of course, already witnessed the destruction of the flat world.

The most comprehensive prophecy concerning the ending and remaking of the world is the Second Prophecy of Mandos, which appears at the very end of the *Quenta Silmarillion*, written immediately prior to work on *The Lord of the Rings*. This prophecy also predicts the Last Battle where Morgoth would come forth and be beaten by Túrin, and so all the wrongs against Men would be avenged. The earth would be broken and the lost Silmarils found, Eärendil would surrender his and all the dead Elves would arise, although here the fate of Men is said not to be known. Stated as being Númenórean in origin and certainly unknown to Andreth, the prophecy reappeared, with minor alterations, in the *Later Quenta Silmarillion* written after *The Lord of the Rings*, and, although omitted from the published *Silmarillion*, a hint of it remains in the prediction that a great Music shall be made '*by the choirs of the Ainur and the Children of Ilúvatar after the end of days*' [64]. This prediction is virtually unchanged from the very earliest version and is one which does suggests an important future role for both kindreds.

Finrod, too, concludes that Men will be Eru's primary instrument for the healing of Arda Marred, and that Arda '*will be destroyed by wicked Men (or the wickedness in Men); but healed through the goodness in Men*' [65]. The Elves role in this healing will be limited to restoring the love of the world to Men. According to the *Athrabeth*, however, Men were originally destined to be the sole agents for the healing of Arda, but, because of their fall, they cannot now fulfil this role without receiving healing themselves, which brings us back to Andreth's 'Old Hope' that Eru himself will one day come among Men and provide this healing. Aragorn's role as the healer-king of Middle-earth could be taken as a foreshadowing and a microcosm of the role of Men as a whole in the ultimate healing of the world.

According to Tolkien, it is our yearning for this unmarred world which is at the root of all desire. In his lecture *On Fairy-Stories*, Tolkien claims that this desire stems from a time commensurate with the fall when we were not separated from the rest of Creation. A yearning of this nature also chimes with the cause of the sea-longing of Elves and Men being the echo of the Music of the Ainur that can still be detected within water. Later Tolkien described 'desire' as an indication of our true, unmarred nature so that the experiencing of a *'stirring of joy'* [66] would be a sign of being on the right path to enlightenment. It is something of this nature which explains the *'lightening of the heart'* [67] experienced by those who inhale the unsullied fragrance of athelas, which, when administered by the hands of Lúthien's descendants, has a purifying role suggestive of incense.

Furthermore, in the *Later Quenta Silmarillion*, Tolkien suggests that the Unmarred Arda of Man's distant past can be discerned by those receptive to this echo, and that it is Man's yearning for this past that is the ground upon which Hope is built. In a debate between Manwë and his fellow Valar, Manwë refers to this as the *'Hope that sustaineth'* [68]. This Hope comes from both the ability to discern the Unmarred which can still be recognised within the present world of Arda Marred - Ælfwine's 'flawless loveliness' - and from a yearning for Arda Healed, the unmarred existence still to come. Could these glimpses of the Unmarred world have been the ultimate source of Hope that sustained Aragorn throughout his life? Most importantly, at Aragorn's death, when his estel needed to be at its strongest, could this be why he was able to die in such peace and with desire for what was yet to come? Aragorn does not seem excited or especially eager to depart this world, yet he is remarkably calm and accepting, easily resisting his wife's pleas to reconsider. One has to wonder to what extent he felt the pull of his true home and how strong was his desire to go there. He possessed the openness of heart and mind to be receptive to such mystical urgings, and he had the ability to tap into 'the other side' as shown by his recalling those with the Black Breath. His hope and his desire at that moment would certainly put a different interpretation on Galadriel's parting words to the king at Dol Baran: *'Elfstone, through darkness you have come to your hope, and have now all your desire'* [69].

~oo0oo~

Hope, then, for both Elves and Men is a fundamental concept that straddles Tolkien's entire mythology. Tolkien provides no certainties in his eschatology, yet he deftly manages to weld his 'pagan' story to religious doctrine without compromising either his Christian beliefs or the internal integrity of his own legendarium. Ultimately, for all the sadness which infuses the history of Middle-earth, the final message is always one of hope. Finrod, although heading for war and defeat, nonetheless says to Andreth at their parting, *'you are not for Arda. Whither you go may you find light. Await us there, my brother - and me'* [70], suggesting that this Elf at least possessed hope that Men and Elves would one day be reunited. Tolkien chose not to confirm this possibility, but such a hope might have lessened the grief of Melian at her parting from Lúthien, or of Elrond at his farewell to Arwen whose separation was said to *'endure beyond the ends of the world'* [71]. And had Arwen possessed the hope of her foremother, whose own story is one of hope of escape from the bondage of time, she, in turn, might have born the loss of her husband without her own terrible despair. Instead, it fell to Lúthien's more distant descendant to demonstrate the true importance of hope.

Through Aragorn, Tolkien was able to illustrate hope at its must profound, and, had *The Tale of Aragorn and Arwen* indeed formed the final part of *The Lord of the Rings*, as Christopher Tolkien suggests, Aragorn's gracious departure would have provided our abiding memory of the entire story. Aragorn's death affords an opportunity to touch upon a subject that has far wider implications than the demise of an aging king, no matter how esteemed. Tolkien always maintained that the purpose of his work was to entertain, but its deeper function of providing a lens through which we come to view our own world, our own faith and fates, is unmistakable. As Tolkien notes, if a fairy-story is to resonate with readers, it must reflect things that are important and relevant to their lives. It must contain a *'mode of reflecting 'truth', different from allegory'* [72]. Aragorn's role in fulfilling this criterion is, without doubt, the most important function of the character. What could be more relevant to the lives of each and every one of us than the manner of our passing, and the fulfilment of our hopes for an existence beyond death? As Tolkien said of the story of Christ, there is none that men would rather find is true. We would all aspire to share Aragorn's unflinching acceptance of our fate and be as blessed as this great warrior as he prepares to face the ultimate battle awaiting all of humankind. Aragorn's example as he conquers even death itself remains one of Tolkien's greatest gifts to us all.

Footnotes

Introduction

1. Tolkien, J.R.R.: *The Letters of J.R.R. Tolkien.*
   [HarperCollins*Publishers* 2006] no.199 p 258

Chapter One: The Riddle of Strider

1. Tolkien, J.R.R.: *The Fellowship of the Ring.*
   [Grafton, an imprint of HarperCollins*Publishers* 1991] p230
2. Ibid. p232
3. Ibid. p232
4. Ibid. p265
5. Ibid. p269
6. Ibid. p269
7. Ibid. p289
8. Ibid. p323
9. Ibid. p324
10. Ibid. p350
11. Ibid. p445
12. Ibid. p439
13. Tolkien, J.R.R.: *The Two Towers.*
    [Grafton, an imprint of HarperCollins*Publishers* 1991] p40
14. Tolkien, J.R.R.: *The Fellowship of the Ring.*
    [Grafton, an imprint of HarperCollins*Publishers* 1991] p457
15. Ibid. p487
16. Ibid. p488
17. Tolkien, J.R.R.: *The Two Towers.*
    [Grafton, an imprint of HarperCollins*Publishers* 1991] pp37-38
18. Ibid. p130
19. Ibid. p208
20. Tolkien, J.R.R.: *The Return of the King.*
    [Grafton, an imprint of HarperCollins*Publishers* 1991] p51
21. Ibid. p48
22. Ibid. p62
23. Ibid. p170

24. Ibid. p425
25. Tolkien, J.R.R.: *The Letters of J.R.R. Tolkien.*
    [HarperCollins*Publishers* 2006] no.181 p237

*Chapter Two: **Trotter***

1. Tolkien, J.R.R.: *The Letters of J.R.R. Tolkien.*
   [HarperCollins*Publishers* 2006] no.163 p216
2. Tolkien, J.R.R.: *The Peoples of Middle-earth.*
   [HarperCollins*Publishers* 2002] p5
3. Tolkien, J.R.R.: *The Return of the Shadow.*
   [HarperCollins*Publishers* 2002] p369
4. Ibid. p137
5. Ibid. pp137-138
6. Ibid. p153
7. Tolkien, J.R.R.: *The Letters of J.R.R. Tolkien.*
   [HarperCollins*Publishers* 2006] no.19 p26
8. Tolkien, J.R.R.: *The Return of the Shadow.*
   [HarperCollins*Publishers* 2002] p20
9. Ibid. p132
10. Tolkien, J.R.R.: *The Hobbit.* George Allen and Unwin [1975] p 52
11. Tolkien, J.R.R.: *The Return of the Shadow.*
    [HarperCollins*Publishers* 2002] p128
12. Ibid.
13. Ibid. p129
14. Ibid. p184
15. Ibid. p186
16. Ibid. p208
17. Tolkien, J.R.R.: *The Hobbit.*
    [George Allen and Unwin 1975] p16
18. Tolkien, J.R.R.: *The Return of the Shadow.*
    [HarperCollins*Publishers* 2002] p331
19. Ibid.
20. Ibid.
21. Ibid. p332
22. Ibid.
23. Ibid. p374
24. Ibid. p393
25. Ibid. p408

26. Ibid. p414
27. Tolkien, J.R.R.: *The Letters of J.R.R. Tolkien.* [HarperCollins*Publishers* 2006] no.347 p426
28. Tolkien, J.R.R.: *The Treason of Isengard.* [HarperCollins*Publishers* 2002] p8
29. Tolkien, J.R.R.: *The Return of the Shadow.* [HarperCollins*Publishers* 2002] p431
30. Ibid. p193
31. Tolkien, J.R.R.: *The Treason of Isengard.* [HarperCollins*Publishers* 2002] p50
32. Ibid. p51
33. Ibid. p120
34. Ibid.
35. Ibid. p121
36. Ibid. p148
37. Ibid. p221
38. Ibid. p227
39. Ibid. p246
40. Ibid. p258
41. Ibid. p.360
42. Tolkien, J.R.R.: *The Return of the Shadow.* [HarperCollins*Publishers* 2002] p215
43. Tolkien, J.R.R.: *The Treason of Isengard.* [HarperCollins*Publishers* 2002] p105
44. Ibid p278
45. Ibid p385
46. Ibid p396
47. Ibid p394
48 Tolkien, J.R.R.: *The Two Towers.* [Grafton, an imprint of HarperCollins*Publishers* 1991] p41
49. Tolkien, J.R.R.: *The Treason of Isengard.* [HarperCollins*Publishers* 2002] p445
50. Ibid. p447
51. Ibid. p448
52. Tolkien, J.R.R.: *The Letters of J.R.R. Tolkien.* [HarperCollins*Publishers* 2006] no.244 p323
53. Tolkien, J.R.R.: *The Treason of Isengard.* [HarperCollins*Publishers* 2002] p448
54. Tolkien, J.R.R.: *The War of the Ring.* [HarperCollins*Publishers* 2002] p20

55. Ibid. p73
56. Tolkien, J.R.R.: *The Letters of J.R.R. Tolkien.*
    [HarperCollins*Publishers* 2006] no.199 p258
57. Tolkien, J.R.R.: *The War of the Ring.*
    [HarperCollins*Publishers* 2002] p236
58. Ibid. p249
59. Ibid. p263
60. Ibid.
61. Ibid.
62 Ibid. p300
63. Tolkien, J.R.R.: *The Return of the King.*
    [George Allen and Unwin 1955] p53
64. Hammond Wayne G. and Scull, Christina: *The Lord of the Rings:*
    A Reader's Companion. [HarperCollins*Publishers* 2005] p529
65. Tolkien, J.R.R.: *The War of the Ring.*
    [HarperCollins*Publishers* 2002] p406
66. Tolkien, J.R.R.: *Sauron Defeated.*
    [HarperCollins*Publishers* 2002] p15
67. Ibid. p16
68. Tolkien, J.R.R.: *The War of the Ring.*
    [HarperCollins*Publishers* 2002] p412
69. Ibid. p425 note 34
70. Tolkien, J.R.R.: *The Lost Road.*
    [HarperCollins*Publishers* 2002] p319
71. Tolkien, J.R.R.: *The Fellowship of the Ring.*
    [Grafton, an imprint of HarperCollins*Publishers* 1991] p487
72. Tolkien, J.R.R.: *The War of the Ring.*
    [HarperCollins*Publishers* 2002] p374
73. Ibid. p360
74. Ibid. p389
75. Ibid. p394
76. Tolkien, J.R.R.: *Sauron Defeated.*
    [HarperCollins*Publishers* 2002] p56
77. Tolkien, J.R.R.: *The Return of the King.*
    [George Allen and Unwin 1955] p249
78. Tolkien, J.R.R.: *The Return of the King.*
    [Grafton, an imprint of HarperCollins*Publishers* 1991] p302
79. Flieger, V.: *Frodo and Aragorn: The Concept of the Hero*; in Zimbardo,
    Rose A. and Isaacs, Neil D., ed: *Understanding The Lord of the Rings.*
    [Houghton Mifflin Company 2004] p129

80. Tolkien, J.R.R.: *The Return of the King.*
    [Grafton, an imprint of HarperCollins*Publishers* 1991] p416
81. Tolkien, J.R.R.: *The Peoples of Middle-earth.*
    [HarperCollins*Publishers* 2002] p263
82. Ibid.
83. Ibid.
84. Ibid. p264
85. Ibid. p268
86. Ibid.
87. Ibid.
88. Ibid.
89. Tolkien, J.R.R.: *The Return of the Shadow.*
    [HarperCollins*Publishers* 2002] p7
90. St Clair, Glorianna: *Tolkien as Reviser: A Case Study: Proceedings of the J.R.R. Tolkien Centenary Conference.*
    [The Tolkien Society 1995] p146

Chapter 3: *The Númenor Dilemma*

1. Tolkien, J.R.R.: *The Fellowship of the Ring.*
   [Grafton, an imprint of HarperCollins*Publishers* 1991] p199
2. Tolkien, J.R.R.: *The Letters of J.R.R. Tolkien.*
   [HarperCollins*Publishers* 2006] no.151 p186
3. Tolkien, J.R.R.: *The Fellowship of the Ring.*
   [Grafton, an imprint of HarperCollins*Publishers* 1991] p11
4. Tolkien, J.R.R.: *The Letters of J.R.R. Tolkien.*
   [HarperCollins*Publishers* 2006] no.257 p347
5. Ibid.
6. Ibid.
7. Tolkien, J.R.R.: *The Letters of J.R.R. Tolkien.*
   [HarperCollins*Publishers* 2006] no.276 p361
8. Tolkien, J.R.R., *The Return of the King.*
   [Grafton, an imprint of HarperCollins*Publishers* 1991] p291
9. Tolkien, J.R.R.: *The Letters of J.R.R. Tolkien.*
   [HarperCollins*Publishers* 2006] no.257 p347
10. Byock, J: *The Prose Edda.* [Penguin Books 2005] p3
11. Tolkien, J.R.R., *The Book of Lost Tales Part II.*
    [HarperCollins*Publishers* 2002] p319
12. Tolkien, J.R.R.: *The Letters of J.R.R. Tolkien.*
    [HarperCollins*Publishers* 2006] no.257 p347

13. Ibid. p378

14. Ibid. p145

15. Tolkien, J.R.R.: *The Lost Road.*
    [HarperCollins*Publishers* 2002] p68

16. Ibid. p60

17. Ibid.

18. Ibid. p26

19. Hammond, Wayne G. and Skull, Christina: *The Lord of the Rings: A Reader's Companion.* [HarperCollins*Publishers* 2005] p4

20. Tolkien, J.R.R.: *The Peoples of Middle-earth.*
    [HarperCollins*Publishers* 2002] p254

21. Tolkien, J.R.R.: *The Letters of J.R.R. Tolkien.*
    [HarperCollins*Publishers* 2006] no.131 p154

22. Ibid.

23. Ibid.

24. Ibid.

25. Ibid. p324

26. Tolkien, J.R.R.: *Sauron Defeated.*
    [HarperCollins*Publishers* 2002] p334

27. Tolkien, J.R.R.: *The Book of Lost Tales Part I.*
    [HarperCollins*Publishers* 2002] p32

28. Tolkien, J.R.R.: *The Lost Road.*
    [HarperCollins*Publishers* 2002] p246

29. Ibid. p276

30. Tolkien, J.R.R.: *The Book of Lost Tales Part II.*
    [HarperCollins*Publishers*[2002] p159

31. Tolkien, J.R.R.: *The Lost Road.*
    [HarperCollins*Publishers* 2002] p276

32. Tolkien, J.R.R.: *The Book of Lost Tales Part II.*
    [HarperCollins*Publishers* 2002] p142

33. Tolkien, J.R.R.: *The Lost Road.*
    [HarperCollins*Publishers*[2002] p320

34. Tolkien, J.R.R.: *The Book of Lost Tales Part I.*
    [HarperCollins*Publishers* 2002] p235

35. Hammond, Wayne G. and Skull, Christina: *The Lord of the Rings: A Reader's Companion.* [HarperCollins*Publishers* 2005] p229

36. Tolkien, J.R.R.: *The Peoples of Middle-earth.*
    [HarperCollins*Publishers* 2002] p226

37. Tolkien, J.R.R.: *Unfinished Tales.*
    [HarperCollins*Publishers* 1998] p370

38. Tolkien, J.R.R.: *The War of the Jewels*.
    [HarperCollins*Publishers* [2002] p224

39. Tolkien, J.R.R.: *The Lost Road*.
    [HarperCollins*Publishers* 2002] p276

40. Tolkien, J.R.R.: *The Peoples of Middle-earth*.
    [HarperCollins*Publishers* 2002] p167

41. Tolkien, J.R.R.: *The War of the Jewels*.
    [HarperCollins*Publishers* 2002] p224

42. Tolkien, J.R.R.: *The Lost Road*.
    [HarperCollins*Publishers* 2002] p276

43. Ibid.

44. Tolkien, J.R.R.: *The War of the Jewels*.
    [HarperCollins*Publishers* 2002] p224

45. Tolkien, J.R.R.: *The Letters of J.R.R. Tolkien*.
    [HarperCollins*Publishers* 2006] no.257 p347

46. Tolkien, J.R.R.: *The Lost Road*.
    [HarperCollins*Publishers* 2002] p332

47. Tolkien, J.R.R.: *The Return of the Shadow*.
    [HarperCollins*Publishers* 2002] p193

48. Ibid. p379

49. Tolkien, J.R.R.: *The Letters of J.R.R. Tolkien*.
    [HarperCollins*Publishers* 2006] no.131 p144

50. Tolkien, J.R.R.: *The Silmarillion*.
    [HarperCollins*Publishers* 1999] *Foreword* p vi

51. Tolkien, J.R.R.: *The Two Towers*.
    [Grafton, an imprint of HarperCollins*Publishers* 1991] p39

52. Flieger, F. and Hostetter, Carl F.: *Tolkien's Legendarium*.
    [Greenwood Press 2000] p188

53. Ibid.

54. Tolkien, J.R.R.: *The Lost Road*.
    [HarperCollins*Publishers* 2002] p103

55. Tolkien, J.R.R.: *Morgoth's Ring*.
    [HarperCollins*Publishers* 2002] p370

56. Ibid. p373

57. Tolkien, J.R.R.: *The Lost Road*.
    [HarperCollins*Publishers* 2002] p296

58. Tolkien, J.R.R.: *The War of the Jewels*.
    [HarperCollins*Publishers* 2002] p243

59. Tolkien, J.R.R.: *Morgoth's Ring*.
    [HarperCollins*Publishers* 2002] p401

60. Ibid. p370
61. Tolkien, J.R.R.: *The Fellowship of the Ring*.
    [Grafton, an imprint of HarperCollins*Publishers* 1991] p35
62. Tolkien, J.R.R.: *The Peoples of Middle-earth*.
    [HarperCollins*Publishers* 2002] p143
63. Tolkien, J.R.R.: *Unfinished Tales*.
    [HarperCollins*Publishers* 1998] p289
64. Tolkien, J.R.R.: *The Fellowship of the Ring*.
    [Grafton, an imprint of HarperCollins*Publishers* 1991] p36

Chapter Four: **The Divine Plan**

1. Tolkien, J.R.R.: *The Letters of J.R.R. Tolkien*.
   [HarperCollins*Publishers* 2006] no153,p194
2. Tolkien, J.R.R.: *The Letters of J.R.R. Tolkien*.
   [HarperCollins*Publishers* 2006] no.319 p407; Rateliff, John D.:
   Return to Bag End. [HarperCollins*Publishers* 2007] p864
3. Tolkien, J.R.R.: *The Lost Road*.
   [HarperCollins*Publishers* 2002] p247
4. Tolkien, J.R.R.: *The Letters of J.R.R. Tolkien*.
   [HarperCollins*Publishers* 2006] no.153 p189
5. Tolkien, J.R.R.: *The Book of Lost Tales Part II*.
   [HarperCollins*Publishers* 2002] p11
6. Ibid. p164
7. Ibid. p185
8. Tolkien, J.R.R.: *The Silmarillion*.
   [HarperCollins*Publishers* 1999] p357
9. Tolkien, J.R.R.: *The Return of the King*.
   [Grafton, an imprint of HarperCollins*Publishers* 1991] p422
10. Tolkien, J.R.R.: *The Shaping of Middle-earth*.
    [HarperCollins*Publishers* 2002] p38
11. Ibid. pp38-39
12. Ibid. p162
13. Tolkien, J.R.R.: *The Fellowship of the Ring*.
    [Grafton, an imprint of HarperCollins*Publishers* 1991] p184
14. Tolkien, J.R.R.: *The Fellowship of the Ring*.
    [Grafton, an imprint of HarperCollins*Publishers* 1991] p260
15. Ibid. p329
16. Tolkien, J.R.R.: *The Two Towers*.
    [Grafton, an imprint of HarperCollins*Publishers* 1991] p346

17. Tolkien, J.R.R.: *The Peoples of Middle-earth.*
    [HarperCollins*Publishers* 2002] p203

18. Tolkien, J.R.R.: *The Return of the King.*
    [Grafton, an imprint of HarperCollins*Publishers* 1991] p153

19. Tolkien, J.R.R.: *The Book of Lost Tales Part II.*
    [HarperCollins*Publishers* 2002] p164

20. Tolkien, J.R.R.: *The Return of the King.*
    [Grafton, an imprint of HarperCollins*Publishers* 1991] p380

21. Tolkien, J.R.R.: *The Peoples of Middle-earth.*
    [HarperCollins*Publishers* 2002] pp244-245

22. Tolkien, J.R.R.: *The Lost Road.*
    [HarperCollins*Publishers* 2002] p304

23. Tolkien, J.R.R.: *The Letters of J.R.R. Tolkien.*
    [HarperCollins*Publishers* 2006] no.256 p344

24. Stratford, Caldecott and Honegger, Thomas: *Tolkien's The Lord of the
    Rings: Sources of Inspiration.* [Walking Tree Publishers 2008] p221

25. Tolkien, J.R.R.: *The Lost Road.*
    [HarperCollins*Publishers* 2002] p48

26. Ibid. p82

27. Tolkien, J.R.R.: *Sauron Defeated.*
    [HarperCollins*Publishers* 2002] p281

28. Ibid. p267

29. Ibid. pp 270-271

30. Tolkien, J.R.R.: *The Letters of J.R.R. Tolkien.*
    [HarperCollins*Publishers* 2006] no.163 p212

31. Tolkien, J.R.R.: *The Lost Road.*
    [HarperCollins*Publishers* 2002] p92

32. Giles, J.A.: *Six Old English Chronicles.*
    [Bohn, London 1848] p. 24

33. Tolkien, J.R.R.: *The Lost Road.*
    [HarperCollins*Publishers* 2002] p90

34. Tolkien, J.R.R.: *The Letters of J.R.R. Tolkien.*
    [HarperCollins*Publishers* 2006] no.227 p303

35. Tolkien, J.R.R.: *The Letters of J.R.R. Tolkien.*
    [HarperCollins*Publishers* 2006] no. 92 p105

36. Tolkien, J.R.R.: *Sauron Defeated.*
    [HarperCollins*Publishers* 2002] p275

37. Ibid. p273

38. Sisam, Kenneth: *Anglo-Saxon Royal Genealogies. Proceedings of
    the British Academy. Vol 39* [Oxford University Press 1953] p308

39. Giles, J.A.: *Six Old English Chronicles.*
    [Bohn, London 1848] p. 24
40. Tolkien, J.R.R.: *The Letters of J.R.R. Tolkien.*
    [HarperCollins*Publishers* 2006] no.257 p347
41. Tolkien J.R.R.: *Finn and Hengest.*
    [HarperCollins*Publishers* 2006] p56
42. Tolkien, J.R.R.: *The Lost Road.*
    [HarperCollins*Publishers* 2002] p86
43. Ibid.
44. Tolkien, J.R.R.: *Sauron Defeated.*
    [HarperCollins*Publishers* 2002] p276
45. Ibid. p273
46. Tolkien, J.R.R.: *The Peoples of Middle-earth.*
    [HarperCollins*Publishers* 2002] p245

Chapter Five: *A Peerless Hero*

1. Flieger, V.: *Frodo and Aragorn: The Concept of the Hero* in Zimbardo, Rose A. and Isaacs, Neil D., ed: *Understanding The Lord of the Rings.*
    [Houghton Mifflin Company 2004] p134
2. Tolkien, J.R.R.:*The Monsters and the Critics.*
    [HarperCollins*Publishers* 1997] p120
3. Ibid. pp134-135
4. Skull, Christina and Hammond, Wayne: *The J.R.R. Tolkien Companion and Guide: Chronology.* [HarperCollins*Publishers* 2006] p249
5. Byock, J: *The Prose Edda.* [Penguin Books 2005] p62
6. Ibid. p60
7. Magnússon, Eiríkr and Morris, William: *Völsunga Saga.*
    [The Scott Library. Walter Scott, Ltd 1888] pp38-39
8. Tolkien, J.R.R.: *The Return of the King.*
    [Grafton, an imprint of HarperCollins*Publishers* 1991] p416
9. Magnússon, Eiríkr and Morris, William: *Völsunga Saga.*
    [The Scott Library. Walter Scott, Ltd 1888] p42
10. Ibid. p79
11. Tolkien, J.R.R.: *The Return of the King.*
    [Grafton, an imprint of HarperCollins*Publishers* 1991] p50
12. Byock, J: *The Prose Edda.* [Penguin Books 2005] p79
13. Campbell, Joseph: *The Hero with a Thousand Faces.*
    [Fontana Press 1993] p30

14. Magnússon, Eiríkr and Morris, William: *Völsunga Saga.*
    [The Scott Library. Walter Scott, Ltd 1888] p77
15. Ibid. p78
16. Tolkien, J.R.R.: *The Legend of Sigurd and Gudrún.*
    [HarperCollins*Publishers* 2009] p125
17. Tolkien, J.R.R.: *The Return of the King.*
    [Grafton, an imprint of HarperCollins*Publishers* 1991] p422
18. Tolkien, J.R.R.: *The Legend of Sigurd and Gudrún.*
    [HarperCollins*Publishers* 2009] p222
19. Ibid.
20. Byock, J.: *The Prose Edda.* [Penguin Books 2005] p85
21. Tolkien, J.R.R.: *The Two Towers.*
    [Grafton, an imprint of HarperCollins*Publishers* 1991] p358
22. Drout, Michael C.: *J.R.R. Tolkien Encyclopedia: scholarship and critical assessment.* [Routledge, New York 2007] p59
23. Heaney, Seamus: *Beowulf.* [Faber and Faber Limited 2000] p8
24. Ibid. p21
25. Tolkien, J.R.R.: *The Two Towers.*
    [Grafton, an imprint of HarperCollins*Publishers* 1991] p146
26. Heaney, Seamus: *Beowulf.*
    [Faber and Faber Limited 2000] p21
27. Tolkien, J.R.R.: *The Fellowship of the Ring.*
    [Grafton, an imprint of HarperCollins*Publishers* 1991] p232
28. Heaney, Seamus: *Beowulf.* [Faber and Faber Limited 2000] p15
29. Tolkien, J.R.R.: *The Fellowship of the Ring.*
    [Grafton, an imprint of HarperCollins*Publishers* 1991] p325
30. Heaney, Seamus: *Beowulf.* [Faber and Faber Limited 2000] p59
31. Ibid. p69
32. Ibid. p79
33. Ibid. p99
34. Tolkien, J.R.R.: *Tree and Leaf. The Homecoming of Beorhtnoth.*
    [HarperCollins*Publishers* 2001] p146
35. Heaney, Seamus: *Beowulf.* [Faber and Faber Limited 2000] p91
36. Tolkien, J.R.R.: *Tree and Leaf. The Homecoming of Beorhtnoth.*
    [HarperCollins*Publishers* 2001] p144
37. Ibid. p141
38. Ibid. p143
39. Tolkien, J.R.R.: *The Return of the King.*
    [Grafton, an imprint of HarperCollins*Publishers* 1991] p272

40. Tolkien, J.R.R.: *The Book of Lost Tales Part II.*
[HarperCollins*Publishers* 2002] p76
41. Tolkien, J.R.R.: *The Children of Hurin.*
[HarperCollins*Publishers* 2007] p88
42. Tolkien, J.R.R.: *The Book of Lost Tales Part II.*
[HarperCollins*Publishers* 2002] p107
43. Ibid. p106
44. Tolkien, J.R.R.: *The Letters of J.R.R. Tolkien.*
[HarperCollins*Publishers* 2006] no.244 p324
45. Tolkien, J.R.R.: *The Letters of J.R.R. Tolkien.*
[HarperCollins*Publishers* 2006] no.131 p144
46. Giles, J.A.: *William of Malmesbury's Chronicle if the Kings of England.*
[Bohn, London 1847] p11
47. Lupack, Alan: *Oxford Guide to Arthurian Literature and Legend.*
[Oxford University Press 2007] p 13
48. Shippey, Tom: *The Road to Middle-earth.*
[HarperCollins*Publishers* 2005] p239;
Frye, Northrop. *Anatomy of Critcism. Four Essays.*
[Princeton University Press 1992]
49. Tolkien, J.R.R.: *The Lost Road.*
[HarperCollins*Publishers* 2002] p317
50. Carpenter, Humphrey: *J.R.R. Tolkien: A Biography.*
[HarperCollins*Publishers* 2002] p45
51. Geoffrey of Monmouth: *The History of the Kings of Britain.*
[Penguin Books 1966] p212
52. Ibid. p221
53. Tolkien, J.R.R.: *The Fellowship of the Ring.*
[Grafton, an imprint of HarperCollins*Publishers* 1991] p487
54. Geoffrey of Monmouth: *The History of the Kings of Britain.*
[Penguin Books 1966] pp 188-189
55. Hammond Wayne G. and Scull, Christina: *The Lord of the Rings: A Reader's Companion.* [HarperCollins*Publishers* 2005] p698
56. Tolkien, J.R.R.: *Unfinished Tales.*
[HarperCollins.*Publishers* 1998] p323
57. Carpenter, Humphrey: *J.R.R. Tolkien: A Biography.*
[HarperCollinsPublishers 2002] p225
58. Flieger, V.: *Interrupted Music.*
[The Kent State University Press 2005] p60
59. Tolkien, J.R.R.: *The Letters of J.R.R. Tolkien.*
[HarperCollins*Publishers* 2006] no.294 p376

60. Shippey, Tom: *Roots and Branches*.
    [Walking Tree Publishers 2007] p282
61. Tolkien, J.R.R.: *The Letters of J.R.R. Tolkien*.
    [HarperCollins*Publishers* 2006] no.153 pp190-195
62. Tolkien, J.R.R.: *The Letters of J.R.R. Tolkien*.
    [HarperCollins*Publishers* 2006] no.153 p195
63. Malory, Sir Thomas: *Le Morte Darthur*.
    [Wordsworth Classics of World Literature 1996] p734
64. Tolkien, J.R.R.: *The Letters of J.R.R. Tolkien*.
    [HarperCollins*Publishers* 2006] no.155 p200
65. Tolkien, J.R.R.: *The Return of the King*.
    [Grafton, an imprint of HarperCollins*Publishers* 1991] p167
66. Ibid.
67. Ibid. p282
68. Tolkien, J.R.R.: *The Letters of J.R.R. Tolkien*.
    [HarperCollins*Publishers* 2006] no.155 p200
69. Kelly, Bob: *Worth Repeating : More Than 5,000 Classic and Contemporary Quotes*. [Kregel Publications US 2003] p169
70. Tolkien, J.R.R.: *The Letters of J.R.R. Tolkien*.
    [HarperCollins*Publishers* 2006] no.183 p240
71. Tolkien, J.R.R.: *The Two Towers*.
    [Grafton, an imprint of HarperCollins*Publishers* 1991] p357
72. Flieger, V.: *Frodo and Aragorn: The Concept of the Hero* in Zimbardo, Rose A. and Isaacs, Neil D., ed: *Understanding The Lord of the Rings*. [Houghton Mifflin Company 2004] p127
73. Ready, William: *Understanding Tolkien and The Lord of the Rings*.
    [Warner Books 1978] pp57-58
74. Campbell, Joseph: *The Hero with a Thousand Faces*.
    [Fontana Press 1993] p356

Chapter six: **The Importance of Hope**

1. Tolkien, J.R.R.: *The Return of the King*.
   [Grafton, an imprint of HarperCollins*Publishers* 1991] p 423
2. Ibid. p 419
3. Tolkien, J.R.R.: *The Fellowship of the Ring*.
   [Grafton, an imprint of HarperCollins*Publishers* 1991] p236
4. Ibid. p255
5. Ibid. p268
6. Ibid. p432

7. Tolkien, J.R.R.: *The Two Towers*.
   [Grafton, an imprint of HarperCollins*Publishers* 1991] p20
8. Tolkien, J.R.R.: *The Two Towers*.
   [Grafton, an imprint of HarperCollins*Publishers* 1991] p119
9. *Good News Bible.* [Collins/Fontana 1976] Luke 2:34-35
10. Tolkien, J.R.R.: *The Return of the King*.
    [Grafton, an imprint of HarperCollins*Publishers* 1991] p272
11. Tolkien, J.R.R.: *The Letters of J.R.R. Tolkien*.
    [HarperCollins*Publishers* 2006] no.181 p237
12. Tolkien, J.R.R.: *The Letters of J.R.R. Tolkien*.
    [HarperCollins*Publishers* 2006] no.186 p246
13. Tolkien, J.R.R.: *The Return of the King*.
    [Grafton, an imprint of HarperCollins*Publishers* 1991] p425
14. Hammond Wayne G. and Scull, Christina: *The Lord of the Rings:
    A Reader's Companion.* [HarperCollins*Publishers* 2005] p702
15. Tolkien, J.R.R.: *The Letters of J.R.R. Tolkien*.
    [HarperCollins*Publishers* 2006] no142 p172
16. Tolkien, J.R.R.: *The Letters of J.R.R. Tolkien*.
    [HarperCollins*Publishers* 2006] no.183 p 243
17. Tolkien, J.R.R.: *The Lost Road.* [HarperCollins*Publishers* 2002] p18
18. Tolkien, J.R.R.: *Sauron Defeated.*
    [HarperCollins*Publishers* 2002] p338
19. Tolkien, J.R.R.:*The Monsters and the critics.*
    [HarperCollins*Publishers* 1997] p18
20. Tolkien, J.R.R.: *The Return of the King*.
    [Grafton, an imprint of HarperCollins*Publishers* 1991] p396
21. Tolkien, J.R.R.: *The Letters of J.R.R. Tolkien*.
    [HarperCollins*Publishers* 2006] no.212 p286
22. Tolkien, J.R.R.: *The Letters of J.R.R. Tolkien*.
    [HarperCollins*Publishers* 2006] no.185 p246
23. Tolkien, J.R.R., *The Book of Lost Tales Part II.*
    [HarperCollins*Publishers* 2002] p255
24. Shippey, Tom: *The Road to Middle-earth.*
    [HarperCollins*Publishers* 2005] p229
25. Tolkien, J.R.R.: *The Letters of J.R.R. Tolkien*.
    [HarperCollins*Publishers* 2006] no.212 pp285-286
26. Tolkien, J.R.R.: *Morgoth's Ring.*
    [HarperCollins*Publishers* 2002] p341
27. *Commentary on Denys the Areopagite On the Divine Names.*
    [Marietti: Turin 1950] p. 115

28. *Good News Bible.* [Collins/Fontana 1976] Romans 2:12-16
29. Tolkien, J.R.R.: *The Fellowship of the Ring.*
    [Grafton, an imprint of HarperCollins*Publishers* 1991] p457
30. Tolkien, J.R.R.: *The Letters of J.R.R. Tolkien.*
    [HarperCollins*Publishers* 2006] no.297 p387
31. Tolkien, J.R.R.: *The Letters of J.R.R. Tolkien.*
    [HarperCollins*Publishers* 2006] no.131 p147
32. Tolkien, J.R.R.: *Morgoth's Ring.*
    [HarperCollins*Publishers* 2002] p311
33. Ibid. p314
34. Ibid. p318
35. Tolkien, J.R.R.: *The Letters of J.R.R. Tolkien.*
    [HarperCollins*Publishers* 2006] no.156 p205
36. Tolkien, J.R.R.: *The Silmarillion.*
    [HarperCollins*Publishers* 1999] p36
37. Tolkien, J.R.R.: *The Letters of J.R.R. Tolkien.*
    [HarperCollins*Publishers* 2006] no.208 p267
38. Tolkien, J.R.R.: *Morgoth's Ring.*
    [HarperCollins.*Publishers* 2002] p320
39. Tolkien, J.R.R.: *The Fellowship of the Ring.*
    [Grafton, an imprint of HarperCollins*Publishers* 1991] p432
40. Tolkien, J.R.R.: *The Return of the King.*
    [Grafton, an imprint of HarperCollins*Publishers* 1991] p187
41. Ibid. p422
42. Ibid. p51
43. Tolkien, J.R.R.: *Sauron Defeated.*
    [HarperCollins*Publishers* 2002] p346
44. Tolkien, J.R.R.: *The Silmarillion.*
    [HarperCollins*Publishers* 1999] p317
45. Tolkien, J.R.R.: *The Letters of J.R.R. Tolkien*
    [HarperCollins*Publishers* 2006] no.181 p237
46. Tolkien, J.R.R.: *The Letters of J.R.R. Tolkien.*
    [HarperCollins*Publishers* 2006] no.156 p206
47. Tolkien, J.R.R.: *The Return of the King.*
    [Grafton, an imprint of HarperCollins*Publishers* 1991] p145
48. Rogers, Deborah C,: *Everyclod and Everyhero: The Image of Man
    in Tolkien* in Lobdell, Jared, ed.: *The Tolkien Compass.*
    [Ballantine Books 1975] p80
49. Drout, Michael C.: *J.R.R. Tolkien Encyclopedia: scholarship and
    critical assessment.* [Routledge, New York 2007] p112

50. Carpenter, Humphrey: *J.R.R. Tolkien: A Biography.*
    [HarperCollins*Publishers* 2002] p92
51. *Good News Bible.* [Collins/Fontana 1976] Revelations 22.16
52. Tolkien, J.R.R.: *The Letters of J.R.R. Tolkien.*
    [HarperCollins*Publishers* 2006] no.297 p387
53. Tolkien, J.R.R.: *The Two Towers.*
    [Grafton, an imprint of HarperCollins*Publishers* 1991] p174
54. Tolkien, J.R.R.: *The Book of Lost Tales Part II.*
    [HarperCollins*Publishers* 2002] p321
55. Tolkien, J.R.R.: *The Silmarillion.*
    [HarperCollins*Publishers* 1999] p35
56. Tolkien, J.R.R.: *Sauron Defeated.*
    [HarperCollins*Publishers* 2002] p398
57. Tolkien, J.R.R.: *The Letters of J.R.R. Tolkien.*
    [HarperCollins*Publishers* 2006] no.96 pp109-110
58. Tolkien, J.R.R.: *Morgoth's Ring.*
    [HarperCollins*Publishers* 2002] p316
59. Tolkien, J.R.R.: *The Silmarillion.*
    [HarperCollins*Publishers* 1999] p316
60. Tolkien, J.R.R.: *The Book of Lost Tales Part II.*
    [HarperCollins*Publishers* 2002] p285,
61. Tolkien, J.R.R.: *The Fellowship of the Ring.*
    [Grafton, an imprint of HarperCollins*Publishers* 1991] p195
62. Tolkien, J.R.R.: *The Hobbit.* [George Allen and Unwin 1975] p240
63. Tolkien, J.R.R.: *The Return of the King.*
    [Grafton, an imprint of HarperCollins*Publishers* 1991] p297/298
64. Tolkien, J.R.R.: *The Silmarillion.* [HarperCollins*Publishers* 1999] p4
65. Tolkien, J.R.R.: *Morgoth's Ring.*
    [HarperCollins*Publishers* 2002] p343
66. Ibid.
67. Ibid.
68. Ibid. p245
69. Tolkien, J.R.R.: *The Return of the King.*
    [Grafton, an imprint of HarperCollins*Publishers* 1991] p316
70. Tolkien, J.R.R.: *Morgoth's Ring.*
    [HarperCollins*Publishers* 2002] p326
71. Tolkien, J.R.R.: *The Return of the King.*
    [Grafton, an imprint of HarperCollins*Publishers* 1991] p310
72. Tolkien, J.R.R.: *The Letters of J.R.R. Tolkien.*
    [HarperCollins*Publishers* 2006] no.181 p233

Bibliography

Anderson, Douglas A.: *Tales Before Tolkien*.
[Random House Publishing Group 2003]

Auden, W.H.: *The Quest Hero* in Zimbardo, Rose A. and Isaacs,
Neil D., ed: *Understanding The Lord of the Rings*.
[Houghton Mifflin Company 2004]

Bede: *The Ecclesiastical History of the English People*.
[Oxford University Press 2008]

Blackman, Robert S.: *Tolkien and the Perils of War*.
[The History Press 2011]

Brennan Croft, Janet: *Tolkien and Shakespeare*.
[McFarland & Company, Inc 2007]

Bruce, Alexander M.: *Scyld and Scef Expanding the Analogues*.
[Routledge 2002]

Byock, J.: *The Prose Edda*. [Penguin Books 2005]

Campbell, Joseph: *The Hero with a Thousand Faces*.
[Fontana Press 1993]

Carpenter, Humphrey: *J.R.R. Tolkien: A Biography*.
[HarperCollins*Publishers* 2002]

Carpenter, Humphrey: *The Inklings*. [HarperCollins*Publishers* 2006]

Chance, Jane: *Tolkien's Art*.
[University Press of Kentucky 2001]

Chance, Jane: *Tolkien and the Invention of Myth*.
[University Press of Kentucky 2004]

Colvin, Michael J.: *Frozen Nature: Abiding Technology in Tolkien's World*: *Proceedings of the Tolkien 2005 Conference Volume Two*. [The Tolkien Society 2008]

Commentary on Denys the Areopagite On the Divine Names. [Marietti: Turin 1950]

Crossley-Holland, Kevin: *Norse Myths Gods of the Vikings*. [Penguin Books 1980]

Davies, Sioned: *The Mabinogion*. [Oxford University Press 2007]

De Troyes, Chrétien: *Arthurian Romances*. [Penguin Books 1991]

Drout, Michael C.: *J.R.R. Tolkien Encyclopedia: scholarship and critical assessment*. [Routledge, New York 2007]

Ebbutt, M.I.: *Hero-myths of legends of the British race*. [George G. Harrap 1910]

Fimi, Dimitra: *Tolkien, Race and Cultural History*. [Palgrave Macmillan 2009]

Fitton, J. Lesley: *The Minoans*. [The Folio Society 2004]

Flieger, V.: *Interrupted Music*. [The Kent State University Press 2005]

Flieger, V.: *Frodo and Aragorn: The Concept of the Hero* in Zimbardo, Rose A. and Isaacs, Neil D., ed: *Understanding The Lord of the Rings*. [Houghton Mifflin Company 2004]

Flieger, V. and Hostetter, Carl F.: *Tolkien's Legendarium*. [Greenwood Press 2000]

Ford, Judy Ann and Reid, Robin Anne: *Councils and Kings: Aragorn's Journey Towards Kingship in J.R.R. Tolkien's The Lord of the Rings and Peter Jackson's The Lord of the Rings*: *Tolkien Studies vol. 6*. [West Virginia University Press 2009]

Frye, Northrop: *Anatomy of Criticism: Four Essays*. [Princeton University Press 1992]

Garmonsway, G.N.: *The Anglo-Saxon Chronicle*.
[Dent & Sons Ltd 1975]

Garth, John: *Tolkien and the Great War*. [HarperCollins*Publishers* 2003]

Geoffrey of Monmouth: *The History of the Kings of Britain*.
[Penguin Books 1966]

Geoffrey of Monmouth: *The Life of Merlin*. [Forgotten Books 2008]

Gerritsen, Willem P. and Anthony G. van Melle: *A Dictionary of Medieval Heroes*. [Boydell Press 2000]

Giles, J.A.: *Six Old English Chronicles*. [Bohn, London 1848]

Giles, J.A.: *William of Malmesbury's Chronicle if the Kings of England*. [Bohn, London 1847]

Gilson, Christopher: *Words, Phrases and Passages in various tongues in The Lord Of The Rings*: *Parma Eldalamberon XVII*.
[The Mythopoeic Society 2007]

Glyer, Diana Pavlac: *The Company They Keep*.
[Kent State University Press 2008]

Good News Bible. [Collins/Fontana 1976]

Graves, Robert: *The Greek Myths*. [The Folio Society 1996]

Guerber, H.A: *Myths and legends of the Middle Ages*.
[George G. Harrap 1911]

Hammond Wayne G. and Scull, Christina: *The Lord of the Rings: A Reader's Companion*. [HarperCollins*Publishers* 2005]

Heaney, Seamus: *Beowulf*. [Faber and Faber Limited 2000]

Hiswelókë's Sindarin dictionary: www.jrrvf.com/hisweloke/sindar/

Hume, David: *The History of England from the Invasion of Julius Caesar to the Revolution in 1688. Volume I.* [Indianapolis: Liberty Fund 1983]

Hutton, Richard H.: *Cardinal Newman.* [Methuen and Co. 1891]

Ingram, James: *The Anglo-Saxon Chronicle.* [The Echo Library 2007]

Kelly, Bob: *Worth Repeating : More Than 5,000 Classic and Contemporary Quotes.* [Kregel Publications US 2003]

Keynes, Simon and Lapudge, Michael: *Alfred the Great: Asser's Life of King Alfred.* [Penguin Books 2004]

Kocher, Paul H.: *Master of Middle-earth.* [Thames and Hudson 1973]

Larrington, Caroline: *The Poetic Edda.* [Oxford University Press 2008]

Lewis, Alex and Curry, Elizabeth: *The Epic Realm of Tolkien.* [ADC Publications Ltd 2009]

Lewis, C.S.: *That Hideous Strength.* [Pan Books in association with The Bodley Head Ltd 1989]

Lönnrot, Elias: *The Kalevala.* [Oxford University Press 2008]

Loomis, Roger Sherman: *Arthurian Literature in the Middle Ages.* [Oxford at the Clarendon Press 1959]

Lupack, A.: *Oxford Guide to Arthurian Literature and Legend.* [Oxford University Press 2007]

Maclean, Magnus: *The Literature of the Celts.* [Senate, an imprint of Tiger Books International PLC 1998]

Magnússon, Eiríkr and Morris, William: *Völsunga Saga.* [The Scott Library. Walter Scott, Ltd 1888]

Malory, Sir Thomas: *Le Morte Darthur.* [Wordsworth Classics of World Literature 1996]

Nennius: *History of the Britons*. [Lightening Source UK Ltd 2009]

Nicholson, Lewis E.: *An Anthology of Beowulf Criticism*. [University of Notre Dame Press 1963]

Petty, Anne: *Tolkien in the Land of Heroes*. [Gold Spring Press 2003]

Plato: *Timaeus and Critias: A new translation by Robin Waterfield*. [Oxford University Press 2008]

Rateliff, John D.: *The History of the Hobbit part one: Mr Baggins*. [HarperCollins*Publishers* 2007]

Rateliff, John D.: *The History of the Hobbit part two: Return to Bag End*. [HarperCollins*Publishers* 2007]

Ready, William: *Understanding Tolkien and The Lord of the Rings*. [Warner Books 1978]

Ritchie, Lyn; Lacon, Ruth and Surtees, Angela: *The History of the Northern Kingdom*.

Rogers, Deborah C,: *Everyclod and Everyhero: The Image of Man in Tolkien* in Lobdell, Jared, ed.: *The Tolkien Compass*. [Ballantine Books 1975]

Rolleston, T.W.: *Myths and Legends of the Celtic Race*. [George G. Harrap 1911]

Rosebury, Brian: *Tolkien A Cultural Phenomenon*. [Palgrave Macmillan 2003]

Sale, Roger: *Modern Heroism*. [University of California Press 1973]

Schweicher, Eric: *Aspects of the Fall in the Silmarillion: Proceedings of the J.R.R. Tolkien Centenary Conference*. [The Tolkien Society 1995]

Shippey, Tom: *J.R.R. Tolkien Author of the Century*. [Houghton Mifflin Company 2001]

Shippey, Tom: *The Road to Middle-earth*. [HarperCollins*Publishers* 2005]

Shippey, Tom: *Roots and Branches*. [Walking Tree Publishers 2007]

Simpson Nikakis, Karen: *Sacral kingship: Aragorn as the rightful and sacrificial king in The Lord of the Rings: Mythlore no.99/100.* [Mythopoeic Society 2007]

Sisam, Kenneth: *Anglo-Saxon Royal Genealogies. Proceedings of the British Academy. Vol 39.* [Oxford University Press 1953]

Skene, William: *The Four Ancient Books of Wales*. [Forgotten Books 2007]

Skull, Christina and Hammond, Wayne: *The J.R.R. Tolkien Companion and Guide: Chronology.* [HarperCollins*Publishers* 2006]

St Clair, Glorianna: *Tolkien as Reviser: A Case Study: Proceedings of the J.R.R. Tolkien Centenary Conference.* [The Tolkien Society 1995]

Stratford, Caldecott and Honegger, Thomas: *Tolkien's The Lord of the Rings: Sources of Inspiration.* [Walking Tree Publishers 2008]

Sturluson, Snorri: *The Prose Edda*. [Penguin Books 2005]

Tennyson, Alfred Lord: *Idylls of the King*. [Penguin Books 1996]

Tolkien, J.R.R.: *The Fellowship of the Ring*.
[George Allen and Unwin 1955]

Tolkien, J.R.R.: *The Two Towers*. [George Allen and Unwin 1955]

Tolkien, J.R.R.: *The Return of the King*. [George Allen and Unwin 1955]

Tolkien, J.R.R.: *The Adventures of Tom Bombadil*.
[George Allen and Unwin 1962]

Tolkien, J.R.R.: *Smith of Wootton Major*.
[Houghton Mifflin Company 1967]
Tolkien, J.R.R.: *Farmer Giles of Ham*. [George Allen and Unwin. 1974]

Tolkien, J.R.R.: *The Hobbit*. [George Allen and Unwin 1975]

Tolkien, J.R.R.: *The Fellowship of the Ring*.
[Grafton, an imprint of HarperCollins*Publishers* 1991]

Tolkien, J.R.R.: *The Two Towers*.
[Grafton, an imprint of HarperCollins*Publishers* 1991]

Tolkien, J.R.R.: *The Return of the King*.
[Grafton, an imprint of HarperCollins*Publishers* 1991]

Tolkien, J.R.R.: *The Monsters and the Critics*.
[HarperCollins*Publishers* 1997]

Tolkien, J.R.R.: *Unfinished Tales*. [HarperCollins*Publishers* 1998]

Tolkien, J.R.R.: *The Silmarillion*. [HarperCollins*Publishers* 1999]

Tolkien, J.R.R.: *Tree and Leaf. The Homecoming of Beorhtnoth*.
[HarperCollins*Publishers* 2001]

Tolkien, J.R.R.: *The Book of Lost Tales Part I*.
[HarperCollins*Publishers* 2002]

Tolkien, J.R.R.: *The Book of Lost Tales Part II*.
[HarperCollins*Publishers* 2002]

Tolkien, J.R.R.: *The Lays of Beleriand*. [HarperCollins*Publishers* 2002]

Tolkien, J.R.R.: *The Shaping of Middle-earth*.
[HarperCollins*Publishers* 2002]

Tolkien, J.R.R.: *The Lost Road*. [HarperCollins*Publishers* 2002]

Tolkien, J.R.R.: *The Return of the Shadow*.
[HarperCollins*Publishers* 2002]

Tolkien, J.R.R.: *The Treason of Isengard*. [HarperCollins*Publishers* 2002]
Tolkien, J.R.R.: *The War of the Ring*. [HarperCollins*Publishers* 2002]

Tolkien, J.R.R.: *Sauron Defeated*. [HarperCollins*Publishers* 2002]

Tolkien, J.R.R.: *Morgoth's Ring*. [HarperCollins*Publishers* 2002]

Tolkien, J.R.R.: *The War of the Jewels*. [HarperCollins*Publishers* 2002]

Tolkien, J.R.R.: *The Peoples of Middle-earth*.
[HarperCollins*Publishers* 2002]

Tolkien J.R.R.: *Finn and Hengest*. [HarperCollins*Publishers*[2006]

Tolkien, J.R.R.: *Sir Gawain and the Green Knight*.
[HarperCollins*Publishers* 2006]

Tolkien, J.R.R.: *The Letters of J.R.R. Tolkien*.
[HarperCollins*Publishers* 2006]

Tolkien, J.R.R.: *The Children of Húrin*. [HarperCollins*Publishers* 2007]

Tolkien, J.R.R.: *The Legend of Sigurd and Gudrún*.
[HarperCollins*Publishers* 2009]

Tolkien, J.R.R. and Gordon, E.V.: *Sir Gawain and the Green Knight*.
[Oxford at the Clarendon Press 1946]

Wood, Ralph C.: *J.R.R. Tolkien: Our Post-modern Contemporary:
Proceedings of the Tolkien 2005 Conference Volume One*.
[The Tolkien Society 2008]

Wytenbroek, J.R.: *Apocalyptic Vision in The Lord of the Rings: Mythlore
54* [The Mythopoeic Society 1988]

Yates, Jessica: *Tolkien the Anti-totalitarian: Proceedings of the J.R.R.
Tolkien Centenary Conference*. [The Tolkien Society 1995]

Zimbardo, Rose A. and Isaacs, Neil D: *Understanding The Lord of the
Rings*. [Houghton Mifflin Company 2004]

Index

A

C

D

F

G

H

M

N

O

$\mathcal{P}$

$\mathcal{T}$

U